ASHAMED OF THE GOSPEL

ASHAMED OF THE GOSPEL

When the Church Becomes Like the World

John F. MacArthur, Jr.

CROSSWAY BOOKS • WHEATON, ILLINOIS
A DIVISION OF GOOD NEWS PUBLISHERS

Ashamed of the Gospel:
When the Church Becomes Like the World

Copyright © 1993 by John F. MacArthur, Jr.

Published by Crossway Books
        A division of Good News Publishers
        1300 Crescent Street
        Wheaton, Illinois 60187

Cover design: The Puckett Group

First printing, 1993

First trade paperback edition, 1999

Printed in the United States of America

ISBN 1-58134-077-X

All Scripture quotations in this book, except those noted otherwise, are from the *New American Standard Bible,* © 1960, 1962, 1963, 1968, 1971, 1972, 1973, 1975, and 1977 by The Lockman Foundation, and are used by permission. Quotations marked KJV are from the King James Version.

Appendix 3, "Carnal vs. Spiritual Wisdom," is an excerpt from "A Soliloquy on the Art of Man-Fishing," by Thomas Boston, adapted for modern readers. This version, © 1993 by Phil Johnson, is used by permission.

Library of Congress Cataloging-in-Publication Data
MacArthur, John, 1939–
    Ashamed of the gospel : when the Church becomes like the
  world / John F. MacArthur, Jr.
      p.   cm.
    Includes bibliographical references.
    ISBN 1-58134-077-X
    1. Evangelicalism. 2. Church. 3. Pastoral theology. 4. Preaching.
  5. Spurgeon, C. H. (Charles Haddon), 1834–1892. I. Title.
  BR1640.M243   1993
  270.8'2—dc20   93-23849
                                        CIP

15 14 13 12 11 10 09 08 07 06 05 04 03 02 01 00 99
15 14 13 12 11 10 9 8 7 6 5 4 3 2

*To Rick Draa, my faithful and
beloved friend and the servant of the
Lord on my behalf — who for more
than twenty years has recorded my voice
and spread it across the globe*

I am not ashamed of the gospel, for it is the power of God for salvation to everyone who believes, to the Jew first and also to the Greek.

ROMANS 1:16

Do not be ashamed of the testimony of our Lord, or of me His prisoner; but join with me in suffering for the gospel according to the power of God. . . . I also suffer these things, but I am not ashamed; for I know whom I have believed and I am convinced that He is able to guard what I have entrusted to Him until that day.

2 TIMOTHY 1:8, 12

Whoever is ashamed of Me and My words in this adulterous and sinful generation, the Son of Man will also be ashamed of him when He comes in the glory of His Father with the holy angels.

MARK 8:38

CONTENTS

PREFACE

Everywhere there is apathy. Nobody cares whether that which is preached is true or false. A sermon is a sermon whatever the subject; only, the shorter it is the better.

CHARLES HADDON SPURGEON[1]

THOSE WORDS from Spurgeon were written more than a hundred years ago. He might have been describing the state of evangelicalism at the end of the twentieth century.

Last summer I stood by his tomb in London—a heavy stone vault, blended into the cemetery between a road and a large building. If I hadn't had someone to lead me there, I would not have found it. Spurgeon's and his wife's names are engraved in stone, but there is no information on the tomb itself about who he was. The average sightseer might miss the stone vault (there are larger, more impressive ones all around), or on seeing it, not realize it is the burial place of a man who in his time was perhaps more well-known and more influential than England's Prime Minister.

As I stood by Spurgeon's grave, I couldn't help thinking how much the church needs men like him today. Spurgeon was not afraid to stand boldly for the truth, even when it meant he stood alone. Preaching the Word of God was his sole passion. He believed the church's tolerance of preaching was beginning to decline, while some ministers were experimenting with alternative approaches and abbreviated messages. He saw in that a great danger, and his concern thrust him into a battle that ultimately led to his death. He had been placed in that grave exactly a hundred years before my visit.

Contrast Spurgeon's attitude toward preaching with the prevailing opinion of our day. In fact, Spurgeon's lament is diametrically opposite the perspective expressed in a column that appeared a few years ago in a popu-

---

[1]"Preface," *The Sword and the Trowel* (1888 complete volume), iii.

lar Christian magazine. A well-known preacher was venting his own *loathing* for long sermons. January 1 was coming, so he resolved to do better in the coming year. "That means wasting less time listening to long sermons and spending much more time preparing short ones," he wrote. "People, I've discovered, will forgive even poor theology as long as they get out before noon."[2]

Unfortunately, that perfectly sums up the predominant attitude behind much of modern ministry. Bad doctrine is tolerable; a long sermon most certainly is not. The timing of the benediction is of far more concern to the average churchgoer than the content of the sermon. Sunday dinner and the feeding of our mouths takes precedence over Sunday school and the nourishment of our souls. Long-windedness has become a greater sin than heresy.

The church has imbibed the worldly philosophy of pragmatism, and we're just beginning to taste the bitter results.

WHAT IS PRAGMATISM?

Pragmatism is the notion that meaning or worth is determined by practical consequences. It is closely akin to *utilitarianism*, the belief that usefulness is the standard of what is good. To a pragmatist/utilitarian, if a technique or course of action has the desired effect, it is good. If it doesn't seem to work, it must be wrong.

Pragmatism as a philosophy was developed and popularized at the end of the last century by philosopher William James, along with such other noted intellectuals as John Dewey and George Santayana. It was James who gave the new philosophy its name and shape. In 1907, he published a collection of lectures entitled *Pragmatism: A New Name for Some Old Ways of Thinking*, and thus defined a whole new approach to truth and life.

Pragmatism has roots in Darwinism and secular humanism. It is inherently relativistic, rejecting the notion of absolute right and wrong, good and evil, truth and error. Pragmatism ultimately defines truth as that which is useful, meaningful, and helpful. Ideas that don't seem workable or relevant are rejected as false.

What's wrong with pragmatism? After all, common sense involves a measure of legitimate pragmatism, doesn't it? If a dripping faucet works fine after you replace the washers, for example, it is reasonable to assume

---

[2]Jamie Buckingham, "Wasted Time," *Charisma* (December 1988), 98.

that bad washers were the problem. If the medicine your doctor prescribes produces harmful side effects or has no effect at all, you need to ask if there's a remedy that works. Such simple pragmatic realities are generally self-evident.

But when pragmatism is used to make judgments about right and wrong, or when it becomes a guiding philosophy of life, theology, and ministry, inevitably it clashes with Scripture. Spiritual and biblical truth is not determined by testing what "works" and what doesn't. We know from Scripture, for example, that the gospel often does not produce a positive response (1 Cor. 1:22, 23; 2:14). On the other hand, satanic lies and deception can be quite effective (Matt. 24:23, 24; 2 Cor. 4:3, 4). Majority reaction is no test of validity (cf Matt. 7:13, 14), and prosperity is no measure of truthfulness (cf Job 12:6). Pragmatism as a guiding philosophy of ministry is inherently flawed. Pragmatism as a test of truth is nothing short of satanic.

Nevertheless, an overpowering surge of ardent pragmatism is sweeping through evangelicalism. Traditional methodology—most notably preaching—is being discarded or downplayed in favor of newer means, such as drama, dance, comedy, variety, side-show histrionics, pop-psychology, and other entertainment forms. The new methods supposedly are more "effective"—that is, they draw a bigger crowd. And since for many the chief criterion for gauging the success of a church has become attendance figures, whatever pulls in the most people is accepted without critical analysis as *good*. That is pragmatism.

Perhaps the most visible signs of pragmatism are seen in the convulsive changes that have revolutionized the church worship service in the past decade. Some of evangelicalism's largest and most influential churches now boast Sunday services that are designed purposely to be more rollicking than reverent.

Even worse, *theology* now takes a back seat to *methodology*. One author has written, "Formerly, a doctrinal statement represented the reason for a denomination's existence. Today, methodology is the glue that holds churches together. A statement of ministry defines them and their denominational existence."[3] Incredibly, many believe this is a positive trend, a major advance for the contemporary church.

---

[3]Elmer L. Towns, *An Inside Look at 10 of Today's Most Innovative Churches* (Ventura, Calif.: Regal, 1990), 249.

Some church leaders evidently think the four priorities of the early church—the apostles' teaching, fellowship, the breaking of bread, and prayer (Acts 2:42)—make a lame agenda for the church in this day and age. Churches are allowing drama, music, recreation, entertainment, self-help programs, and similar enterprises to eclipse traditional Sunday worship and fellowship. In fact, everything seems to be in fashion in the church today *except* biblical preaching. The new pragmatism sees preaching—particularly expository preaching—as passé. Plainly declaring the truth of God's Word is regarded as unsophisticated, offensive, and utterly ineffective. We're now told we can get better results by first amusing people or giving them success tips and pop-psychology, thus wooing them into the fold. Once they feel comfortable, they'll be ready to receive biblical truth in small, diluted doses.

Pastors are turning to books on marketing methods in search of new techniques to help churches grow. Many seminaries have shifted their pastoral training emphasis from Bible curriculum and theology to counseling technique and church-growth theory. All these trends reflect the church's growing commitment to pragmatism.

As Martyn Lloyd-Jones pointed out,

> These proposals that we should preach less, and do various other things more, are of course not new at all. People seem to think that all this is quite new, and that it is the hallmark of modernity to decry or to depreciate preaching, and to put your emphasis on these other things. The simple answer to that is that there is nothing new about it. The actual form may be new, but the principle is certainly not a new one at all; indeed it has been the particular emphasis of this present century.[4]

IS PRAGMATISM REALLY A SERIOUS THREAT?

I am convinced that pragmatism poses precisely the same subtle threat to the church in our age that modernism represented nearly a century ago. Modernism was a movement that embraced higher criticism (an approach to Scripture that discards the notion the Bible is God's Word) and liberal theology while denying nearly all the supernatural aspects of Christianity. But modernism did not first surface as an overt attack on orthodox doc-

---

[4]*Preaching and Preachers* (Grand Rapids, Mich.: Zondervan, 1971), 33.

trine. The earliest modernists seemed concerned primarily with inter-denominational unity. They were willing to downplay doctrine for that goal, because they believed doctrine was inherently divisive and a fragmented church would become irrelevant in the modern age. To heighten Christianity's relevance, modernists sought to synthesize Christian teachings with the latest insights from science, philosophy, and literary criticism. Modernism began as a methodology but soon evolved into a unique theology.

Modernists viewed doctrine as a secondary issue. They emphasized brotherhood and experience and de-emphasized doctrinal differences. Doctrine, they believed, should be fluid and adaptable—certainly not something worth fighting for. In 1935 John Murray gave this assessment of the typical modernist:

> The modernist very often prides himself on the supposition that he is concerned with life, with the principles of conduct and the making operative of the principles of Jesus in all departments of life, individual, social, ecclesiastical, industrial, and political. His slogan has been that Christianity is life, not doctrine, and he thinks that the orthodox Christian or fundamentalist, as he likes to name him, is concerned simply with the conservation and perpetuation of outworn dogmas of doctrinal belief, a concern which makes orthodoxy in his esteem a cold and lifeless petrification of Christianity.[5]

When harbingers of modernism began to appear in the late 1800s, few Christians were troubled. The most heated controversies in those days were relatively small backlashes against men like Charles Spurgeon—men who were trying to warn the church about the threat. Most Christians—particularly church leaders—were completely unreceptive to such warnings. After all, it wasn't as if *outsiders* were imposing new teachings on the church; these were people from within the denominations—and scholars at that. Certainly they had no agenda to undermine the core of orthodox theology or attack the heart of Christianity itself. Divisiveness and schism seemed far greater dangers than apostasy.

But whatever the modernists' motives at first, their ideas *did* repre-

---

[5]"The Sanctity of the Moral Law," *Collected Writings of John Murray*, 4 vols. (Edinburgh: Banner of Truth, 1976), 1:193.

sent a grave threat to orthodoxy, as history has proved. The movement spawned teachings that decimated practically all the mainline denominations in the first half of this century. By downplaying the importance of doctrine, modernism opened the door to theological liberalism, moral relativism, and rank unbelief. Most evangelicals today tend to equate the word "modernism" with full-scale denial of the faith. It is often forgotten that the aim of the early modernists was simply to make the church more "modern," more unified, more relevant, and more acceptable to a skeptical modern age.

Just like the pragmatists today.

Like the church of a hundred years ago, we live in a world of rapid changes—major advances in science, technology, world politics, and education. Like the brethren of that generation, Christians today are open, even eager, for change in the church. Like them, we yearn for unity among the faithful. And like them, we are sensitive to the hostility of an unbelieving world.

Unfortunately, there is at least one other parallel between the church today and the church in the late nineteenth century: many Christians seem completely unaware—if not unwilling to see—that serious dangers threaten the church from within. Yet if church history teaches us anything, it teaches us that the most devastating assaults on the faith have always begun as subtle errors arising from inside the body itself.

Living in an unstable age, the church cannot afford to be vacillating. We minister to people desperate for answers, and we cannot soft-pedal the truth or extenuate the gospel. If we make friends with the world, we set ourselves at enmity with God. If we trust worldly devices, we automatically relinquish the power of the Holy Spirit.

These truths are repeatedly affirmed in Scripture: "Do you not know that friendship with the world is hostility toward God? Therefore whoever wishes to be a friend of the world makes himself an enemy of God" (Jas. 4:4). "Do not love the world, nor the things in the world. If anyone loves the world, the love of the Father is not in him" (1 John 2:15).

"The king is not saved by a mighty army; a warrior is not delivered by great strength. A horse is a false hope for victory; nor does it deliver anyone by its great strength" (Ps. 33:16, 17). "Woe to those who go down to Egypt for help, and rely on horses, and trust in chariots because they are many, and in horsemen because they are very strong, but they do not look to the Holy One of Israel, nor seek the Lord!" (Isa. 31:1).

"'Not by might nor by power, but by My Spirit,' says the Lord of hosts" (Zech. 4:6).

The whole point about Israel's being a light to the world (Isa. 42:6; 49:6) is that they were supposed to be *different*. They were explicitly forbidden to imitate the Gentiles' manner of dress, grooming, foods, religion, and other aspects of the culture. God told them, "You shall not do what is done in the land of Egypt where you lived, nor are you to do what is done in the land of Canaan where I am bringing you; you shall not walk in their statutes" (Lev. 18:3). And as Martyn Lloyd-Jones pointed out, "Our Lord attracted sinners because He was different. They drew near to Him because they felt that there was something different about Him. . . . And the world always expects us to be different. This idea that you are going to win people to the Christian faith by showing them that after all you are remarkably like them, is theologically and psychologically a profound blunder."[6]

IS WORLDLINESS STILL A SIN?

Worldliness is rarely even mentioned today, much less identified for what it is. The word itself is beginning to sound quaint. Worldliness is the sin of allowing one's appetites, ambitions, or conduct to be fashioned according to earthly values. "All that is in the world, the lust of the flesh and the lust of the eyes and the boastful pride of life, is not from the Father, but is from the world. And the world is passing away, and also its lusts; but the one who does the will of God abides forever" (1 John 2:16, 17).

Yet today we have the extraordinary spectacle of church programs designed explicitly to cater to fleshly desire, sensual appetites, and human pride—"the lust of the flesh and the lust of the eyes and the boastful pride of life." To achieve this worldly appeal, church activities often go beyond the merely frivolous. For several years a colleague of mine has been collecting a "horror file" of clippings that report how churches are employing innovations to keep worship services from becoming dull. In the past half decade, some of America's largest evangelical churches have employed worldly gimmicks like slapstick, vaudeville, wrestling exhibitions, and even mock striptease to spice up their Sunday meetings. No brand of horseplay, it seems, is too outrageous to

---

[6]*Preaching and Preachers*, 140.

be brought into the sanctuary. Burlesque is fast becoming the liturgy of the pragmatic church.

Moreover, many in the church believe this is the *only* way we will ever reach the world. If the unchurched multitudes don't want biblical preaching, we are told, we must give them what they want. Hundreds of churches have followed precisely that theory, actually surveying unbelievers to learn what it would take to get them to attend.

Subtly the overriding goal is becoming church attendance and worldly acceptability rather than a transformed life. Preaching the Word and boldly confronting sin are seen as archaic, ineffectual means of winning the world. After all, those things actually drive most people away. Why not entice people into the fold by offering what they want, creating a friendly, comfortable environment, and catering to the very desires that constitute their strongest urges? As if we might get them to accept Jesus by somehow making Him more likable or making His message less offensive.

That kind of thinking badly skews the mission of the church. The Great Commission is not a marketing manifesto. Evangelism does not require salesmen, but prophets. It is the Word of God, not any earthly enticement, that plants the seed for the new birth (1 Peter 1:23). We gain nothing but God's displeasure if we seek to remove the offense of the cross (cf Gal. 5:11).

IS ALL INNOVATION WRONG?

Please do not misunderstand my concern. It is not innovation per se that I oppose. I recognize that styles of worship are always in flux. I also realize that if the typical seventeenth-century Puritan walked into Grace Community Church (where I am pastor) he might be shocked by our music, probably dismayed to see men and women seated together, and quite possibly disturbed that we use a public address system. Spurgeon himself would not appreciate our organ. But I am not in favor of a stagnant church. And I am not bound to any particular musical or liturgical style. Those things in and of themselves are not issues Scripture even addresses. Nor do I think my own personal preferences in such matters are necessarily superior to the tastes of others. I have no desire to manufacture some arbitrary rules that govern what is acceptable or not in church services. To do so would be the essence of legalism.

My complaint is with a philosophy that relegates God and His Word to a subordinate role in the church. I believe it is unbiblical to elevate entertainment over biblical preaching and worship in the church service. And I stand in opposition to those who believe salesmanship can bring people into the kingdom more effectively than a sovereign God. That philosophy has opened the door to worldliness in the church.

"I am not ashamed of the gospel," the apostle Paul wrote (Rom. 1:16). Unfortunately, "ashamed of the gospel" seems more and more apt as a description of some of the most visible and influential churches of our age.

I see striking parallels between what is happening in the church today and what happened a hundred years ago. The more I read about that era, the more my conviction is reinforced that we are seeing history repeat itself. Throughout this book, I will highlight features of late nineteenth-century evangelicalism that correspond to contemporary issues. I will particularly focus on an episode from the life of Spurgeon that has come to be known as "The Down-Grade Controversy." And I will quote frequently from Spurgeon's writings on these matters.

I share at least two things in common with Charles Spurgeon: Both of us were born on June 19, and like me, he pastored one congregation for virtually all of his ministry. The more I read of his writing and preaching, the more I sense a kindred spirit.

By no means, however, do I view myself as Spurgeon's equal. Surely no preacher in the history of the English language has had Spurgeon's facility with words, his ability to convey the authority of the divine message, his passion for truth, or his grasp of preaching combined with such knowledge of theology. He was also a churchman par excellence, innately gifted as a leader. Pastoring in troubled times, Spurgeon filled his 5,500-seat auditorium several times a week. His own flock's esteem for him remained undiminished until his death. I sit at his feet, not by his side.

Certainly, I do not desire to ignite the kind of altercation Spurgeon touched off in the Down-Grade Controversy. Spurgeon himself blamed the conflict for his death. Departing for a rest on the French Riviera in 1891, he told friends, "The fight is killing me."[7] Three months later word came back from France that Spurgeon was dead. He had not sought a fight. But refusing to compromise what he felt were biblical convictions, he could not avoid the controversy that ensued.

---

[7]Iain Murray, *The Forgotten Spurgeon* (Edinburgh: Banner of Truth, 1966), 163.

Controversy frankly is distasteful to me. Those who know me personally will affirm that I do not enjoy any kind of dispute. Yet there is a fire in my bones that constrains me to speak plainly regarding my biblical convictions. I cannot keep silent when so much is at stake.

It is in that spirit that I offer this book. I hope no one will perceive it as an attack on any person or ministry in particular. It is not. It is a plea to the whole church regarding matters of principle, not personalities. And while I expect there will be widespread disagreement with much of what I say, I have tried to write without being disagreeable.

These are issues about which many people have deep convictions. When such matters are broached—particularly when contrary opinions are stated forthrightly—people sometimes become angry. I do not write in anger, and I would ask readers to receive what I write with the spirit in which it is offered.

My prayer is that this book will challenge your thinking in a way that will drive you to the Scriptures "to see whether these things [are] so" (cf Acts 17:11). And I pray that the Lord will deliver His church from the same kind of downhill slide into worldliness and unbelief that devoured the church and exhausted her spiritual stamina exactly a hundred years ago.

1

Christianity on the
Down-Grade

Doth that man love his Lord who would be willing to see Jesus wearing a crown of thorns, while for himself he craves a chaplet of laurel? Shall Jesus ascend to his throne by the cross, and do we expect to be carried there on the shoulders of applauding crowds? Be not so vain in your imagination. Count you the cost, and if you are not willing to bear Christ's cross, go away to your farm and to your merchandise, and make the most of them; only let me whisper this in your ear, "What shall it profit a man if he gain the whole world and lose his own soul?"

CHARLES HADDON SPURGEON[1]

IF YOU'RE familiar with the life of Charles Haddon Spurgeon, you have probably heard of "the Down-Grade Controversy." Spurgeon spent the final four years of his life at war against the trends of early modernism, which he rightly saw as a threat to biblical Christianity.

The name by which history remembers the controversy comes from the title of a series of articles Spurgeon published in his monthly magazine, *The Sword and the Trowel.* (See Appendix for an overview of the "Down-Grade" articles and a fuller account of the ensuing controversy.) Spurgeon wanted to admonish his flock about the dangers of moving away from the historic positions of biblical Christianity. Biblical truth is like the pinnacle of a steep, slippery mountain, Spurgeon suggested. One step away, and you find yourself on the down-grade. Once a church or indi-

---

[1]"Holding Fast the Faith," *The Metropolitan Tabernacle Pulpit*, Vol. 34 (London: Passmore and Alabaster, 1888), 78. This sermon was preached 5 February 1888, at the height of the Down-Grade Controversy, just after Spurgeon's censure by the Baptist Union (see Appendix).

vidual Christian gets on the down-grade, Spurgeon said, momentum takes over. Recovery is unusual and occurs only when Christians get on the "up-line" through spiritual revival.

In the controversy that transpired, Spurgeon resigned from the Baptist Union. Later, he was the subject of an official censure by the Union. Within a few years the Baptist Union was hopelessly lost to the new theology and Spurgeon was dead. In 1900, Spurgeon's wife, Susannah, wrote,

> So far as the Baptist Union was concerned, little was accomplished by Mr. Spurgeon's witness-bearing and withdrawal. . . . But, in other respects, I have had abundant proofs that the protest was not in vain. Many, who were far gone on the 'Down-grade,' were stopped in their perilous descent, and, by God's grace, were brought back to the 'Up-line'; others, who were unconsciously slipping, were made to stand firmly on the Rock; while, at least for a time, in all the churches, Evangelical doctrines were preached with a clearness and emphasis which had long been lacking.[2]

She believed the Lord would ultimately make clear how right her husband had been in his "protest against false doctrine and worldliness."[3]

To this day, church historians debate whether Spurgeon was right to withdraw from the Union. Many believe he should have stayed and fought to keep it orthodox. He considered that option, but concluded it would have been futile. I am inclined to believe Spurgeon was right to withdraw. But whether we agree with his course of action or not, we must acknowledge that history *has* vindicated Spurgeon's warnings about the down-grade. In the early part of the twentieth century, the spreading "false doctrine and worldliness"—theological liberalism and modernism—ravaged denominational Christianity throughout the world. Most of the mainline denominations were violently if not fatally altered by these influences. The result in Spurgeon's own England was particularly devastating. A hundred years after Spurgeon sounded the alarm, most theological education in England is rank liberal. Church attendance is a fraction of what it was then. Evangelicals are a tiny minority, true bib-

---

[2]*The Autobiography of Charles H. Spurgeon*, 4 vols. (London: Passmore and Alabaster, 1897), 4:255.
[3]*Ibid.*, 4:257.

lical preaching is uncommon even in supposedly Bible-believing churches, and the evangelical movement has been dangerously susceptible to almost every theological fad exported from America. In short, evangelicalism in England never recovered from the modernist/liberal assault that began a century ago.

A hundred years later, we are seeing history repeat itself. The evangelical church has become worldly—and not just worldly, but studiously so. Winds of doctrinal compromise are beginning to stir.

"False doctrine and worldliness"—the same two influences Spurgeon attacked—*always* go hand in hand, with worldliness leading the way. Christians today tend to forget that modernism was not first of all a theological agenda but a methodological one. Early modernists were not trying to hit at the core of biblical faith; they were simply trying to make Christianity more palatable to a cynical world.

The same spirit is rampant in the church today. I am convinced that most of those behind it would not deliberately undermine biblical Christianity. Nevertheless, they have introduced into the church a philosophy of pragmatism and a spirit of worldliness that, if left unchecked, will eventually reap the same bitter harvest as the modernism of a hundred years ago.

MARKET-DRIVEN MINISTRY?

The new philosophy is straightforward: The church is in competition against the world. And the world is very good at capturing people's attention and affections. The church, on the other hand, tends to be very poor at "selling" its product. Evangelism should therefore be viewed as a marketing challenge, and the church should market the gospel the way all modern businesses sell their products. That calls for some fundamental changes. The goal in all marketing is "to make both the producer and consumer satisfied,"[4] so anything that tends to leave the "consumer" unsatisfied must be jettisoned. Preaching—particularly preaching about sin, righteousness, and judgment—is too confrontive to be truly satisfying. The church must learn to couch the truth in ways that amuse and entertain.

One best-selling author has written, "I believe that developing a marketing orientation is precisely what the Church needs to do if we are to make a difference in the spiritual health of this nation for the remainder

---

[4]George Barna, *Marketing the Church* (Colorado Springs, Colo.: NavPress, 1988), 41.

of this century."[5] He adds, "My contention, based on careful study of data and the activities of American churches, is that the major problem plaguing the Church is its failure to embrace a marketing orientation in what has become a marketing-driven environment."[6]

That all may sound very modern, and very shrewd—but it is not biblical. And it has given the church a hard push onto the slippery slope. Marketing principles are becoming the arbiter of truth. Elements of the message that don't fit the promotional plan are simply omitted. Marketing savvy demands that the offense of the cross must be downplayed. Salesmanship requires that negative subjects like divine wrath be avoided. Consumer satisfaction means that the standard of righteousness cannot be raised too high. The seeds of a watered-down gospel are thus sown in the very philosophy that drives many ministries today.

And make no mistake, the new philosophy *is* altering the message the church conveys to the world, although many who propound these ideas think of themselves as loyal to biblical doctrine.

Christianity is on the down-grade again.

TOWARD A BIBLICAL PHILOSOPHY OF MINISTRY

How does market-driven ministry compare with the biblical model? How would Timothy have fared under Paul's tutelage if he had followed the advice of twentieth-century marketers?

We have a thorough answer to that question from the two epistles Paul wrote Timothy in the New Testament. Paul had personally mentored the young pastor, but Timothy encountered severe trials when he was assigned the task of leading the church at Ephesus out of sin and error. He struggled with fear and human weakness. He was evidently tempted to soften his preaching in the face of persecution. At times he seemed ashamed of the gospel. Paul had to remind him to stand up for the faith with boldness, even if it meant suffering: "Do not be ashamed of the testimony of our Lord, or of me His prisoner; but join with me in suffering for the gospel" (2 Tim. 1:8). The two rich epistles from Paul to Timothy outline a ministry philosophy that challenges the prevailing wisdom of today.

---

[5] *Ibid.*, 13.
[6] *Ibid.*, 23.

Paul instructed Timothy that he must:

- Correct those teaching false doctrine and call them to a pure heart, a good conscience, and a sincere faith (1 Tim. 1:3-5).

- Fight for divine truth and for God's purposes, keeping his own faith and a good conscience (1:18, 19).

- Pray for the lost and lead the men of the church to do the same (2:1-8).

- Call women in the church to fulfill their God-given role of submission and to raise up godly children, setting an example of faith, love, and sanctity with self-restraint (2:9-15).

- Carefully select spiritual leaders for the church on the basis of their giftedness, godliness, and virtue (3:1-13).

- Recognize the source of error and those who teach it, and point these things out to the rest of the church (4:1-6).

- Constantly be nourished on the words of Scripture and its sound teaching, avoiding all myths and false doctrines (4:6).

- Discipline himself for the purpose of godliness (4:7-11).

- Boldly command and teach the truth of God's Word (4:12).

- Be a model of spiritual virtue that all can follow (4:12).

- Faithfully read, explain, and apply the Scriptures publicly (4:13, 14).

- Be progressing toward Christlikeness in his own life (4:15, 16).

- Be gracious and gentle in confronting the sin of his people (5:1, 2).

- Give special consideration and care to those who are widows (5:3-16).

- Honor faithful church leaders who work hard (5:17-21).

- Choose church leaders with great care, seeing to it that they are both mature and proven (5:22).

- Take care of his physical condition so he is strong to serve (5:23).

- Teach and preach principles of true godliness, helping his people discern between true godliness and mere hypocrisy (5:24—6:6).

- Flee the love of money (6:7-11).

- Pursue righteousness, godliness, faith, love, perseverance, and gentleness (6:11).
- Fight for the faith against all enemies and all attacks (6:12).
- Keep all the Lord's commandments (6:13-16).
- Instruct the rich to do good, to be rich in good works, and to be generous (6:17-19).
- Guard the Word of God as a sacred trust and a treasure (6:20, 21).

In his second epistle, Paul reminded Timothy to:

- Keep the gift of God in him fresh and useful (2 Tim. 1:6).
- Not be timid but powerful (1:7).
- Never be ashamed of Christ or anyone who serves Christ (1:8-11).
- Hold tightly to the truth and guard it (1:12-14).
- Be strong in character (2:1).
- Be a teacher of apostolic truth so that he may reproduce himself in faithful men (2:2).
- Suffer difficulty and persecution willingly while making the maximum effort for Christ (2:3-7).
- Keep his eyes on Christ at all times (2:8-13).
- Lead with authority (2:14).
- Interpret and apply Scripture accurately (2:15).
- Avoid useless conversation that leads only to ungodliness (2:16).
- Be an instrument of honor, set apart from sin and useful to the Lord (2:20, 21).
- Flee youthful lusts and pursue righteousness, faith, and love (2:22).
- Refuse to be drawn into philosophical and theological wrangling (2:23).
- Not be an arguer but kind, teachable, gentle, and patient even when he is wronged (2:24-26).
- Face dangerous times with a deep knowledge of the Word of God (3:1-15).
- Understand that Scripture is the basis and content of all legitimate ministry (3:16, 17).

- Preach the Word—in season and out of season—reproving, rebuking, and exhorting with great patience and instruction (4:1, 2).

- Be sober in all things (4:5).

- Endure hardship (4:5).

- Do the work of an evangelist (4:5).

Nothing in that list hints at a market-driven philosophy. In fact, most of those commands are impossible to harmonize with the theories that are so popular today. To sum it all up in five categories, Paul commanded Timothy: 1) to be faithful in his preaching of biblical truth; 2) to be bold in exposing and refuting error; 3) to be an example of godliness to the flock; 4) to be diligent and work hard in the ministry; and 5) to be willing to suffer hardship and persecution in his service for the Lord.

Of course, the practical significance of this goes beyond those who are pastors. *Every* Christian is called to a life of ministry and is to follow the example of pastors (1 Tim. 4:11-12). So Paul's instructions to Timothy contain principles that apply to every believer in every form of ministry. When the church is on the down-grade, it means that multitudes of individuals are carried along on the spiritual decline. "False doctrine and worldliness" in the church infect every member of the body. Paul's instructions to Timothy are by no means meant only for the "elite" in Christian leadership or professional ministry. That is to say that ministry philosophy—and the issues we are addressing in this book—should be the concern of every Christian; these matters are by no means the exclusive domain of professional clergy.

Recently I spent some time reading a dozen or so of the latest books on ministry and church growth. Most of those books had long sections devoted to defining a philosophy of ministry. *Not one* of them referred to the instructions Paul outlined so carefully for Timothy. In fact, none of them drew any element of their ministry philosophy from the New Testament pastoral epistles! Most drew principles from modern business, marketing techniques, management theory, psychology, and other similar sources. Some tried to *illustrate* their principles using biblical anecdotes. But not one of them drew their philosophy from Scripture—although much of the New Testament was explicitly written to instruct churches and pastors in these matters!

MINISTERING IN AN AGE OF ITCHING EARS

Unfortunately, the market-driven ministry philosophy appeals to the very worst mood of our age. It caters to people whose first love is themselves and who care not for God—unless they can have Him without disrupting their selfish lifestyles. Promise such people a religion that will allow them to be comfortable in their materialism and self-love, and they will respond in droves.

Paul foresaw such a time. Near the end of his second epistle to Timothy, after outlining the principles we have listed above, Paul abridged his advice to Timothy in this well-known verse: "Preach the word; be ready in season and out of season; reprove, rebuke, exhort, with great patience and instruction" (2 Tim. 4:2). Then the apostle added this prophetic warning: "For the time will come when they will not endure sound doctrine; but wanting to have their ears tickled, they will accumulate for themselves teachers in accordance to their own desires; and will turn away their ears from the truth, and will turn aside to myths" (4:3, 4). The King James Version translates the passage like this: "After their own lusts shall they heap to themselves teachers, having itching ears; and they shall turn away their ears from the truth."

Clearly there was no room in Paul's philosophy of ministry for the give-people-what-they-want theory that is so prevalent today. He did not urge Timothy to conduct a survey to find out what his people wanted. He did not suggest that he study demographic data or do research on the "felt needs" of his people. He commanded him to preach the Word—faithfully, systematically, reprovingly, patiently—and let it confront the spirit of the age head-on.

HOW DO WE DEFINE SUCCESS?

Notice that Paul said nothing to Timothy about how people might respond. He did not lecture Timothy on how large his church was, how much money it took in, or how influential it was. He did not suggest that the world was supposed to revere, esteem, or even accept Timothy. In fact, Paul said nothing whatever about external success. Paul's emphasis was on *commitment*, not success.

Contemporary ministry philosophy is infatuated with worldly standards of success. The churches most often judged "successful" are the large, rich megachurches with multimillion-dollar facilities, spas, handball courts, day-care centers, and so on. But not one church in a thousand falls into that category. That means one of two things: most churches are piti-ful failures, or the gauge of success in ministry must be something besides material prosperity.

The answer is obvious to anyone who knows Scripture. External cri-teria such as affluence, numbers, money, or positive response have never been the biblical measure of success in ministry. Faithfulness, godliness, and spiritual commitment are the virtues God esteems—and such qual-ities should be the building blocks of any ministry philosophy. That is true in both small and large churches. Size does not signify God's bless-ing. And popularity is no barometer of success. In fact, it can be a reason for condemnation. God told Jeremiah, "An appalling and horrible thing has happened in the land: The prophets prophesy falsely, and the priests rule on their own authority; and My people love it so!" (Jer. 5:30, 31).

Look again at Paul's instructions to Timothy. Instead of urging Timothy to devise a ministry that would garner accolades from the world, he warned him about suffering and hardship—hardly the stuff of modern church-growth experts' aspirations! In Scripture external success is *never* a valid goal. Paul was not telling Timothy how to be "successful," he was encouraging him to pursue the divine standard.

That, of course, is what defines true success. Real success is not get-ting results at any cost. It is not prosperity, power, prominence, popular-ity, or any of the other worldly notions of success. Real success is doing the will of God regardless of the consequences.

Or, using the terms as the world often employs them, the appropri-ate goal is not success, but excellence.[7] Paul was encouraging Timothy to be all that God had called and gifted him to be. He was not advising Timothy to seek success; he was urging him to pursue excellence.

THE FOUNDATION OF AN EXCELLENT MINISTRY

Let's look a little more closely at these few verses from the beginning of 2 Timothy 4:

> I solemnly charge you in the presence of God and of Christ Jesus, who is to judge the living and the dead, and by His appearing and His king-dom: preach the word; be ready in season and out of season; reprove, rebuke, exhort, with great patience and instruction. For the time will

---

[7] A helpful contrast between *success* and *excellence* may be found in Jon Johnston, *Christian Excellence: Alternative to Success* (Grand Rapids, Mich.: Baker, 1985).

come when they will not endure sound doctrine; but wanting to have their ears tickled, they will accumulate for themselves teachers in accordance to their own desires; and will turn away their ears from the truth, and will turn aside to myths. But you, be sober in all things, endure hardship, do the work of an evangelist, fulfill your ministry (vv. 1-5).

That brief passage defines biblical ministry. It includes nine reminders from Paul to Timothy that no minister dare disregard. Those who are derelict in these duties are on the down-grade, whether they realize it or not.

REMEMBER YOUR CALLING

"I solemnly charge you in the presence of God and of Christ Jesus, who is to judge the living and the dead, and by His appearing and His Kingdom"—thus Paul begins this final section of the last inspired epistle he ever wrote. He was a prisoner, near the end of his own life, anticipating his own execution (v. 16). He knew he would soon stand before God to give an account. These thoughts were heavy on his mind. And so he reminded Timothy of the seriousness of the young pastor's own commission.

He counseled Timothy to live and work in light of impending judgment. Timothy needed to concern himself with what *God* thought of his ministry, not what *people* thought. Notice that Paul invoked "the *presence* of God and of Christ Jesus, who is to judge the living and the dead." He wanted Timothy to understand that the One who would judge him is the One in whose presence he was then ministering. God judges by His own criteria, not by what people think.

Elsewhere Paul says, "We shall all stand before the judgment seat of God. . . . So then each one of us shall give account of himself to God" (Rom. 14:10, 12). That is the point he wants to make with Timothy. He must not be ministering to please men, but to please God.

PREACH THE WORD

What kind of ministry pleases God? "Preach the Word" (v. 2). Obedience to that simple command *must* be the centerpiece of every truly biblical ministry philosophy. The preacher's task is to proclaim Scripture and give the sense of it (cf Neh. 8:8). All other content is extraneous.

My father is a pastor, and when I first told him years ago that I believed God had called me to a life of ministry, he gave me a Bible in which he had written, "Dear Johnny, preach the Word. 2 Timothy 4:2." That simple statement became the compelling stimulus in my heart. I have never forgotten that simple biblical instruction from my dad—preach the Word. What else is there to preach?

Preaching the Word is not always easy. The message we are required to proclaim is often offensive. Christ Himself is a stone of stumbling and a rock of offense (Rom. 9:33; 1 Peter 2:8). The message of the cross is a stumbling block to some (1 Cor. 1:23; Gal. 5:11), mere foolishness to others (1 Cor. 1:23). "[The] natural man does not accept the things of the Spirit of God; for they are foolishness to him, and he cannot understand them, because they are spiritually appraised" (1 Cor. 2:14). Why do you suppose Paul wrote, "I am not ashamed of the gospel" (Rom. 1:16)? Surely it is because so many Christians *are* ashamed of the very message we are commanded to proclaim.

As we have noted, Timothy evidently struggled with the temptation to be ashamed. Paul admonished him not to be "ashamed of the testimony of our Lord" or ashamed of Paul (2 Tim. 1:8). Timothy seems to have become a timid soul, exhibiting "a spirit of timidity," not at all like the strong and courageous apostle Paul. He was young, and some people demeaned him because of that (1 Tim. 4:12). He knew full well that even being associated with Paul was dangerous. Publicly proclaiming God's truth could land him in prison with Paul. At the very least, he was sure to incur hostility and debates from Jews who were antagonistic to the Gospel.

What is more, Timothy apparently struggled with the impulses of youthful lust (2:22). He may have felt he was not all he should be.

Those were some compelling reasons for Timothy to silence his proclamation. So when Paul commanded him to preach, he was demanding that he go against his own inclinations and inhibitions.

What was the Word that Timothy was to preach? Paul had made this clear at the end of chapter 3: "*All Scripture* is inspired by God and profitable for teaching, for reproof, for correction, for training in righteousness" (2 Tim. 3:16, emphasis added). This is the Word to be preached: the whole counsel of God (cf Acts 20:27). In chapter 1 Paul had told Timothy, "Retain the standard of sound words which you have heard from me" (v. 13). He was speaking of the revealed words of Scripture—all of it. He urged Timothy to "Guard . . . the treasure which has been entrusted to you" (v. 14). Then in chapter 2 he told him to study the Word and handle it accurately (2:15). Now he is telling him to proclaim it. So the entire task of the faithful minister revolves around the Word of God—guarding it, studying it, and proclaiming it.

In Colossians 1 the apostle Paul, describing his own ministry philosophy, writes, "Of this church I was made a minister according to the stewardship from God bestowed on me for your benefit, *that I might fully carry out the preaching of the word of God*" (v. 25, emphasis added). In 1 Corinthians he goes a step further: "When I came to you, brethren, I did not come with superiority of speech or of wisdom, proclaiming to you the testimony of God. For I determined to know nothing among you except Jesus Christ, and Him crucified" (1 Cor. 2:1, 2). In other words, his goal as a preacher was not to entertain people with his rhetorical style, or to amuse them with cleverness, humor, novel insights, or sophisticated methodology—he simply preached Christ crucified.

There have always been those in the pulpit who gathered crowds because they are gifted orators, interesting storytellers, entertaining speakers, dynamic personalities, shrewd crowd-manipulators, rousing speech-makers, popular politicians, or erudite scholars. Such preaching may be *popular*, but it is not necessarily *powerful*. No one can preach with supernatural power who does not preach the Word. And no faithful preacher will water down or neglect the whole counsel of God. Proclaiming the Word—all of it—is the pastor's calling.

And so preaching the Word *must* be the very heart of our ministry philosophy. Any other philosophy replaces the voice of God with human wisdom. Philosophy, politics, humor, psychology, homespun advice, and human opinion can never accomplish what the Word of God does. Those things may be interesting, informative, entertaining, and sometimes even helpful—but they are not spiritually transforming, and they are not the business of the church. The preacher's task is not to be a conduit for human wisdom; he is God's voice to speak to the congregation. No human message comes with the stamp of divine authority—only the Word of God. I frankly do not understand preachers who are willing to abdicate this solemn privilege. Moral lectures and motivational talks are no substitute for God's Word. Why should we proclaim the wisdom of men when we have the privilege of preaching the Word of God?

BE FAITHFUL IN AND OUT OF SEASON

Paul next reminds Timothy that this duty is a never-ending task. Not only is he to preach the Word, he is to do it regardless of the climate of opinion around him. He is to be faithful when such preaching is tolerated—but also when it is not.

Let's face it—right now preaching the Word is out of season. Humanity is experiencing God's wrath as He gives people over to the consequences of sinful choices (Rom. 1:24, 26, 28), "the due penalty of their error." Society may be feeling this divine abandonment in our age more than ever before. And the decline of preaching in the church can actually contribute to people's sense of helplessness. Martyn Lloyd-Jones argued that "in many ways it is the departure of the Church from preaching that is responsible in a large measure for the state of modern society.... The Church, having abandoned her real task, has left humanity more or less to its own devices."[8]

This is certainly no time for weak men, weak messages, and weak ministries. What is needed is moral strength and courage, and uncompromising proclamation of the truth that can set people free. "So far from saying that we must have less preaching and turn more and more to other devices and expedients, I say that we have a heaven-sent opportunity for preaching."[9]

But the market-driven philosophy currently in vogue says that plainly declaring biblical truth is outmoded. Biblical exposition and theology are seen as antiquated and irrelevant. "Churchgoers don't want to be preached to anymore," this philosophy says. "The baby-boom generation won't just sit in the pew while someone up front preaches. They are products of a media-driven generation, and they need a church experience that will satisfy them on their own terms."

But Paul says the excellent minister must be faithful to preach the Word even when it is not in fashion. The expression he uses is, "be ready." The Greek term (*ephistēmi*) literally means "to stand beside." It has the idea of eagerness. It was often used to describe a military guard, always at his post, prepared for duty. Paul was speaking of an explosive eagerness to preach, like that of Jeremiah, who said that the Word of God was a fire in his bones. That's what he was demanding of Timothy. Not reluctance but readiness. Not hesitation but fearlessness. No cool talk but the fire of the Word of God.

REPROVE, REBUKE, AND EXHORT

Paul also gives Timothy instructions about the *tone* of his preaching. He uses two words that carry negative connotations and one that is positive:

---

[8] *Preaching and Preachers* (Grand Rapids: Zondervan, 1971), 35.
[9] *Ibid.*, 42.

reprove, rebuke, and exhort (2 Tim. 4:2). All valid ministry must have a balance of positive *and* negative. The preacher who fails to reprove and rebuke is not fulfilling his commission.

I recently listened to a radio interview with a preacher who assiduously avoids any mention of sin in his preaching because he feels people are burdened with too much guilt anyway. The interviewer asked how he could justify such a policy. The pastor replied that he had made the decision to focus on meeting people's needs, not attacking their sin.

But people's deepest need is to confess and overcome their sin. So preaching that fails to confront and correct sin through the Word of God does *not* meet people's need. It may make them feel good. And they may respond enthusiastically to the preacher, but that does not mean such preaching meets real needs.

To reprove, rebuke, and exhort is to preach the Word, for those are the very same ministries Scripture accomplishes: "All Scripture is inspired by God and profitable for teaching, for reproof, for correction, for training in righteousness" (2 Tim. 3:16). Notice the same balance of positive and negative tone. Reproof and correction are negative; teaching and training are positive.

The positive tone is crucial, too. The word "exhort" (*parakaleō*) means "encourage." The excellent preacher confronts sin and then encourages repentant sinners to behave righteously. He is to do this "with great patience and instruction" (4:2). In 1 Thessalonians 2:11, Paul talks about "exhorting and encouraging and imploring . . . as a father would his own children." This often requires great patience and much instruction. But the excellent minister cannot neglect these aspects of his calling.

DON'T COMPROMISE IN DIFFICULT TIMES

There is an urgency in Paul's charge to young Timothy: "For the time will come when they will not endure sound doctrine; but wanting to have their ears tickled, they will accumulate for themselves teachers in accordance to their own desires" (2 Tim. 4:3). That is a prophecy reminiscent of those found in 2 Timothy 3:1 ("Realize this, that in the last days difficult times will come") and 1 Timothy 4:1 ("The Spirit explicitly says that in later times some will fall away from the faith.") This, then, is Paul's third prophetic warning to Timothy about the difficult times to come. Note the progression: The first one said that the time would come when people would depart from the faith. The second one warned Timothy that dangerous times were coming for the church. Now the third one suggests that the time would come when those *in the church* would not endure sound doctrine, but desire instead to have their ears tickled.

Fearless preaching is all the more necessary in such dangerous times. When people will not tolerate the truth, that's when courageous, outspoken preachers are most desperately needed to speak it.

Why are people unwilling to endure sound teaching? It is because they love sin. Sound preaching, as we have seen, confronts and rebukes sin, and people in love with sinful lifestyles will not tolerate such teaching. They want to have their ears tickled (v. 3).

Paul employs the expression "sound teaching" in 1 Timothy 1 as well. In verses 9 and 10 of that chapter, he speaks of "those who are lawless and rebellious, for the ungodly and sinners, for the unholy and profane, for those who kill their fathers or mothers, for murderers and immoral men and homosexuals and kidnappers and liars and perjurers, *and whatever else is contrary to sound teaching*" (emphasis added). A society filled with and influenced by liars, perjurers, murderers, and homosexuals is by no means tolerant of sound teaching.

Note that Paul does *not* suggest that the way to reach such a society is to soften the message so that such people will be comfortable with it. Just the opposite is true. Such ear-tickling is abominable. Paul urges Timothy to be willing to suffer for the truth's sake, and keep preaching the Word faithfully. That's the only way intolerant people can be exposed to the truth, which alone can soften their hearts.

Incidentally, the interpretive question raised by this passage hinges on the word "they" in verse 3. To whom does the word refer? To the world? Or to the church? Surely it includes the world—unregenerate people seldom are willing to tolerate sound teaching. But here Paul is speaking of people to whom Timothy preaches. This seems to refer to people in the church. It suggests that a time would come when professing Christians in Ephesus would not stand for sound preaching.

But isn't that also the state of the church in our society today? In fact, it is precisely what marketing experts are pointing out to church leaders. The whole basis of their philosophy is that people don't want to hear the truth proclaimed; they want to be entertained. The marketing plan says, give them what they want. Scripture says otherwise.

There are thousands of supposedly evangelical churches worldwide that cannot stomach sound doctrine. They would not tolerate for two weeks strong biblical teaching that refutes their doctrinal error, confronts their sin, convicts them, and calls them to obey the truth. They don't want to hear healthy teaching. Why? Because people in the church want to own God without giving up sinful lifestyles, and they will not endure someone telling them what God's Word says about it.

What *do* they want to hear? "Wanting to have their ears tickled, they will accumulate for themselves teachers in accordance to their own desires" (v. 3). Ironically, they seek out *teachers*. In fact, they *heap to themselves* teachers—but not sound ones. They choose the teachers who tell them what they want to hear. They want what tickles their ears and feeds their lusts. They want what makes them feel good about themselves. Preachers who offend them, they reject. They accumulate a mass of teachers who feed their insatiable, selfish appetites. And the preacher who brings the message they most need to hear is the one they least like to hear.

Unfortunately, preachers with ear-tickling messages are all too abundantly available. "In periods of unsettled faith, scepticism, and mere curious speculation in matters of religion, teachers of all kinds swarm like the flies in Egypt. The demand creates the supply. The hearers invite and shape their own preachers. If the people desire a calf to worship, a ministerial calf-maker is readily found."[10]

This appetite for ear-tickling preaching has a terrible end. Verse 4 says these people will ultimately "turn away their ears from the truth and will be turned aside to myths." They become the victims of their own refusal to hear the truth. The phrase "they will turn away" is in the active voice. The people willfully choose this action. "Will be turned aside to myths" is in the passive voice. It describes what happens to them. Having turned from the truth, they become victims of deception. As soon as they turn away from the truth, they become pawns of Satan. The absence of light is darkness.

This is happening in the church today. Evangelicalism has lost its tolerance for confrontive preaching. Now the church is flirting with serious doctrinal error. Christians madly pursue extrabiblical revelation in the form of prophecies and dreams. Preachers deny or ignore the reality of hell. The modern gospel promises heaven apart from holiness. Churches ignore the biblical teaching on women's roles, homosexuality, and other politically-charged issues. The human medium has overtaken the divine

---

[10]Marvin R. Vincent, *Word Studies in the New Testament*, 4 vols. (New York: Scribner's, 1900), 4: 321.

message. This is evidence of serious doctrinal compromise. If the church does not repent and return to the up-line (as Spurgeon would say), these errors and others like them will become epidemic.

Look again at the key phrase in verse 3: "wanting to have their ears tickled." Why won't they endure sound doctrine? Why do they heap to themselves teachers? Why do they turn away from the truth? Because down deep inside they simply want to have their ears tickled. They don't want to be confronted. They don't want to be convicted. They want to be entertained. They want preaching that produces pleasant sensations. They want to feel good. They want their ears tickled with anecdotes, humor, psychology, motivational lectures, reassurance, positive thinking, self-congratulation, ego-massaging sermonettes, and agreeable small talk. Biblical reproof, rebuke, and exhortation are unacceptable.

But the truth of God does not tickle our ears; it boxes them. It burns them. It *first* reproves, rebukes, convicts—*then* exhorts and encourages. Preachers of the Word must be careful to maintain that balance.

In John 6, after Jesus had delivered a particularly hard message, Scripture tells us, "As a result of this many of His disciples withdrew, and were not walking with Him anymore" (v. 66). As the crowds left, our Lord turned to His disciples and asked, "You do not want to go away also, do you?" (v. 67). Peter's reply on behalf of the Twelve is significant: "Lord, to whom shall we go? You have words of eternal life" (v. 68). That was the right response. It revealed the difference between true disciples and hangers-on: their hunger for *the Word*. Jesus said, "If ye continue in my word, then are ye my disciples indeed" (John 8:31, KJV). People seeking to be entertained or fed, curiosity-seekers, and people who just follow the crowd are by no means true disciples. It is those who love the Word that are true followers of Christ. They will not desire preachers who tickle their ears.

BE SOBER IN ALL THINGS

The attitude of the excellent minister must be one of thoughtful sobriety. "Be sober in all things" (v. 5) is not merely a warning against drunkenness. Nor is Paul suggesting that Timothy should be somber, joyless, gloomy, morose. *Sober* means self-controlled, steady, attentive. It describes a state of mental alertness and control of one's faculties.

The excellent minister is a solid person, a stable person, like an athlete who has brought all his passions and appetites and nerves under complete control to perform at a maximum level. To put it in the negative, a preacher is not to be flaky, not to be trendy, not to be a pursuer of whims. In the face of a changing world, in the midst of a vacillating church, in the context of a rocking and reeling society, ministers had better be rooted, steadfast, stable, rock-solid. We cannot compromise when the pressure is on.

The church has had enough erratic, trendy, whimsical preachers whose style depends on the mood of the mob. What is most needed now are those who remain totally steadfast in an unstable world, and who know their priorities. We need ministers whose heads are clear of deceit, false teaching, and unorthodox notions. We need preachers who will courageously declare the whole counsel of God. How wearisome it must be to God to hear His inspired Word replaced by insipid, innocuous pablum dribbled out of pulpits!

The noble preacher is balanced, consistent, solid. He is unmoved by the cries of those who beg to have their ears tickled.

ENDURE HARDSHIP

Obviously, excellent ministers cannot be those who yearn for earthly applause. Neither can they be lovers of earthly comfort. The life of ministry is not a life of leisure. Timothy needed to be willing to endure hardship (v. 5). He could not have the kind of ministry God desired of him unless he was willing to go through some suffering.

No ministry of any value comes without pain. I often encounter young men headed for ministry who are looking for a church without problems, a ministry without challenges, a congregation that will make life easy. There is no such place for the faithful preacher of the Word. The notion that ministry can be both effective and painless is a lie. You *will* encounter hardship if you preach the unadulterated Word. And when adversity strikes, you have two choices. You can endure and remain steadfast, or you can compromise. The faithful minister holds the line for the truth. You cannot do that and escape suffering. "Indeed, all who desire to live godly in Christ Jesus will be persecuted" (2 Tim. 3:12). Thus faithfulness and hardship go hand in hand.

This is a repeated theme in 2 Timothy. In 2:1, 3, Paul wrote, "You therefore, my son, be strong in the grace that is in Christ Jesus. . . . Suffer hardship with me, as a good soldier of Christ Jesus." Now he reminds Timothy again that suffering is as much a part of the faithful minister's duty as any other aspect of the work.

Did Timothy follow Paul's counsel? Evidently he did. Hebrews

13:23, an obscure little verse, says, "Take notice that our brother Timothy has been released, with whom, if he comes soon, I shall see you." The writer of Hebrews obviously knew Timothy well and loved him. He tells the Hebrews that Timothy had been "released." Released from what? The Greek word used there suggests that Timothy had been released from prison. We can assume that when the suffering came, Timothy endured it. He did not compromise. He remained faithful, even though it evidently meant imprisonment. He did not try to find a cheap way out.

DO THE WORK OF AN EVANGELIST

At first sight it might seem that the command to "do the work of an evangelist" is an abrupt change of direction. But it is not. Paul was encouraging Timothy to reach out beyond the comfort level of his own flock and boldly proclaim the Word to unbelievers. Paul was not suggesting that Timothy's *office* was that of an evangelist. He was telling him that part of his duty as a pastor was to evangelize unbelievers.

Again, Paul was commanding Timothy to declare the truth boldly. Timothy may have been tempted to seek a haven in the comfort of the flock. Paul was urging him to minister instead on the front line. He wanted Timothy to face the world courageously and preach Christ crucified. He wanted him to proclaim sin, righteousness, judgment, and God's law. He wanted him to declare the depravity, not the dignity, of humankind. He wanted him to herald the Second Coming and warn of eternal judgment. He wanted him to magnify the cross, the resurrection, the atonement, grace, and faith. He was urging Timothy to be solemn and persuasive in confronting unbelief.

FULFILL YOUR MINISTRY

Paul's brief charge to Timothy ends with a final imperative: "Fulfill your ministry" (v. 5). "Fulfill" means accomplish, fill it up, do it all. He might have said, "Don't serve God halfheartedly; do it with all your might." Paul was coming to the end of his own life, and he was able to say, "I am already being poured out as a drink offering, and the time of my departure has come. I have fought the good fight, I have finished the course, I have kept the faith; in the future there is laid up for me the crown of righteousness, which the Lord, the righteous Judge, will award to me on that day; and not only to me, but also to all who have loved His appearing" (4:6-8). He wanted Timothy to reach the same point someday.

Remember, this charge from Paul to Timothy has implications for every Christian. We are all to be ministers in some sphere of service. Whether you are a mother ministering to her own children, or pastor of a huge congregation, these principles apply to you. There is no room for compromise. There is no place for timidity. There is no time for delay. There is no need for fear. Fill up your service to the Lord; accomplish it all. That is possible only if the ministry is done right.

HOLDING FAST THE FAITH

At the height of the Down-Grade Controversy, two weeks after he was censured by the Baptist Union, Charles Spurgeon preached a message entitled "Holding Fast the Faith," in which he said,

> We must never hide our colours. There are times when we must dash to the front and court the encounter, when we see that our Captain's honour demands it. Let us never be either ashamed or afraid. Our Lord Jesus deserves that we should yield ourselves as willing sacrifices in defence of his faith. Ease, reputation, life itself, must go for the name and faith of Jesus. If in the heat of the battle our good name or our life must be risked to win the victory, then let us say, "In this battle some of us must fall; why should not I? I will take part and lot with my Master, and bear reproach for his sake." Only brave soldiers are worthy of our great Lord. Those who sneak into the rear, that they may be comfortable, are not worthy of the kingdom. . . .
>
> Brethren, we must be willing to bear ridicule for Christ's sake, even that peculiarly envenomed ridicule which "the cultured" are so apt to pour upon us. We must be willing to be thought great fools for Jesus' sake. . . . For my part, I am willing to be ten thousand fools in one for my dear Lord and Master, and count it to be the highest honour that can be put upon me to be stripped of every honour, and loaded with every censure for the sake of the grand old truth which is written on my very heart. . . .
>
> Before I could quit my faith . . . I should have to be ground to powder, and every separate atom transformed.[11]

Spurgeon closed with these words:

---

[11]"Holding Fast the Faith," 78, 83.

Everybody admires Luther! Yes, yes; but you do not want any one else to do the same to-day. When you go to the Zoological Gardens you all admire the bear; but how would you like a bear at home, or a bear wandering loose about the street? You tell me that it would be unbearable, and no doubt you are right.

So, we admire a man who was firm in the faith, say four hundred years ago; the past ages are a sort of bear-pit or iron cage for him; but such a man to-day is a nuisance, and must be put down. Call him a narrow-minded bigot, or give him a worse name if you can think of one. Yet imagine that in those ages past, Luther, Zwingle, Calvin, and their compeers had said, "The world is out of order; but if we try to set it right we shall only make a great row, and get ourselves into disgrace. Let us go to our chambers, put on our night-caps, and sleep over the bad times, and perhaps when we wake up things will have grown better."

Such conduct on their part would have entailed upon us a heritage of error. Age after age would have gone down into the infernal deeps, and the pestiferous bogs of error would have swallowed all. These men loved the faith and the name of Jesus too well to see them trampled on. Note what we owe them, and let us pay to our sons the debt we owe our fathers.

It is to-day as it was in the Reformers' days. Decision is needed. Here is the day for the man, where is the man for the day? We who have had the gospel passed to us by martyr hands dare not trifle with it, nor sit by and hear it denied by traitors, who pretend to love it, but inwardly abhor every line of it. The faith I hold bears upon it marks of the blood of my ancestors. Shall I deny their faith, for which they left their native land to sojourn here? Shall we cast away the treasure which was handed to us through the bars of prisons, or came to us charred with the flames of Smithfield?

Personally, when my bones have been tortured with rheumatism, I have remembered Job Spurgeon, doubtless of my own stock, who in Chelmsford Jail was allowed a chair, because he could not lie down by reason of rheumatic pain. That Quaker's broad-brim overshadows my brow. Perhaps I inherit his rheumatism; but that I do not regret if I have his stubborn faith, which will not let me yield a syllable of the truth of God.

When I think of how others have suffered for the faith, a little scorn or unkindness seems a mere trifle, not worthy of mention. An ancestry of lovers of the faith ought to be a great plea with us to abide by the Lord God of our fathers, and the faith in which they lived. As for me, I must hold the old gospel: I can do no other. God helping me, I will endure the consequences of what men think obstinacy.

Look you, sirs, *there are ages yet to come.* If the Lord does not speedily appear, there will come another generation, and another, and all these generations will be tainted and injured if we are not faithful to God and to his truth to-day. We have come to a turning-point in the road. If we turn to the right, mayhap our children and our children's children will go that way; but if we turn to the left, generations yet unborn will curse our names for having been unfaithful to God and to his Word. I charge you, not only by your ancestry, but by your posterity, that you seek to win the commendation of your Master, that though you dwell where Satan's seat is, you yet hold fast his name, and do not deny his faith. God grant us faithfulness, for the sake of the souls around us! How is the world to be saved if the church is false to her Lord? How are we to lift the masses if our fulcrum is removed? If our gospel is uncertain, what remains but increasing misery and despair? Stand fast, my beloved, in the name of God! I, your brother in Christ, entreat You to abide in the truth. Quit yourselves like men, be strong. The Lord sustain you for Jesus' sake. Amen.[12]

Spurgeon did his part. He passed the baton to another generation, and they passed it to another. They finished their course having kept the faith, and now it is our turn. Will we keep the faith? Will we fulfill our ministry? Are we willing to suffer hardship for being faithful? Are we committed to a biblical ministry of preaching the Word without shame?

We who love the Lord and His church must not sit by while the church gains momentum on the down-grade of worldliness and compromise. Men and women before us have paid with their blood to deliver the faith intact to us. Now it is our turn to guard the truth. It is a task that calls for courage, not compromise. And it is a responsibility that demands unwavering devotion to a very narrow purpose.

In the same sermon I have been quoting from, Spurgeon included this reminder:

Dear friends, this name, this faith, these are our *message.* Our only business here below is to cry, "Behold the Lamb." Are any of you sent of God with any other message? It cannot be. The one message which God has given to his people to proclaim is salvation through the

---

[12]*Ibid.,* 83-84.

Lamb—salvation by the blood of Jesus. . . . To tell of Jesus is our occupation, we have nothing to say which is not comprised in the revelation made to us by God in Jesus Christ. He who is our comfort is our one theme.[13]

That echoes Paul's words to Timothy: "Preach the Word." We have nothing else worth saying. There is no other message. There is no other valid ministry. Until the church recovers the centrality of that truth and that single-minded commitment to our calling, evangelicalism will continue to be pulled relentlessly further into the down-grade.

---

[13]*Ibid.*, 81.

2

The User-Friendly Church?

At a certain meeting of ministers and church officers, one after another doubted the value of prayer-meetings; all confessed that they had a very small attendance, and several acknowledged without the slightest compunction that they had quite given them up. What means this? Are churches in a right condition when they have only one meeting for prayer in a week, and that a mere skeleton?

CHARLES HADDON SPURGEON[1]

THE CONTEMPORARY church is undergoing a revolution in worship styles unprecedented since the Protestant Reformation. Ministry has married marketing philosophy, and this is the monstrous offspring. It is a studied effort to change the way the world perceives the church. Church ministry is being completely revamped in an attempt to make it more appealing to unbelievers.

The experts are now telling us that pastors and church leaders who want to be successful must concentrate their energies in this new direction. Provide non-Christians with an agreeable, inoffensive environment. Give them freedom, tolerance, and anonymity. Always be positive and benevolent. If you must have a sermon, keep it brief and amusing. Don't be preachy or authoritative. Above all, keep everyone entertained. Churches following this pattern will see numerical growth, we're assured; those that ignore it are doomed to decline.

The kinds of innovation being tried are extraordinary, even radical. For example, some churches now offer their largest services on Friday or

---

[1]"Another Word Concerning the Down-Grade," *The Sword and the Trowel* (August 1887), 397-98.

Saturday night instead of Sunday morning. These services are usually heavy on music and entertainment, offering people an alternative to the theater or social circuit. Church members can now "get church out of the way" early, then have the rest of the weekend to use as they wish. One Saturday churchgoer explained why these alternative services are so important: "If you go to Sunday school at 9:00 A.M., then to the 11 A.M. service and leave about 1 P.M., your day is pretty well shot."[2]

Judging from attendance figures, *lots* of church members feel spending the Lord's Day in church is tantamount to blowing the whole day. Non-Sunday alternative services in some churches are more heavily attended than traditional Sunday worship services.

That's not all. Many of these services offer no preaching whatsoever. Instead they rely on music, skits, multimedia, and other means of communication to convey the message. "This is the generation that grew up on television," one pastor told *Time* magazine. "You have to present religion to them in a creative and visual way." Some churches are taking that philosophy a step further, cutting out preaching on Sunday morning as well.

Even the music and skits are carefully chosen to try to make unbelievers comfortable. Almost nothing is dismissed as inappropriate: rock 'n' roll oldies, disco tunes, heavy metal, rap, dancing, comedy, clowns, mime artists, and stage magic have all become part of the evangelical repertoire. In fact, one of the few things judged out of place in church these days is clear and forceful preaching.

The whole point is to make the church "user-friendly." That is a term borrowed from the computer industry. It was first employed to describe software and hardware that is easy for the novice to operate. Applied to the church, it usually describes a ministry that is benign and utterly non-challenging. In practice, it has become an excuse for importing worldly amusements into the church in an attempt to try to attract non-Christian "seekers" or "unchurched Harrys" by appealing to their fleshly interests. The obvious fallout of this preoccupation with the unchurched is a corresponding deemphasis on those who are the true church. The spiritual needs of believers are often neglected to the hurt of the body.

---

[2]Cited in John Dart, "Protestant Churches Join the Fold, Fill Pews with Saturday Services," *Los Angeles Times* (15 September 1991), B3.

POUNDING THE PULPIT?

Not that preaching has been entirely abandoned. Some of the user-friendly churches offer at least one service a week (often a midweek service) where a spoken message is the centerpiece. But even in those meetings the style is frequently psychological and motivational rather than biblical. Above all, the emphasis is on user-friendliness. I recently read through a stack of newspaper and magazine articles about the user-friendly phenomenon, and a common thread began to emerge. Here are some quotations from clippings describing the preaching in user-friendly churches:

- "There is no fire and brimstone here. No Bible-thumping. Just practical, witty messages."

- "Services at [the church featured in the article] have an informal feeling. You won't hear people threatened with hell or referred to as sinners. The goal is to make them feel welcome, not drive them away."

- "As with all clergymen [this pastor's] answer is God—but he slips Him in at the end, and even then doesn't get heavy. No ranting, no raving. No fire, no brimstone. He doesn't even use the H-word. Call it Light Gospel. It has the same salvation as the Old Time Religion, but with a third less guilt."

- "The sermons are relevant, upbeat, and best of all, short. You won't hear a lot of preaching about sin and damnation and hell fire. Preaching here doesn't sound like *preaching*. It is sophisticated, urbane, and friendly talk. It breaks all the stereotypes."

- "[The pastor] is preaching a very upbeat message. . . . It's a salvationist message, but the idea is not so much being saved from the fires of hell. Rather, it's being saved from meaninglessness and aimlessness in this life. It's more of a soft-sell."

- "The idea, [the pastor] says, is to get people through the front doors, then disprove the stereotype of the sweating, loosened necktied, Bible-thumping preacher who yells and screams about burning in hell for eternity."

So the new rules may be summed up as follows: Be clever, informal, positive, brief, and friendly. Never loosen your necktie. Never let them see you sweat. And never, never use the H-word.

Most of the above quotations represent what outside observers have said about user-friendly churches, not how they portray their own ministries. Many of them would vehemently deny that they downplay or deny any point of evangelical doctrine. In fact, George Barna's bestselling book *User-Friendly Churches* includes this disclaimer twice: "None of the successful churches described in this book is interested in being user friendly in the sense of compromising the gospel or the historic faith of the church just to make friends with the age."[3]

But in fact the truth of Scripture is being compromised if it is decentralized and if in order to forge a friendship with the world hard truths are avoided, vapid amusements are set in place of sound teaching, and semantic gymnastics are employed to avoid mention of the difficult truths of Scripture. If the design is to make the seeker comfortable, isn't that rather incompatible with the biblical teaching on sin, judgment, hell, and several other important topics? So the biblical message is inevitably distorted by the philosophy. And what about the believer who should be fed?

Please understand, I'm not suggesting preachers *ought* to be sweaty, unkempt ranters and ravers who scream, yell, pound the pulpit, and thump the Bible. But let's face it, except in very narrow, hyper-fundamentalist sects, such preachers are hardly in abundance these days. The imagery of the Bible-thumper has become an easy stereotype that is often used against those who simply believe straightforward proclamation of truth is more important than making "unchurched Harry" comfortable.

The weakness of the pulpit today does not stem from frantic cranks who harangue about hell; it is the result of men who compromise and who fear to speak God's Word powerfully, with conviction. The church is certainly not suffering from an overabundance of forthright preachers; rather, it seems glutted with men-pleasers (cf Gal. 1:10).

THE CUSTOMER IS SOVEREIGN

At the heart of the market-driven, user-friendly church is the goal of giving people what they want. Advocates of the philosophy are quite candid about this. I noted in Chapter 1 that consumer satisfaction is the stated goal of the new philosophy. One key resource on market-driven ministry says, "This is what marketing the church is all about: providing our product (relationships) as a solution to people's felt need."[4]

"Felt needs" thus determine the road map for the modern church

---

[3](Ventura, Calif.: Regal, 1991), 1, 15-16.
[4]George Barna, *Marketing the Church* (Colorado Springs, Colo.: NavPress, 1988), 51.

marketing plan. The idea is a basic selling principle: you satisfy an existing desire rather than trying to persuade people to buy something they don't want.

Accurately assessing people's felt needs is therefore one of the keys to modern church-growth theory. Church leaders are advised to poll potential "customers" and find out what they are looking for in a church—then offer that. Demographic information, community surveys, door-to-door polls, and congregational questionnaires are the new tools. Information drawn from such sources is considered *essential* to building a workable marketing plan. Ministers today are told they cannot reach people effectively without it.

Worst of all, it seems people's emotional "felt needs" are taken more seriously than the real but unfelt spiritual deficiencies Scripture addresses. "Felt needs" include issues like loneliness, fear of failure, "codependency," a poor self-image, depression, anger, resentment, and similar inward-focused inadequacies. Some of these are real, and some are fabricated by the psychological sales pitch. These problems, we are told, are behind drug addiction, sex addiction, and several dozen other syndromes. The *real* problem—the root of all such troubles—is human depravity, an issue that is carefully skirted (though seldom overtly denied) in the teaching of the typical user-friendly church.

No longer are pastors trained to declare to people what God demands of them. Instead, they are counseled to find out what the people's demands are, then do whatever is necessary to meet them. The audience is regarded as "sovereign," and the wise preacher will "shape his communications according to their needs in order to receive the response he [seeks]."[5]

The effect of such a philosophy is apparent; more and more people-pleasers fill the pulpits of our churches. Moreover, Scripture is overruled by the marketing plan as the authoritative guide for ministry. One textbook on church marketing includes this statement: "The marketing plan is the Bible of the marketing game; everything that happens in the life of the product occurs because the plan wills it."[6] Applied to church ministry, that means a human strategy—not the Word of God—becomes the fountain of all church activity, and the standard by which ministry is measured.

---

[5] *Ibid.*, 33.
[6] *Ibid.*, 45.

That approach to ministry is so obviously convoluted and so grossly unbiblical that I am amazed so many pastors are influenced by it. But it has become an extremely influential philosophy. Thousands of churches have overhauled their entire ministry and are now attempting to cater to the masses.

In fact, the user-friendly-church movement has become so large that many secular newspapers have begun to take note of the trend. One article in the *Los Angeles Times* described how a megachurch grew out of a door-to-door survey conducted for a "marketing study" when this church was not yet formed. "Customer Poll Shapes a Church" was the title of the article—and it is fitting. The story described how the pastor "tailored the church's program to the needs and gripes people registered in his door-to-door survey."[7] Of course, the article said, his messages are brief, low-key, upbeat, and topical, with titles like "The Changing American Dream." He spices his sermonettes with quotations from news and financial magazines.

Another Southern California newspaper ran an article entitled, "Marketing the Maker." It describes several local churches that have employed the market-driven philosophy—and seem to be booming. One church "bought time on classic rock stations for an ad that sounded more like a pitch for a social club than an invitation to join a church. And newspaper ads were placed in the entertainment section, not the religion section."[8]

There is nothing wrong, of course, with a church placing ads in the entertainment section. But it *is* wrong for a church to promise—and deliver—a "church service" that is merely a form of entertainment. And that is precisely what many of these churches are doing. "A *celebration*—not a service" is how this particular church promotes its meetings, held, appropriately, in a movie theater.

One "church" has taken the concept to its logical conclusion—"a church service created for the medium of television. Our sanctuary has no pews . . . our sanctuary is [the] viewers' television set."[9] Created by the founder of the Home Shopping Network, "Worship" is a 24-hour "non-stop Christian church service." How can a "church" like that offer

---

[7]Russell Chandler (11 December 1989), A1.
[8]Mike McIntyre, *The San Diego Union* (6 November 1988), D8.
[9]"Designed by the Holy Spirit to Forever Change Christian Television" (advertisement), *Religious Broadcasting* (October 1992), 4-5.

meaningful fellowship? you ask. The founders of "Worship" feel they have that covered. "At *Worship*, fellowship is a significant part of each service, but this, too, is handled in a unique way through modern tools of communication. . . . *Worship* employs the latest technology in digital telephone equipment to enable viewers from around the country to quickly connect to a Fellowship partner."[10]

And so the "customer" achieves ultimate sovereignty. If he doesn't like what he sees, he can simply turn off the set. If he doesn't enjoy the "fellowship," he can hang up the phone.

TURNING CHURCH-GROWTH THEORY UPSIDE DOWN

Scripture says the early Christians "turned the world upside down" (Acts 17:6, KJV). In our generation the world is turning the church upside down. Biblically, God is sovereign, not "unchurched Harry." The Bible, not a marketing plan, is supposed to be the sole blueprint and final authority for all church ministry. Ministry should meet people's real needs, not salve their selfishness. And the Lord of the church is Christ, not some couch potato with the remote control in his hand.

I never hear the term "user-friendly church" without thinking of Acts 5 and Ananias and Sapphira. What happened there flies in the face of almost all contemporary church-growth theory. The Jerusalem church certainly wasn't very user-friendly. In fact, it was exactly the opposite; Luke tells us this episode inspired "great fear . . . upon the whole church, and upon all who heard of these things" (v. 11). The church service that day was so disturbing that none of the unchurched people "dared to associate with them." The thought of attending such a church struck terror in their hearts, even though "the people held them in high esteem" (Acts 5:13). The church was definitely not a place for sinners to be comfortable—it was a frightening place!

Let's look carefully at this passage and try to understand it in the proper context. To do that we must go back into Acts 4. Remember, the church was newborn, in all its pristine beauty and freshness and vitality. It was yet unstained by gross sin or human failure. The people were intensely studying the apostles' doctrine. Those early days of church history were bright, happy days, full of love and real fellowship. The joy was overwhelming, and the love was deep and all-inclusive; consequently

---

[10]"In Spirit and in Truth," *Religious Broadcasting* (December 1992), 12.

their testimony was loud and clear. The results were that some fifteen to twenty thousand had come to faith in Jesus Christ in just a few weeks' time. Already Satan had tried by persecution to thwart the purpose of the church. It made no difference; the believers only prayed for more boldness. God answered that prayer, and even more people were saved. God was very real; Christ was very much alive; and the Holy Spirit was displayed in great power in those days.

But Satan was already plotting a more dangerous attack. If he couldn't destroy the church by an external assault of persecution, he would try the more subtle internal approach. And that is exactly what happened.

SIN IN THE CAMP

This is the first recorded occasion of sin in the church. Of all the firsts in Acts, it is the saddest. Satan's strategy of infiltrating the church began at this time, and it is still continuing today.

This entire account is a classic example of the Bible's stubborn honesty. God could have given us a soft-focus picture of the church with all the imperfections hidden. But Scripture never leaves the truth out—even when it is painful and ugly. The church is not perfect and never has been. Some people use that as an excuse to stay away: "I'd go to church, but there are too many hypocrites." I always think, *Well, we have room for one more.* The objection itself is hypocritical. Of course there are hypocrites in the church. That's one of the truths we glean from this account in Acts 5. So there's a sense in which a passage like this can be an encouragement. Not that we are encouraged by sin. But it is encouraging to know that the early church grappled with exactly the same kind of problems we have today.

Even the apostle Paul must have sometimes been discouraged by problems he encountered in the churches. In 2 Corinthians 11:24-27, he gave a list of all the kinds of trials and persecution he had endured:

> Five times I received from the Jews thirty-nine lashes. Three times I was beaten with rods, once I was stoned, three times I was shipwrecked, a night and a day I have spent in the deep. I have been on frequent journeys, in dangers from rivers, dangers from robbers, dangers from my countrymen, dangers from the Gentiles, dangers in the city, dangers in the wilderness, dangers on the sea, dangers among false brethren; I have been in labor and hardship, through many sleepless nights, in hunger and thirst, often without food, in cold and exposure.

Then in conclusion he adds this, the supreme trial of all: "Apart from such external things, there is the daily pressure upon me of concern for all the churches" (v. 28). He wasn't talking about administration; he was speaking of the battle to bring believers to maturity.

Beginning with this incident in Acts 5, the sins of the saints became a perpetual problem for the church. Every epistle Paul wrote in the New Testament included something of major consequence about sin in the church. In Romans 16:17, 18 he wrote, "Now I urge you, brethren, keep your eye on those who cause dissensions and hindrances contrary to the teaching which you learned, and turn away from them. For such men are slaves, not of our Lord Christ but of their own appetites; and by their smooth and flattering speech they deceive the hearts of the unsuspecting." The Corinthian church was overrun with problems: divisions, strife, immorality, misuse of spiritual gifts, and so on. The Galatians were tolerant of false teaching and legalism (cf Gal. 3:1-4). Paul had to entreat the Ephesians to walk in a manner worthy of their calling, to be humble and gentle, patiently showing forbearance to one another in love, being diligent to preserve the unity of the Spirit in the bond of peace (4:1-4). He had to urge the Philippians to be like-minded, united in peace, intent on one purpose (2:1, 2). He even named two women, Euodia and Syntyche, whom he wanted to get along with one another (4:2, 3). In Colossians 3 Paul repeats a whole list of spiritual deficiencies, capped by a command for the Colossians to clean up their lives. He unrelentingly waged war against sin in the church.

A SHARING COMMUNITY

The church had begun as a sharing community. Acts 4:32-37 says,

> The congregation of those who believed were of one heart and soul; and not one of them claimed that anything belonging to him was his own; but all things were common property to them. And with great power the apostles were giving witness to the resurrection of the Lord Jesus, and abundant grace was upon them all. For there was not a needy person among them, for all who were owners of land or houses would sell them and bring the proceeds of the sales, and lay them at the apostles' feet; and they would be distributed to each, as any had need. And Joseph, a Levite of Cyprian birth, who was also called Barnabas by the apostles (which translated means, Son of Encouragement), and who owned a tract of land, sold it and brought the money and laid it at the apostles' feet.

THEY HAD TRUE SPIRITUAL UNITY

The congregation had already burgeoned and blossomed to include thousands of people, and they were continually multiplying. Nevertheless, they "were of one heart and soul." It was not just that they all belonged to the same organization, but that they had true spiritual unity. They believed as one. They thought as one. They were in the truest sense a body, a single organism with one heartbeat and one soul (cf Phil. 1:27). They were preoccupied with each other and with winning the world. They were too busy with those priorities to worry about their own selves. Everyone was caring for everyone else, so everyone's needs were met. Selfishness was therefore rendered unnecessary. What a beautiful kind of preoccupation that was! How rich and sweet their fellowship must have been!

THEY SHARED ALL THEIR POSSESSIONS

Many people misunderstand this passage. "All things were common property to them" does not mean these people lived in a commune. Remember, at Pentecost, Jerusalem was filled with pilgrims who came for the feast. During religious feasts, as many as a million people would come to Jerusalem. They obviously needed housing and food, and there weren't enough inns to accommodate everyone. So it was customary for believers to open their homes and allow people to live with them. Suddenly, at Pentecost on this particular year, hundreds of these people embraced Christ, and then began to win their friends and families to Him. Surely many of them remained in Jerusalem to sit under the apostles' teaching.

The financial pressures on these people and their hosts must have been tremendous. In addition, there were many poor people in Jerusalem. And some believers' income may have been cut off when they testified of their faith in Christ. To deal with these things, all believers were willing to share what they had.

This was not a commune. People did not drop out of society, quit their jobs, pool their money, and live in a common building or camp. Acts 2 describes what they were doing:

> And all those who had believed were together, and had all things in common; and they began selling their property and possessions, and were sharing them with all, as anyone might have need. And day by day continuing with one mind in the temple, and breaking bread from house to house, they were taking their meals together with gladness and sincerity of heart, praising God, and having favor with all the peo-

ple. And the Lord was adding to their number day by day those who were being saved (vv. 44-47).

This was a spiritual community, not a cloister. Christians still owned their own houses—they continued "breaking bread from house to house" (v. 46). That is, they broke bread, or had communion, in private homes. "Selling" and "sharing" in verse 45 are perfect-tense verbs, suggesting that the selling and sharing were going on all the time. There was no one point when the community of believers sold all they had and pooled their funds. A continuous process was going on whereby people who had resources were sharing them with believers who did not. They did not live in a communal shelter or put up barracks to accommodate everyone. That would have undermined the God-ordained priority of the family unit, which God designed to be independent and to function as the building block of society and the means of passing truth and righteousness from generation to generation.

People were selling their possessions—their land holdings and their portable goods—and sharing the proceeds when they knew others had needs. Paul commanded giving in this same spirit. He urged the Corinthians to be generous in giving to the needs of the saints in Macedonia, "your abundance being a supply for their want, that their abundance also may become a supply for your want, that there may be equality" (2 Cor. 8:14). Is that any different from what we do today? Not if our churches are healthy. Christians who see a brother or sister in need should have a natural desire to supply the need (cf 1 John 3:16). That's what these early Christians were doing. Those who sold possessions did so completely voluntarily. This becomes a crucial point when we examine the sin of Ananias and Sapphira.

THEY WERE NOURISHED BY POWERFUL PREACHING

"With great power the apostles were giving witness to the resurrection" (4:33). The preaching was bold and powerful. They were not ashamed of the gospel, though there was much persecution in those days. In fact, it specifically says they were preaching about the resurrection. That is the very truth that got them in the most trouble. At the beginning of this same chapter we learn that the priests, the captain of the temple guard, and the Sadducees, "being greatly disturbed because they were teaching the people and proclaiming in Jesus the resurrection from the dead" (v. 2), seized Peter and John and threw them in jail. Peter and John weren't trying to win approval from the Sadducees and priests by preaching a message they wanted to hear! They boldly proclaimed the very thing that most offended them! They refused to tone down the great doctrines of the Word of God to eliminate the offense. They never suppressed the biblical message because someone might be offended.

The apostles' preaching ministry included teaching as well as evangelism. Acts 2:42 says that those who believed "were continually devoting themselves to the apostles' teaching." This was a well-fed but voracious flock.

The Jerusalem church would have been a wonderful place of fellowship. They did not follow any of the contemporary user-friendly marketing techniques, but the fellowship was warm and real. They lovingly met one another's actual needs. And they had rich and ample teaching. Acts 2:42 tells us, "They were continually devoting themselves to the apostles' teaching and to fellowship, to the breaking of bread and to prayer." *None of that was designed to attract unbelievers.* Nevertheless, new people kept coming, because the Lord kept adding to the church day by day those who were being saved (v. 47).

A POSITIVE ROLE MODEL

Luke records how resources were shared among needy believers. Those with surplus property and possessions sold them, then placed the proceeds at the apostles' feet (4:34, 35). The apostles distributed the funds to those who had needs. Through that simple system, all the needs were met (v. 34). That is essentially the same system we use today when we take an offering in the church. The money goes into a common fund, where the leaders of the church have the responsibility for stewardship of it.

Barnabas is the specific example Luke chose to show a spiritual role model. *Barnabas* was a nickname, meaning "son of encouragement." Apparently this man, "Joseph, a Levite of Cyprian birth," had the gift of exhortation, so he was given a nickname that fit. Barnabas later accompanied the apostle Paul on his first missionary journey.

Barnabas was a Levite, a member of the priestly tribe of Israel. It is unlikely that he, a priest, would have been a very wealthy man. But somehow he had acquired a piece of property. He sold it. Then he brought the money to the apostles to be distributed. He didn't ask for recognition. He didn't try to control how the money was used. He just turned it over. What is clear from Acts chapter 4 is that Barnabas gave from love out of a pure heart—just for the blessedness of giving. And we can assume that a whole lot of others in the Jerusalem church did the same thing.

A NEGATIVE ROLE MODEL

But not everyone. The story that follows makes a startling contrast to the tone of Acts 4. It is shocking to see sin in this church. It is appalling to see the brazen falsehood Ananias and Sapphira conspired to tell. Most of all, it is astonishing to see how severely the Lord dealt with their sin:

> But a certain man named Ananias, with his wife Sapphira, sold a piece of property, and kept back some of the price for himself, with his wife's full knowledge, and bringing a portion of it, he laid it at the apostles' feet. But Peter said, "Ananias, why has Satan filled your heart to lie to the Holy Spirit, and to keep back some of the price of the land? While it remained unsold, did it not remain your own? And after it was sold, was it not under your control? Why is it that you have conceived this deed in your heart? You have not lied to men, but to God." And as he heard these words, Ananias fell down and breathed his last; and great fear came upon all who heard of it. And the young men arose and covered him up, and after carrying him out, they buried him.
>
> Now there elapsed an interval of about three hours, and his wife came in, not knowing what had happened. And Peter responded to her, "Tell me whether you sold the land for such and such a price?" And she said, "Yes, that was the price." Then Peter said to her, "Why is it that you have agreed together to put the Spirit of the Lord to the test? Behold, the feet of those who have buried your husband are at the door, and they shall carry you out as well." And she fell immediately at his feet, and breathed her last; and the young men came in and found her dead, and they carried her out and buried her beside her husband. And great fear came upon the whole church, and upon all who heard of these things (Acts 5:1-11).

As generous and sacrificial and selfless as the saints at Jerusalem were, there was an exception. Ananias' sin was spawned by the seeds of greed and deceit. It is to the book of Acts what Achan's sin is to the book of Joshua. Both were deceitful, miserly, selfish acts that interrupted the victorious progress of God's people and brought sin into the camp at the height of great triumph.

The saints in Jerusalem were giving out of a Spirit-filled heart. Ananias' sin revealed a Satan-filled heart (v. 3). The contrast between the end of the fourth chapter and the beginning of the fifth could hardly be more dramatic.

Ananias' name means "the Lord is gracious"; Sapphira means "beautiful." Their deed was anything but gracious or beautiful. Seeing that others were selling property and giving the money to the apostles, they pledged to do the same. Verse 2 tells us, however, that when the time came to give, they "kept back some of the price." It is clear that both of them were in on the plot.

THE LEAVEN OF THE PHARISEES

What was their motive? They wanted a little spiritual prestige. They wanted to *appear* to be giving sacrificially, yet keep some of the money for themselves. That suggests they loved money. And "the love of money is a root of all sorts of evil," Paul wrote Timothy. "Some by longing for it have wandered away from the faith, and pierced themselves with many a pang" (1 Tim. 6:10). That was certainly true of Ananias and Sapphira. The book of Hebrews says "Let your character be free from the love of money, being content with what you have; for He Himself has said, 'I will never desert you, nor will I ever forsake you'" (13:5).

Here were two characters so tainted with the love of money that they were willing to conspire together to commit public hypocrisy. They sold their land, but rather than giving all the proceeds to the Lord as they had promised, they gave only a portion to the Lord under the pretense that it was the whole price. They must have thought they could gain spiritual esteem *and* some cash through the charade.

Their sin was not that they did not give everything. There was no divine requirement that they give everything. They had a perfect right to keep or give whatever they desired. They didn't even have to sell their property. It was all voluntary, as is all giving spoken of in the New Testament.

The sin was their lie. They had evidently made a vow to the Holy Spirit publicly in front of the congregation. They lied to the entire congregation, but worse still, they lied to God (Acts 5:4). Perhaps they thought of this as a secret sin, but it didn't stay secret long. God Himself exposed it to the entire congregation.

Now let's be honest. This kind of hypocrisy is not a particularly uncommon sin. Nor is it the kind of evil we tend to think of as heinous. Lots of people give money under false pretenses. This is the moral equivalent of the man who rolls up a few dollar bills so it will look like he's putting a large wad into the collection plate. Or the woman who makes a great show of depositing an offering envelope, when there's only a quarter inside. It's like the Pharisees who had someone blow a trumpet in the synagogues and streets when they gave alms, so that everyone would notice (Matt. 6:2).

Jesus says of such people, "they have their reward in full" (Matt. 6:2, 5, 16). They want people to see their show of good works; people notice. That's their reward. They seek glory from people, not from God, so the human recognition is the only reward they will ever get. "But when you give alms, do not let your left hand know what your right hand is doing that your alms may be in secret; and your Father who sees in secret will repay you" (6:3, 4). This sin may seem petty to us, but not to God. God hates hypocrisy and feigned holiness. Jesus called it "the leaven of the Pharisees" (Luke 12:1).

Now this leaven was threatening to infect the infant church. God would deal with it harshly and abruptly, sending signals to everyone about the seriousness of life in the church.

PETER'S RESPONSE

Peter, under the inspiration of the Spirit of God, saw through their hypocrisy. Imagine the shock that hit Ananias! He came before the apostles, laid his money at their feet, and smugly told them it was all the money he got from selling his property. He probably stood there a moment, basking in what he thought was their approval. He must have assumed that they were looking at him as a spiritual example, a generous and godly man.

Suddenly Peter said to him, "Ananias, why has Satan filled your heart to lie to the Holy Spirit, and to keep back some of the price of the land?" (Acts 5:3)—a rather confrontive thing to say in a church service.

In many churches Ananias would have received the approval he sought, no matter what his motives. A pragmatic church leader might reason, *After all, this is a substantial sum of money. OK, his motives aren't pure, but, hey, he's not a bad guy, and we can use the money. We can't embarrass him in front of all the people. If we do that, we'll never get another dime from him.*

Not Peter. He confronted the sin directly. "Why has Satan filled your heart?" Notice that Peter was putting the blame on Ananias, not Satan. "Why?" he asked. Then again in verse 4: "Why is it that you have conceived this deed in your heart?"

Peter made clear that the sin was Ananias' hypocrisy, not his keeping half the money: "While it remained unsold, did it not remain your own? And after it was sold, was it not under your control?" (v. 4). He could have done whatever he wanted with the money. He could have kept his land. There was no requirement for him to do otherwise. It would not have been sinful if Ananias had said, "I sold my property; here is part of the money." He had every right to give as much or as little as he wanted. But he sinned by claiming he was giving everything when he had actually kept some for himself.

And he lied to God, not just to men. More specifically, this was a blatant lie to the Holy Spirit.[11] How had he lied to the Holy Spirit? He had vowed to give the full value of his property and failed to follow through. The Old Testament sage wrote, "When you make a vow to God, do not be late in paying it, for He takes no delight in fools. Pay what you vow! It is better that you should not vow than that you should vow and not pay" (Eccl. 5:4, 5). Moses' law contained a similar warning: "When you make a vow to the Lord your God, you shall not delay to pay it, for it would be sin in you, and the Lord your God will surely require it of you. However, if you refrain from vowing, it would not be sin in you. You shall be careful to perform what goes out from your lips, just as you have voluntarily vowed to the Lord your God, what you have promised" (Deut. 23:21-23).

GOD'S JUDGMENT

God's response to the situation was immediate, severe, and final. He struck Ananias dead on the spot. "As he heard these words, Ananias fell down and breathed his last" (Acts 5:5). This was a judicial act of the Most Holy God. Perhaps Ananias' heart simply stopped out of sheer terror. Right in front of the entire church.

User-friendly? Hardly. In fact, the effect was that "great fear came upon all who heard of it" (v. 5). God had made Ananias an example to others who might be tempted to trifle with Him and taint the purity of the church.

Does God always judge sin this way? Obviously not, but like Nadab and Abihu (Lev. 10), Korah (Num. 16), Achan (Josh. 7), Herod (Acts 12), and others throughout Scripture, Ananias was immediately judged for his sin and paid with his life. God sovereignly chose to strike him dead sum-

---

[11]This passage is one of the proofs for the deity and personality of the Holy Spirit. In verse 3 Peter said Ananias had lied to the Holy Spirit. In verse 4 he tells Ananias, "You have not lied to men, but to God." The Holy Spirit *is* God. By lying to the apostles about what he was doing, Ananias had committed an even greater offense against the Holy Spirit.

marily. He thus became an example to all. The truth is, God *could* judge every sin this way. "The wages of sin is death" (Rom. 6:23). It is only because of the Lord's infinite mercy that we are not all consumed (Lam. 3:22, KJV). Sometimes God does judge sin with physical death. Paul wrote to the Corinthians who were disrupting and defiling the Lord's table, "He who eats and drinks, eats and drinks judgment to himself, if he does not judge the body rightly. For this reason many among you are weak and sick, and a number sleep" (1 Cor. 11:29, 30). "Sleep" in that verse refers to physical death. God was actually judging those irreverent Corinthians by making them physically ill, and some were even dying.

With Ananias, however, there was no illness, no time lapse. He dropped dead on the spot. God's judgment was swift and terrifying.

SAPPHIRA'S SIN

Scripture says, "The young men arose and covered him up, and after carrying him out, they buried him" (Acts 5:6). Sapphira was not present when her husband died. "There elapsed an interval of about three hours, and his wife came in, not knowing what had happened" (v. 7). Sapphira was oblivious to her husband's fate, perhaps thinking she would make a grand entrance, with everyone admiring her for the great act of generosity she and Ananias had done.

Peter immediately confronted her: "Tell me whether you sold the land for such and such a price?" And she said, "Yes, that was the price" (v. 8). This was a deliberate lie, proving that she and her husband had conspired together to commit a premeditated act of hypocrisy.

Peter was as direct as he had been with Ananias: "Why is it that you have agreed together to put the Spirit of the Lord to the test? Behold, the feet of those who have buried your husband are at the door, and they shall carry you out as well" (v. 9). She never even had the opportunity to respond. "She fell immediately at his feet, and breathed her last; and the young men came in and found her dead, and they carried her out and buried her beside her husband" (v. 10).

JUDGMENT MUST BEGIN AT THE HOUSE OF GOD

God is serious about the purity of the church. This was an early and unforgettable lesson about how God views sin among the fellowship of believers. In essence, God was saying, "I am not playing church. I will not trifle with sinners. I am not interested in user-friendliness. I desire righteousness, truth, and sincere hearts." He thus served notice that He is deadly serious. The church is no social gig.

What was the result of this episode? Again, "Great fear came upon the whole church" (5:11). You can be certain there was a lot of careful self-examination going on in the Jerusalem church that day. And that was the point. God was purifying His church. He wanted His people to take sin seriously. He wanted to discourage shallow commitment. He wanted the people to fear Him. The church meets to worship God, and that demands the confrontation of sin. Here the Lord gives us the very basic model for the church's meeting—sin is dealt with fiercely. The issue is not what unbelievers think about such severity; it is what God thinks about such iniquity.

Surely in first-century Jerusalem there were a lot more contemptible sinners than Ananias and Sapphira. What about Herod, for example? Why didn't God strike him dead? As a matter of fact, He ultimately did (cf Acts 12:18-23). But as Peter wrote, "It is time for judgment to begin with the household of God" (1 Peter 4:17). God judges His own people before He turns His wrath on pagans.

Can the church avoid God's judgment? Yes, but only by purifying herself. After warning the Corinthians that God was already judging sinning church members with sickness and death, Paul told them, "If we judged ourselves rightly, we should not be judged" (1 Cor. 11:31). In other words, it is the job of faithful church members to maintain the church's purity. Frankly, this is a far more powerful word to unbelievers about reality than some bland and light-hearted talk intended to make them feel welcome and accepted. This lets the unbeliever know that the church is a holy people and is not for unrepentant sinners, but for the redeemed ones who love righteousness.

We maintain purity by following the process Jesus outlined in the eighteenth chapter of Matthew: "If your brother sins, *go and reprove him in private*; if he listens to you, you have won your brother. But if he does not listen to you, *take one or two more with you*, so that by the mouth of two or three witnesses every fact may be confirmed. And if he refuses to listen to them, *tell it to the church*; and if he refuses to listen even to the church, *let him be to you as a Gentile and a tax-gatherer*" (vv. 15-17, emphasis added). We refer to this process as "church discipline." It may not seem like a very user-friendly concept, but it is what God commands. His design is to purify the church and thus to bless and protect His people from His judgment. Paul wrote, "When we are judged, we are disciplined by the Lord in order that we may not be condemned along with the world" (1 Cor. 11:32).

Jesus went on to say, "Truly I say to you, whatever you shall bind on earth shall be bound in heaven; and whatever you loose on earth shall be loosed in heaven. Again I say to you, that if two of you agree on earth about anything that they may ask, it shall be done for them by My Father who is in heaven. For where two or three have gathered together in My name, there I am in their midst" (Matt. 18:18-20). Remember, in this context our Lord was describing how to deal with sin in the fellowship. The point is that Christ carries out His own will in the church *through the discipline process.* "I am in their midst" means He personally works in and through believers to purify His church as they follow the steps He outlined. The effect is that repentant believers are restored (their sin is "loosed" from them), and hardhearted sinners are exposed and ousted from the fellowship (their sin is "bound" to them). If we don't follow this process and keep the church pure, He will intervene in judgment (1 Cor. 11:30).

KNOWING THE TERROR OF THE LORD,
WE PERSUADE MEN

Here is the salient point for this book: God's judgment against Ananias and Sapphira had an effect beyond the fellowship of believers: "Great fear came upon . . . all who heard of these things" (Acts 5:11). Verse 13 says unbelievers did not dare associate with them! This is precisely the opposite of the user-friendly philosophy that is so popular today. Instead of luring people to church by making them feel comfortable and secure, God used fear to keep unbelievers away.

The fear of God was a central doctrine in the early church, as in the Old Testament. Unbelievers and believers alike were taught to fear Him. None but a rank fool would deal frivolously with God. It was that very fear that drew people for salvation and kept them obedient. Salvation doesn't come from wanting to join the fun and end emotional pain—it comes when the heart cries out for deliverance from sin!

The contemporary user-friendly movement aims for just the opposite. Rather than arousing fear of God, it attempts to portray Him as fun, jovial, easygoing, lenient, and even permissive. Haughty sinners who ought to approach God in terror (cf Luke 18:13) are emboldened to presume on His grace. Sinners hear nothing of divine wrath. This is as wrong as preaching rank heresy.

As we learn from the account of Ananias and Sapphira, God's wrath is not to be taken lightly. Peter wrote, "If [judgment] begins with us first, what will be the outcome for those who do not obey the gospel of God?" (1 Peter 4:17). Paul spoke of divine wrath as one of the primary motivations for evangelism: "Therefore knowing the fear of the Lord, we persuade men" (2 Cor. 5:11).

WHERE IS USER-FRIENDLINESS TAKING THE CHURCH?

The user-friendly philosophy is a sharp turn down a wrong road for the church. I am convinced that the downgrading of worship, Scripture, and theology will ultimately usher in serious doctrinal compromise. In fact, that may already be happening. Christian leaders who identify themselves as evangelical are beginning to question cardinal doctrines such as hell and human depravity.

One of the most popular movements afoot today embraces a doctrine known as "conditional immortality," similiar to annihilationism.[12] It is the idea that unredeemed sinners are simply eradicated rather than spending eternity in hell. A perfect fit for the user-friendly philosophy, this view teaches that a merciful God could not possibly consign created beings to eternal torment. Instead, he obliterates them completely.

Conditional immortality and annihilationism are not new ideas. History shows, however, that most people and movements who adopt annihilationist views do not remain orthodox. Denying the eternality of hell is tantamount to a running start on the down-grade.

Spurgeon attacked conditional immortality as one of the great errors of the nineteenth-century down-grade. He said that those who deny the eternality of hell "have pretty nearly obliterated the hope of such a heaven as we have all along expected. Of course, the reward of the righteous is to be of no longer continuance than the punishment of the wicked. Both are described as 'everlasting' in the same verse [Matt. 25:46], spoken by the same sacred lips; and as the 'punishment' is made out to be only 'age-lasting,' so must the 'life' be."[13]

---

[12]*Conditional immortality* teaches that human souls are not inherently immortal; thus those damned in the judgment pass into oblivion, while the righteous are given immortality. *Annihilationism* is the view that all souls are immortal, but the wicked lose their immortality in the judgment.

[13]"Progressive Theology," *The Sword and the Trowel* (1888), 158.

Scripture says, "The devil who deceived them was thrown into the lake of fire and brimstone, where the beast and the false prophet are also; and they will be tormented day and night forever and ever" (Rev. 20:10). Jesus told of the rich man who "In Hades . . . lifted up his eyes, being in torment, and saw Abraham far away, and Lazarus in his bosom. And he cried out and said, 'Father Abraham, have mercy on me, and send Lazarus, that he may dip the tip of his finger in water and cool off my tongue; for I am in agony in this flame'" (Luke 16:23, 24). It was also Jesus who said, "If your eye causes you to stumble, cast it out; it is better for you to enter the kingdom of God with one eye, than having two eyes, to be cast into hell, where their worm does not die, and the fire is not quenched" (Mark 9:47, 48). And Revelation 14:11 describes the eternal state of those who follow Antichrist in the Tribulation: "The smoke of their torment goes up forever and ever; and they have no rest day and night, those who worship the beast and his image, and whoever receives the mark of his name." The most prolific teacher on hell in all of Scripture was the Lord Jesus Himself. He had more to say about the subject than all the apostles, prophets, and evangelists of Scripture put together.

Preaching that downplays God's wrath does not enhance evangelism; it undermines it. The urgency of the gospel is utterly lost when the preacher denies the reality or severity of everlasting punishment. The authority of Scripture is compromised when so much of Christ's clear message must be denied or explained away. The seriousness of sin is depreciated by this teaching. And therefore the gospel itself is subverted.

How deeply has the tendency to deny hell penetrated evangelicalism? One survey of evangelical seminary students revealed that nearly half—46 percent—felt preaching about hell to unbelievers is in "poor taste."[14] Worse, three out of every ten self-professed "born again" people surveyed believe "good" people will go to heaven when they die—even if they've never trusted Christ.[15] One in every ten evangelicals say they believe the concept of sin is outmoded.

Too many who have embraced the user-friendly trend have not carefully pondered how user-friendliness is incompatible with true biblical theology. It is, at its heart, a pragmatic, not a biblical, outlook. It is based on precisely the kind of thinking that is eating away at the heart of ortho-

---

[14]James Davison Hunter, *Evangelicalism: The Coming Generation* (Chicago: University of Chicago, 1987), 40.

[15]George Barna, *The Barna Report* (Ventura, Calif.: Regal, 1992), 52.

dox doctrine. It is leading evangelicalism into neo-modernism and putting churches in the fast lane on the down-grade.

The answer, of course, is not an *un*friendly church, but a vibrant, loving, honest, committed, worshiping fellowship of believers who minister to one another like the church in Acts chapter 4—but who eschew sin, keep one another accountable, and boldly proclaim the full truth of Scripture. People who have no love for the things of God may not find such a place very user-friendly. But God's blessing will be on the fellowship of true believers, because that is what He ordained the church to be like. And He *will* add to the church, as He promised.

3

Gimme That Show-Time Religion

The fact is, that many would like to unite church and stage, cards and prayer, dancing and sacraments. If we are powerless to stem this torrent, we can at least warn men of its existence, and entreat them to keep out of it. When the old faith is gone, and enthusiasm for the gospel is extinct, it is no wonder that people seek something else in the way of delight. Lacking bread, they feed on ashes; rejecting the way of the Lord, they run greedily in the path of folly.

CHARLES HADDON SPURGEON[1]

TOWARD THE end of the nineteenth century . . . the Age of Exposition began to pass, and the early signs of its replacement could be discerned. Its replacement was to be the Age of Show Business."[2]

While Charles Spurgeon was doing battle in the Down-Grade Controversy, a worldwide trend was beginning to emerge that would set the course of human affairs for all of the twentieth century. It was the emergence of entertainment at the very center of family and cultural life. This trend saw the decline of what Neil Postman terms "the Age of Exposition"—marked by the thoughtful exchange of ideas through print and verbal means (preaching, debates, lectures). And it gave rise to "the age of Show Business"—in which amusements and entertainment have become the most important and time-consuming aspects of human discourse. Drama, film, and finally television have moved show business into

---

[1]"Another Word Concerning the Down-Grade," *The Sword and the Trowel* (August 1887), 398.
[2]Neil Postman, *Amusing Ourselves to Death* (New York: Penguin, 1985), 63.

67

the center of our lives—ultimately right into the middle of our living rooms.

In show business, truth is irrelevant; what really matters is whether we are entertained. Substance counts for little; *style* is everything. In the words of Marshall McLuhan, the medium is the message. Unfortunately, that kind of thinking now rules the church as surely as it does the world.

A. W. Tozer wrote these words in 1955:

> For centuries the Church stood solidly against every form of worldly entertainment, recognizing it for what it was—a device for wasting time, a refuge from the disturbing voice of conscience, a scheme to divert attention from moral accountability. For this she got herself abused roundly by the sons of this world. But of late she has become tired of the abuse and has given over the struggle. She appears to have decided that if she cannot conquer the great god Entertainment she may as well join forces with him and make what use she can of his powers. So today we have the astonishing spectacle of millions of dollars being poured into the unholy job of providing earthly entertainment for the so-called sons of heaven. Religious entertainment is in many places rapidly crowding out the serious things of God. Many churches these days have become little more than poor theaters where fifth-rate "producers" peddle their shoddy wares with the full approval of evangelical leaders who can even quote a holy text in defense of their delinquency. And hardly a man dares raise his voice against it.[3]

By today's standards, the issues that so inflamed Tozer's passions seem trifling. For example, churches were attracting people to Sunday evening services by showing Christian films. Young people's rallies featured up-tempo music and speakers whose specialty was humor. High-energy games and activities were beginning to play a key role in church youth work. Looking back, it may seem difficult to understand Tozer's distress. Hardly anyone these days would be shocked or concerned about any of the methods that seemed radically innovative in the fifties. Most of them are generally regarded as conventional today.

Tozer, however, was not condemning games, music styles, or movies per se. He was concerned with the philosophy underlying what was happening in the church. He was sounding an alarm about a deadly change

---

[3] *The Root of the Righteous* (Harrisburg, Penn.: Christian Publications, 1955), 32-33.

of focus. He saw evangelicals using entertainment as a tool for church growth, and he believed that was subverting the church's priorities. He feared that frivolous diversions and carnal amusements in the church would eventually destroy people's appetites for real worship and the preaching of God's Word.

He was right about that. In fact, Tozer's rebuke is more fitting than ever as the church approaches the end of the century. He—and Spurgeon before him—were identifying a trend that has come into full bloom in our generation. What the church was flirting with in Spurgeon's time became an infatuation in Tozer's. It is now an obsession. Worse yet, the forms of entertainment now used in church are often completely secular—devoid of anything Christian.

An article in *The Wall Street Journal* described one well-known church's bid "to perk up attendance at Sunday evening services." The church "staged a wrestling match, featuring church employees. To train for the event, 10 game employees got lessons from Tugboat Taylor, a former professional wrestler, in pulling hair, kicking shins and tossing bodies around without doing real harm."[4] No harm to the staff members, perhaps, but what is the effect of such an exhibition on the church's message? Is not the gospel itself clouded and badly caricatured by such tomfoolery? Can you imagine what Spurgeon or Tozer would have thought?

That wrestling match is not an obscure example from some eccentric church on the fringe. It took place in the Sunday evening service of one of America's five largest churches. Similar examples could be drawn from many of the leading churches supposedly in the mainstream of evangelical orthodoxy.

Some will maintain that if biblical principles are presented, the medium doesn't matter. That is nonsense. If an entertaining medium is the key to winning people, why not go all out? Why not have a real carnival? A tattooed acrobat on a high wire could juggle chain saws and shout Bible verses while a trick dog balanced on his head. That would draw a crowd. And the *content* of the message would still be biblical. It's a bizarre scenario, but one that illustrates how the medium can cheapen and corrupt the message.

And sadly, it's not terribly different from what is actually being done

---

[4]R. Gustav Niebuhr, "Mighty Fortresses: Megachurches Strive to Be All Things to All Parishioners," *The Wall Street Journal* (13 May 1991), A6.

in some churches. There seems almost no limit to what modern church leaders will do to entice people who aren't interested in worship and preaching. Too many have bought the notion that the church must win people by offering an alternative form of entertainment.

Just how far will the church go in competing with Hollywood? A large church in the southwestern United States has installed a half-million-dollar special-effects system that can produce smoke, fire, sparks, and laser lights in the auditorium. The church sent staff members to study live special effects at Bally's Casino in Las Vegas. The pastor ended one service by ascending to "heaven" via invisible wires that drew him up out of sight while the choir and orchestra added a musical accompaniment to the smoke, fire, and light show.[5] It was just a typical Sunday show for that pastor: "He packs his church with such special effects as . . . cranking up a chain saw and toppling a tree to make a point . . . the biggest Fourth of July fireworks display in town and a Christmas service with a rented elephant, kangaroo and zebra. The Christmas show features 100 clowns with gifts for the congregation's children."[6]

Shenanigans like that would have been the stuff of Spurgeon's worst nightmares. And even Tozer could not have foreseen the extreme to which evangelicals would go in paying homage to the great god Entertainment.

DRIVEN BY PRAGMATISM

There is no denying that these antics seem to work—that is, they draw a crowd. Many churches that have experimented with such methods report growing attendance figures. And a handful of megachurches— those that can afford first-class productions, effects, and facilities—have been able to stimulate enormous numerical growth. Some of them fill huge auditoriums with thousands of people several times every week.

A few of these megachurches resemble elegant country clubs or resort hotels. They feature impressive facilities with bowling lanes, movie theaters, health spas, restaurants, ballrooms, roller-skating rinks, and state-of-the-art multi-court gymnasiums. Recreation and entertainment are inevitably the most visible aspects of these enterprises. Such churches have become meccas for students of church growth.

---

[5] Robert Johnson, "Heavenly Gifts: Preaching a Gospel of Acquisitiveness, a Showy Sect Prospers," *The Wall Street Journal* (11 December 1990), A1-8.
[6] *Ibid.*, A8.

Now evangelicals everywhere are frantically seeking new techniques and new forms of entertainment to attract people. Whether a method is biblical or not scarcely seems to matter to the average church leader today. Does it *work?* That is the new test of legitimacy. And so raw pragmatism has become the driving force in much of the professing church.

IT'S SHOW TIME!

When Charles Spurgeon warned about those who "would like to unite church and stage, cards and prayer, dancing and sacraments," he was belittled as an alarmist. But Spurgeon's prophecy has been fulfilled before our eyes. Modern church buildings are constructed like theaters ("playhouses," Spurgeon called them). Instead of a pulpit, the focus is a stage. Churches are hiring full-time media specialists, programming consultants, stage directors, drama coaches, special-effects experts, and choreographers.

This is all the natural extension of a market-driven church philosophy. If the church is only in business to promote a product, church leaders had *better* pay attention to the methods of Madison Avenue. After all, the church's chief competition is a world filled with secular amusements and a host of worldly goods and services. Therefore, the marketing experts say, we will never win people until we develop effective alternative forms of entertainment to capture people's attention and loyalty away from the world's offerings. That goal thus establishes the nature of the marketing campaign.

What's wrong with that? For one thing, the church has no business marketing its ministry as an alternative to secular amusements (1 Thess. 3:2-6). That corrupts and cheapens the church's real mission. We are not carnival barkers, used-car salesmen, or commercial pitchmen. We are Christ's ambassadors (2 Cor. 5:20). Knowing the terror of the Lord (v. 11), motivated by the love of Christ (v. 14), utterly made new by Him (v. 17), we implore sinners to be reconciled to God (v. 20).

Moreover, instead of confronting the world with the truth of Christ, the market-driven megachurches are enthusiastically promoting the worst trends of secular culture. Feeding people's appetite for entertainment only exacerbates the problems of mindless emotion, apathy, and materialism. Quite frankly, it is difficult to conceive of a ministry philosophy more contradictory to the pattern our Lord gave us.

Proclaiming and explaining the Word for the maturing and holiness of believers should be the heart of every church's ministry. If the world looks at the church and sees an entertainment center, we're sending the wrong message. If Christians view the church as an amusement parlor, the church will die. One dear woman, struggling in a church that has embraced all the modern fads, recently complained, "When is the church going to stop trying to entertain the goats and get back to feeding the sheep?"

Nothing in Scripture indicates the church should lure people to Christ by presenting Christianity as an attractive option. Nothing about the gospel is optional: "There is salvation in no one else . . . there is no other name under heaven that has been given among men, by which we must be saved" (Acts 4:12). Nor is the gospel meant to be attractive in the sense of modern marketing. As we have noted, the message of the gospel is often "a stone of stumbling and a rock of offense" (Rom. 9:33; 1 Peter 2:8). It is disturbing, revolting, upsetting, confrontive, convicting, and offensive to human pride. There's no way to "market" that. Those who try to erase the offense by making it entertaining inevitably corrupt and obscure the crucial aspects of the message. The church must realize that its mission has never been public relations or sales; we are called to live holy lives and declare God's raw truth—lovingly but uncompromisingly—to an unbelieving world.

IS NUMERICAL GROWTH A LEGITIMATE GOAL?

Perhaps I should say that I am no opponent of large churches or of church growth. Grace Community Church was founded more than thirty-five years ago and has experienced tremendous growth through most of its history. On a typical Sunday as many as ten thousand people attend our services. We have experienced cycles of growth followed by plateaus. We're currently in another phase of strong growth.

What I oppose is the pragmatism often advocated by church growth specialists who elevate numerical growth over spiritual growth and who believe they can induce that numerical growth by following whatever techniques seem to be working at the moment. The faddism bred by that philosophy is becoming more and more unruly. It is diverting people from biblical churches and churches from biblical priorities, while producing a handful of megachurches whose growth is dependent on their ability to anticipate and respond to the next cultural trend. The church has been drawn away from true revival and is being seduced by those who advocate the *popularization* of Christianity. Tragically, most Christians seem oblivious to the problem, satisfied with a Christianity that is fashionable and highly visible.

Is numerical growth a legitimate goal in church ministry? Certainly no worthy church leader would seriously argue that numerical growth is inherently undesirable. And no one believes that stagnation or numerical decline are to be sought. But is numerical growth always the best gauge of a church's health?

I agree with George Peters, who wrote,

> Quantitative growth . . . can be deceptive. It may be no more than the mushrooming of a mechanically induced, psychological or social movement, a numerical count, an agglomeration of individuals or groups, an increase of a body without the development of muscle and vital organs. It may be Christendom in the making but not Christianity breaking through. Many mass movements of the past and community and tribal movements have been just that. An example is found in the mass accessions in Europe, particularly in France and Russia, when many were driven to baptism and drawn into the church, resulting in a mass of people professing Christendom but not in a dynamic, vibrant, growing, and responsible church of Jesus Christ. . . . It must be admitted . . . that to a great extent this expansion of the form, profession, and name of Christendom has little resemblance to the Christianity defined in the New Testament and the church portrayed in the book of Acts.
>
> In many ways the expansion of Christendom has come at the expense of the purity of the gospel and true Christian order and life. The church has become infested with pagan beliefs and practices, and is syncretistic in theology. . . . Large segments have become Christo-pagan.[7]

Nothing in Scripture indicates that church leaders should set numerical goals for church growth.[8] Here's how the apostle Paul described the growth process: "I planted, Apollos watered, but *God was causing the growth.*

---

[7] *A Theology of Church Growth* (Grand Rapids, Mich.: Zondervan, 1981), 23-24.
[8] Cf C. Peter Wagner, ed., Donald A. McGavran, *Understanding Church Growth*, third ed. (Grand Rapids, Mich.: Eerdmans, 1990), 265-281. Here Wagner and McGavran argue that numerical goal setting is an essential part of a biblical approach to church growth: "Setting membership goals is in accordance with God's eternal purpose. Goal setting in the service of the Great Commission is pleasing to God. . . . Scripture is solidly on the side of careful planning for church growth" (p. 270). Yet the only passage of Scripture they cite in support of that statement is Acts 18:4, 5, 9, which says nothing about the setting of goals, numerical or otherwise.

So then neither the one who plants nor the one who waters is anything, but *God who causes the growth*" (1 Cor. 3:6, 7, emphasis added).

If we concern ourselves with the *depth* of our ministry, God will see to the *breadth* of it. If we minister for spiritual growth, numerical growth will be what God chooses it to be.

What good, after all, is numerical expansion that is not rooted in commitment to the Lordship of Christ? If people come to church primarily because they find it entertaining, they will surely leave as soon as they stop being amused or something comes along to interest them more. And so the church is forced into a hopeless cycle where it must constantly try to eclipse each spectacle with something bigger and better.

THE PRAGMATIC ROOTS OF THE CHURCH GROWTH MOVEMENT

Pragmatism as a philosophy of ministry has gained impetus from the church growth movement that has flourished over the past fifty years or so. Donald McGavran, the father of the modern church growth movement, was an unabashed pragmatist. He said:

> We devise mission methods and policies in the light of what God has blessed—and what He has obviously not blessed. Industry calls this "modifying operation in light of feedback." Nothing hurts missions overseas so much as continuing methods, institutions, and policies which ought to bring men to Christ—but don't; which ought to multiply churches—but don't. We teach men to be ruthless in regard to method. If it does not work to the glory of God and the extension of Christ's church, throw it away and get something which does. As to methods, we are fiercely pragmatic—doctrine is something else.[9]

As a young missionary in India and the son of missionary parents, McGavran had noticed that it was not unusual for missions organizations to labor in India for years and have little or no fruit to show for it. McGavran's own agency had planted only twenty or thirty small churches in several decades of missionary work.[10] McGavran determined to devise

---

[9]"For Such a Time as This" (unpublished address, 1970), cited in C. Peter Wagner, "Pragmatic Strategy for Tomorrow's Mission," in A. R. Tippet, ed., *God, Man and Church Growth* (Grand Rapids, Mich.: Eerdmans, 1973), 147.
[10]Wagner, ed., *Understanding Church Growth*, viii-ix.

a strategy of missions that took note of which methods seemed to work and which ones didn't. "As he declared in the preface to a book he coauthored in the 1930s, he had dedicated himself to 'discarding theories of church growth which do not work, and learning and practicing productive patterns. . . .'"[11]

McGavran's pragmatism seems to have been initially prompted by a legitimate concern for stewardship. He "became alarmed when he saw all too many of God's resources—personnel and finances—being used without asking whether the kingdom of God was being advanced by the programs they were supporting."[12] But pragmatism became the philosophical basis for nearly all that McGavran taught, and that in turn set the agenda for the whole church growth movement.

McGavran founded the Institute of Church Growth, which in 1965 united with the Fuller School of World Mission. From there the pragmatic precepts of the church growth movement have reached into virtually every mission field worldwide.

C. Peter Wagner, professor of church growth at the Fuller School of World Mission, is Donald McGavran's best-known student. Wagner is the most prolific if not the most influential spokesman in the church growth movement today. He writes of the movement's inherent pragmatism:

> The Church Growth Movement has always stressed pragmatism, and still does even though many have criticized it. It is not the kind of pragmatism that compromises doctrine or ethics or the kind that dehumanizes people by using them as means toward an end. It is, however, the kind of consecrated pragmatism which ruthlessly examines traditional methodologies and programs asking the tough questions. If some sort of ministry in the church is not reaching intended goals, consecrated pragmatism says there is something wrong which needs to be corrected.[13]

Wagner, like most in the church growth movement, claims that the "consecrated pragmatism" he advocates does not allow compromise of doctrine or ethics. "The Bible does not allow us to sin that grace may

---

[11]*Ibid.*, ix.
[12]*Ibid.*
[13]*Leading Your Church to Growth* (Ventura, Calif.: Regal, 1984), 201.

abound or to use whatever means that God has prohibited in order to accomplish those ends He has recommended," he notes correctly.[14]

"But with this proviso," Wagner continues, "we ought to see clearly that the end *does* justify the means. What else possibly could justify the means? If the method I am using accomplishes the goal I am aiming at, it is for that reason a good method. If, on the other hand, my method is not accomplishing the goal, how can I be justified in continuing to use it?"[15]

Is that true? Certainly not. Especially if "the goal I am aiming at" is a numerical goal with no biblical warrant, or if "my method . . . not accomplishing the goal" is the clear preaching of God's Word. That is precisely the kind of thinking that is moving biblical exposition out of Christian ministry and replacing it with vaudeville.

One recent best-seller goes even further:

It is . . . critical that we keep in mind a fundamental principle of Christian communication: the audience, not the message, is sovereign. If our advertising is going to stop people in the midst of hectic schedules and cause them to think about what we're saying, *our message has to be adapted to the needs of the audience.* When we produce advertising that is based on the take-it-or-leave-it proposition, rather than on a sensitivity and response to people's needs, people will invariably reject our message.[16]

What if the Old Testament prophets had subscribed to such a philosophy? Jeremiah, for example, preached forty years without seeing any significant positive response. On the contrary, his countrymen threatened to kill him if he did not stop prophesying (Jer. 11:19-23); his own family and friends plotted against him (12:6); he was not permitted to marry and so had to suffer agonizing loneliness (16:2); plots were devised to kill him secretly (18:20-23); he was beaten and put in stocks (20:1, 2); he was spied on by friends who sought revenge (v. 10); he was consumed with sorrow and shame—even cursing the day he was born (vv. 14-18); and finally, falsely accused of being a traitor to the nation (37:13, 14), Jeremiah was beaten, thrown into a dungeon, and starved many days (vv.

---

[14]*Your Church Can Grow* (Ventura, Calif.: Regal, 1976), 160-61.
[15]*Ibid.*, 161 (emphasis in original).
[16]Barna, *Marketing the Church*, 145 (emphasis added).

15-21). If an Ethiopian Gentile had not interceded on his behalf, Jeremiah would have died there. In the end, tradition says he was exiled to Egypt, where he was stoned to death by his own people. He had virtually no converts to show for a lifetime of ministry.

Suppose Jeremiah had attended a church growth seminar and learned a pragmatic philosophy of ministry. Do you think he would have changed his style of confrontational ministry? Can you imagine him staging a variety show or using comedy to try to win people's affections? He may have learned to gather an appreciative crowd, but he certainly would not have had the ministry God called him to.

The apostle Paul didn't use a system based on merchandising skill either, though some self-appointed experts have tried to make him a model of the new pragmatism. One advocate of marketing technique asserts, "Paul was one of the all-time great tacticians. He perpetually studied strategies and tactics to identify those that would enable him to attract the most 'prospects' and realize the greatest number of conversions."[17] Of course, the Bible says nothing like that. On the contrary, the apostle Paul shunned clever methods and gimmicks that might proselyte people to false conversions through fleshly persuasion. Paul himself wrote,

> When I came to you, brethren, I did not come with superiority of speech or of wisdom, proclaiming to you the testimony of God. For I determined to know nothing among you except Jesus Christ, and Him crucified. And I was with you in weakness and in fear and in much trembling. And my message and my preaching were not in persuasive words of wisdom, but in demonstration of the Spirit and of power, that your faith should not rest on the wisdom of men, but on the power of God (1 Cor. 2:1-5).

He reminded the church at Thessalonica,

> For our exhortation does not come from error or impurity or by way of deceit; but just as we have been approved by God to be entrusted with the gospel, so we speak, not as pleasing men but God, who examines our hearts. For we never came with flattering speech, as you know, nor with a pretext for greed—God is witness—nor did we seek glory from

---

[17]*Ibid.*, 31-32.

men, either from you or from others, even though as apostles of Christ we might have asserted our authority (1 Thess. 2:3-6).

Biblical correctness is the *only* framework by which we must evaluate all ministry methods.

Any end-justifies-the-means philosophy of ministry inevitably *will* compromise doctrine, despite any proviso to the contrary. If we make effectiveness the gauge of right and wrong, how can that fail to color our doctrine? Ultimately the pragmatist's notion of truth is shaped by what seems effective, not by the objective revelation of Scripture.

A look at the methodology of the church growth movement shows how this occurs. The movement studies *all* growing churches—even those with false doctrine at the core of their teaching. Liberal denominational churches, extreme charismatic sects, and militant hyper-fundamentalist dictatorships all are held up to the specialist's scrutiny. Sometimes principles of growth are gleaned even from Mormon assemblies and Jehovah's Witness Kingdom Halls. The church growth expert looks for characteristics common to all growing churches and advocates whatever methods seem to work. And the issue is always numerical growth.

Are we to believe that growth in non-Christian congregations is proof that God is at work? Why would we want to duplicate the methodology of religious groups that corrupt the gospel? Isn't it fair to question whether any growth resulting from such methods is illegitimate, engineered by fleshly means? After all, if a method works as well for a cult as it does for the people of God, there's no reason to assume positive results signify God's blessing.

Utterly missing from most of the church growth literature is any critical analysis of the faulty doctrinal platform on which much contemporary church growth is built. One author has said of Peter Wagner:

> Wagner makes negative assessments about nobody. He has made a career out of finding what is good in growing churches, and affirming it—without asking many critical questions. This enables him to hold up as models of church life not only Wimber's Vineyard, but Schuller's Crystal Cathedral, the entire Southern Baptist denomination, and just about any other church that is growing.[18]

---

[18]Tim Stafford, "Testing the Wine from John Wimber's Vineyard," *Christianity Today* (8 August 1986), 18.

The fact that a church is growing is often mistaken for divine sanction. After all, people reason, why be critical of any teaching that God is blessing with numerical growth? Is it not better to tolerate doctrinal flaws and lapses of orthodoxy for the sake of growth and unity? Thus pragmatism molds and shapes one's doctrinal outlook.

Wagner himself, for example, formerly a non-charismatic, changed his doctrinal views to embrace the signs and wonders of the Third Wave movement—for reasons that are largely pragmatic. He is very candid about this:

> I am proud to be among those who are advocating power evangelism as an important tool for fulfilling the great commission in our day. One of the reasons I am so enthusiastic is that *it is working.* Across the board, the most effective evangelism in today's world is accompanied by manifestations of supernatural power.[19]

Obviously, then, Wagner's pragmatic perspective *has* shaped his doctrine, not vice versa.

Wagner virtually concedes this point. He says the methodology of the church growth movement is "phenomenological," not theological. That approach "may appear altogether too subjective to many traditional theologians," he admits.[20] He continues, "As a starting point, church growth often looks to the 'is' previous to the 'ought.' . . . What Christians experience about God's work in the world and in their lives is not always preceded by careful theological rationalizations. Many times the sequence is just the opposite: theology is shaped by Christian experience."[21]

That being the case, isn't Wagner's assertion that his pragmatism "is not the kind . . . that compromises doctrine"[22] rendered meaningless? After all, if experience suggests signs and wonders are effective tools for church growth, and if it is legitimate to allow our experience to shape our theology, it is quite logical to amend one's doctrine—as Wagner himself did—to accommodate some pragmatic, heuristic observation. One must then simply find a way to reinterpret or adapt Scripture to fit whatever doctrinal scheme pragmatism seems to dictate.

It is folly to think one can be both pragmatic *and* biblical. The pragmatist wants to know *what works now*. The biblical thinker cares only

---

[19] *The Third Wave of the Holy Spirit* (Ann Arbor, Mich.: Vine, 1988), 87.
[20] *Church Growth: State of the Art* (Wheaton, Ill.: Tyndale, 1986), 33.
[21] *Ibid.*
[22] *Leading Your Church to Growth*, 201.

about *what the Bible mandates*. The two philosophies oppose each other at the most basic level.

THE AGE OF PRAGMATISM

Nevertheless, philosophical pragmatism has never been more popular in evangelical churches. The church growth movement, which for years was a major factor in world missionary activity, is now having enormous influence in the backyard of Western evangelicalism. The chickens of pragmatism are coming home to roost. North American churches by the hundreds are experimenting with pragmatic methodologies, and the result has been an explosion of interest in innovative church growth techniques. The church growth movement has formed an unofficial alliance with those who believe evangelism is primarily a marketing venture.

Pragmatism in the church reflects the spirit of our age. Books with titles like *Marketing Your Ministry*, *Marketing the Church*, and *The Development of Effective Marketing and Communication Strategies for Churches* are all the rage. The Christian publishing industry is producing more and more advice for church leaders drawn from secular fields of study—psychology, marketing, management, politics, entertainment, and business—while commentaries, Bible study helps, and books on biblical issues are on the decline.

The role model for contemporary pastors is not the prophet or the shepherd—it is the corporate executive, the politician, or worst of all, the talk-show host. Much of the contemporary church is preoccupied with audience ratings, popularity polls, corporate image, statistical growth, financial profit, opinion surveys, demographic charts, census figures, fashion trends, celebrity status, top-ten lists, and other pragmatic issues. Fast fading is the church's passion for purity and truth. No one seems to care, as long as the response is enthusiastic.

Tozer noticed that pragmatism had crept into the church of his day, too. He wrote, "I say without hesitation that a part, a very large part, of the activities carried on today in evangelical circles are not only influenced by pragmatism but almost completely controlled by it."[23] Tozer described the danger posed to the church by even so-called "consecrated" pragmatism:

---

[23]*God Tells the Man Who Cares* (Harrisburg, Penn.: Christian Publications, 1970), 71.

The pragmatic philosophy . . . asks no embarrassing questions about the wisdom of what we are doing or even about the morality of it. It accepts our chosen ends as right and good and casts about for efficient means and ways to get them accomplished. When it discovers something that works it soon finds a text to justify it, "consecrates" it to the Lord and plunges ahead. Next a magazine article is written about it, then a book, and finally the inventor is granted an honorary degree. After that any question about the scripturalness of things or even the moral validity of them is completely swept away. You cannot argue with success. The method works; *ergo*, it must be good.[24]

A BANKRUPT PHILOSOPHY

Do you see how the new philosophy necessarily undermines sound doctrine? It discards Jesus' own methods—preaching and teaching—as the primary means of ministry. It replaces them with methodologies utterly devoid of substance. It exists independently of any creed or canon. In fact, it avoids dogma or strong convictions as divisive, unbecoming, or inappropriate. It dismisses doctrine as academic, abstract, sterile, threatening, or simply impractical. Rather than teaching error or denying truth, it does something far more subtle, but just as effective from the enemy's point of view. It jettisons content altogether. Instead of attacking orthodoxy head on, it gives lip service to the truth while quietly undermining the foundations of doctrine. Instead of exalting God, it denigrates the things that are precious to Him. In that regard, pragmatism poses dangers more subtle than the liberalism that threatened the church in the first half of the century.

Liberalism attacked biblical preaching. One of the leading liberal figures in early twentieth-century America was Harry Emerson Fosdick, who wrote, "Preachers who pick out texts from the Bible and then proceed to give their historic settings, their logical meaning in the context, their place in the theology of the writer, with a few practical reflections appended, are grossly misusing the Bible."[25] Fosdick was driven to his hatred of biblical exposition by the same pragmatic concern that has invaded evangelicalism today:

---

[24]*Ibid.*, 70.
[25]"What Is the Matter with Preaching?" *Harpers Magazine* (July 1928), 135.

Could any procedure be more surely predestined to dullness and futility? Who seriously supposes that, as a matter of fact, one in a hundred of the congregation cares, to start with, what Moses, Isaiah, Paul, or John meant in those special verses, or came to church deeply concerned about it? Nobody who talks to the public so assumes that the vital interests of the people are located in the meaning of words spoken two thousand years ago.[26]

Fosdick's suggestion was that preachers start with the audience's felt needs: "Let them not end but start with thinking of the auditors' vital needs, and then let the whole sermon be organized around their constructive endeavor to meet those needs."[27]

"All this is good sense and good psychology," Fosdick wrote, appealing to pragmatism as his justification. "Everybody else is using it from first-class teachers to first-class advertisers. Why should so many preachers continue in such belated fashion to neglect it?"[28]

That is exactly the conventional wisdom of the user-friendly, market-driven philosophy. It starts with felt needs and addresses them with topical messages. If Scripture is used at all, it is only for illustrative purposes—precisely as Fosdick advocated. It is sheer accommodation to a society addicted to self-esteem and entertainment. Only now that advice comes from *within* evangelicalism. It follows what is fashionable but reveals little concern for what is true. It was well-suited for the liberalism from whence it came. But it is totally out of place among Christians who profess to believe that Scripture is the inspired Word of God.

One recent best-selling evangelical book warns readers to be on guard against preachers whose emphasis is on *interpreting* Scripture rather than *applying* it. Wait a minute. Is that wise counsel? No, it is not. There is no danger of irrelevant doctrine; the real threat is an undoctrinal attempt at relevance. The nucleus of all that is truly practical is found in the teaching of Scripture. We don't *make* the Bible relevant; it is inherently so, simply because it is God's Word. And after all, how can *anything* God says be irrelevant (2 Tim. 3:16, 17)?

---

[26] *Ibid.*
[27] *Ibid.*
[28] *Ibid.*, 136.

THE CHURCH AS A PUB

The radical pragmatism of the "user-friendly" school robs the church of its prophetic role. It makes the church a populist organization, recruiting members by providing them a warm and friendly atmosphere in which to eat, drink, and be entertained. The church functions more like a saloon than a house of worship.

That is no overstatement. One recent best-selling book advocating pragmatic church-growth ideas included this suggestion:

> Remember how the corner tavern used to be the place where the men of the neighborhood would congregate to watch major sports events, like the World Series or championship boxing matches? While times have changed, that same concept can still be used to great impact by the Church. Most churches have a large hall or auditorium which could be used for special gatherings built around major media events—sports, political debates, entertainment specials and the like.[29]

That entire scenario is built on a set of presuppositions that are patently unbiblical. The church is not a lodge recruiting members. It is not a pub for the neighborhood. It is not a frat house enlisting pledges. It is not a community center where parties are held. It is not a country club for the masses. It is not a city precinct meeting where the community's problems are addressed. It is not a court to rectify society's injustices. It is not an open forum, or a political convention, or even an evangelistic rally.

The church is the body of Christ (1 Cor. 12:27), and church meetings are for corporate worship and instruction. The church's only legitimate goal is "the equipping of the saints for the work of service, to the building up of the body of Christ" (Eph. 4:12)—vital growth, not mere numerical expansion.

The notion that church meetings should be used to tantalize or attract non-Christians is a relatively recent development. Nothing like it is found in Scripture; in fact, the apostle Paul spoke of unbelievers' entering the assembly as an exceptional event (1 Cor. 14:23). Hebrews 10:24, 25 indicates that church services are for the benefit of believers, not

---

[29]George Barna, *The Frog in the Kettle* (Ventura, Calif.: Regal, 1990), 94-95.

unbelievers: "Let us consider how to stimulate one another to love and good deeds, not forsaking our own assembling together."

Acts 2:42 shows us the pattern the early church followed when they met: "They were continually devoting themselves to the apostles' teaching and to fellowship, to the breaking of bread and to prayer." Note that the early church's priorities clearly were to worship God and uplift the brethren. The church came together for worship and edification; it scattered to evangelize the world.

Our Lord commissioned His disciples for evangelism in this way: "Go therefore and make disciples of all the nations" (Matt. 28:19). Christ makes it clear that the church is not to wait for or invite the world to come to its meetings, but to *go* to the world. That is every believer's responsibility. I fear that an approach emphasizing a palatable gospel presentation within the walls of the church absolves the individual believer from his personal obligation to be a light in the world (Matt. 5:16).

Again we emphasize that the proclamation of God's Word is to be central in the church (1 Cor. 1:23; 9:16; 2 Cor. 4:5; 1 Tim. 6:2; 2 Tim. 4:2). "In season and out of season," it is the task of God's ministers to "reprove, rebuke, exhort, with great patience and instruction" (2 Tim. 4:2). The pastor who sets entertainment above forceful biblical preaching abdicates the primary responsibility of an elder: "holding fast the faithful word which is in accordance with the teaching, that he may be able both to exhort in sound doctrine and to refute those who contradict" (Titus 1:9).

The church's strategy has never been to appeal to the world on the world's terms. Churches aren't supposed to compete for the consumer on the same level as Miller Lite or MTV. We can't stimulate genuine growth by clever persuasion or inventive techniques. It is the Lord who adds to the church (Acts 2:47). Human methodologies cannot accelerate or supersede the divine process. Any additional growth they produce is a barren imitation.

Artificial or unnatural growth in the biological realm can cause disfigurement—or worse, cancer. Synthetic growth in the spiritual realm is every bit as unhealthy.

GOOD TECHNIQUE? NO, BAD THEOLOGY.

The philosophy that marries marketing technique with church growth theory is the result of bad theology. It assumes that if you package the gospel right, people will get saved. It is rooted in Arminianism, which makes the human will, not a sovereign God, the decisive factor in salvation. It speaks of conversion as a "decision for Christ." Such language and such doctrine have begun to color modern ministry. The goal of market-driven ministry is an instantaneous human decision, rather than a radical transformation of the heart wrought by Almighty God through the Holy Spirit's convicting work and the truth of His Word. An honest belief in the sovereignty of God in salvation would bring an end to a lot of the nonsense that is going on in the church.

Moreover, this whole ad-agency approach to the church corrupts Christianity and caters to the fleshly lusts that are woven into the very fabric of this world's system (1 John 2:16). We have a society filled with people who want what they want when they want it. They are into their own lifestyle, recreation, and entertainment. They want comfort, happiness, and success. When churches appeal to those selfish desires, they only fuel fires that hinder true godliness.

The church has accommodated our culture by devising a brand of Christianity where taking up one's cross is optional—or even unseemly. Indeed, many members of the church in the Western world suppose they can best serve God by being as non-confrontive to their world as possible.

Having absorbed the world's values, Christianity in our society is now dying. Subtly but surely, worldliness and self-indulgence are eating away the heart of the church. The gospel usually proclaimed today is so convoluted that it offers believing in Christ as nothing more than a means to contentment and prosperity. The offense of the cross (cf Gal. 5:11) has been systematically removed so that the message might be made more acceptable to unbelievers. The church somehow got the idea it could declare peace with the enemies of God.

When on top of that punk-rockers, ventriloquists' dummies, clowns, knife-throwers, professional wrestlers, weight-lifters, body-builders, comedians, dancers, jugglers, ringmasters, rap artists, actors, and show-business celebrities take the place of the preacher, the gospel message is dealt a catastrophic blow. "How shall they hear without a preacher?" (Rom. 10:14).

I do believe we can be innovative and creative in how we present the gospel, but we have to be careful to harmonize our methods with the profound spiritual truth we are trying to convey. It is too easy to trivialize the sacred message. And we must make the message, not the medium, the heart of what we want to convey to the audience.

Don't be quick to embrace the trends of the high-tech megachurches. And don't sneer at conventional worship and preaching. We don't need clever approaches to get people saved (1 Cor. 1:21). We simply need to get back to preaching the truth and planting the seed. If we're faithful in that, the soil God has prepared will bear fruit.

But if the church in America does not get back to biblical Christianity, we will soon see the end of our influence for Christ. Everyone is astonished to see how rapidly the face of the modern world is changing. What so few Christians seem to realize is how frighteningly fast the church is coasting along the down-grade at the same time. We may be witnessing the last days of biblical evangelicalism as a significant force in our nation. It is not really far-fetched to imagine that twenty years hence, missionaries from Eastern Europe might be evangelizing America.

The reality of that possibility greatly alarms me. We who know and love the truth must be the prophetic voice of our God and affirm the holiness of His Name. We must demand that any effort in the name of our Lord manifest the integrity of His nature. He is "Holy, Holy, Holy" (Isa. 6:3) and must be so represented. Anything less is not worthy of our Lord's majesty, awesomeness, and holiness.

THE BREAKING FORTH OF A LEPROSY

Spurgeon saw this same tendency to import amusements into the church at the end of the nineteenth century. As the Down-Grade Controversy was raging in 1889, Spurgeon's health was waning badly, and he missed many Sundays in the pulpit. But on a Thursday evening in April, he gave a message at the Tabernacle in which he said,

> I trust I am not given to finding fault where fault there is not; but I cannot open my eyes without seeing things done in our churches which, thirty years ago, were not so much as dreamed of. In the matter of amusements, professors have gone far in the way of laxity. What is worse, the churches have now conceived the idea that it is their duty to amuse the people. Dissenters who used to protest against going to the theatre, now cause the theatre to come to them. Ought not many [church buildings] to be licensed for stage-plays? If some one were to see to the rigid carrying out of the law, would they not be required to take out a license for theatricals?
>
> I dare not touch upon what has been done at bazaars and fancy fairs. If these had been arranged by decent worldly people, could they have gone further? What folly has been left untried? What absurdity has been too great for the consciences of those who profess to be the

children of God, who are not of the world, but called to walk with God in a separated life?

The world regards the high pretensions of such men as hypocrisy; and truly I do not know another name for them. Think of those who enjoy communion with God playing the fool in costume! They talk of wrestling with the Lord in secret prayer, but they juggle with the world in unconcealed gambling. Can this be right? Have right and wrong shifted places? Surely there is a sobriety of behaviour which is consistent with a work of grace in the heart, and there is a levity which betokens that the spirit of evil is supreme.

Ah, sirs! there may have been a time when Christians were too precise, but it has not been in my day. There may have been such a dreadful thing as Puritanic rigidity, but I have never seen it. We are quite free from that evil now, if it ever existed. We have gone from liberty to libertinism. We have passed beyond the dubious into the dangerous, and none can prophesy where we shall stop. Where is the holiness of the church of God to-day? . . . Now she is dim as smoking flax, and rather the object of ridicule than of reverence.

May not the measure of the influence of a church be estimated by its holiness? If the great host of professing Christians were, in domestic life and in business life, sanctified by the Spirit, the church would become a great power in the world. God's saints may well mourn with Jerusalem when they see spirituality and holiness at so low an ebb! Others may regard this as a matter of no consequence; but we view it as the breaking forth of a leprosy.[30]

The challenge for Christ's church is this: "Let us cleanse ourselves from all defilement of flesh and spirit, perfecting holiness in the fear of God" (2 Cor. 7:1). It isn't the cleverness of our methods, the techniques of our ministry, or the wit of our sermons that puts power in our testimony. It is obedience to a holy God and faithfulness to His righteous standard in our daily lives.

We must wake up. The down-grade is a dangerous place to be. We cannot afford to be indifferent. We cannot continue our mad pursuit of pleasure and self-gratification. We are called to fight a spiritual battle, and we cannot win by appeasing the enemy. A weak church must be made strong, and a needy world must be confronted with the message of sal-

---

[30]"A Dirge for the Down-Grade, and a Song for Faith," *The Metropolitan Tabernacle Pulpit*, Vol. 35 (London: Passmore and Alabaster, 1889), 267-68.

vation, and there may be little time left. As Paul wrote to the church at Rome, "It is already the hour for you to awaken from sleep; for now salvation is nearer to us than when we believed. The night is almost gone, and the day is at hand. Let us therefore lay aside the deeds of darkness and put on the armor of light" (Rom. 13:11, 12).

4

All Things to All Men

The extent to which sheer frivolity and utterly inane amusement have been carried in connection with some places of worship would almost exceed belief.... There can be no doubt that all sorts of entertainments, as nearly as possible approximating to stage-plays, have been carried on in connection with places of worship, and are, at this present time in high favour. Can these things promote holiness, or help in communion with God? Can men come away from such things and plead with God for the salvation of sinners and the sanctification of believers? We loathe to touch the unhallowed subject; it seems so far removed from the walk of faith and the way of heavenly fellowship. In some cases the follies complained of are even beneath the dignity of manhood, and fitter for the region of the imbecile than for thoughtful men.

CHARLES HADDON SPURGEON[1]

I DOUBT there has ever been anyone like Sister Paula in the entire history of Christianity. She describes herself as "an open transsexual Christian, preaching the gospel. . . . Tammy Faye with a 5 o'clock shadow."[2] Sister Paula was born Larry Nielsen, and supposedly became a Christian "in 1950, as a 12-year-old innately effeminate boy." After Larry became Paula in a sex-change operation a few years ago, a female Pentecostal televangelist friend urged Larry/Paula to start a television ministry. *People* magazine described Sister Paula as fifty-three years old, six-feet-one-and-a-half-inches tall, "built like a linebacker."[3]

Can you imagine anything more incongruous or more profane than a transsexual evangelist? Yet Sister Paula believes she can have a more

---

[1]"Restoration of Truth and Revival," *The Sword and the Trowel* (December 1887), 606.
[2]*People* (16 March 1992), 68.
[3]*Ibid.*

effective ministry to people in our generation than the typical "straight" Christian using nothing but the gospel. Sister Paula's ministry philosophy is fundamentally the same strategy the church marketing experts advocate, though thankfully, none of them would want to see it taken to such an extreme.

The notion that the church must become like the world to win the world has taken evangelicalism by storm. Virtually every modern worldly attraction has a "Christian" counterpart. We have Christian motorcycle gangs, Christian bodybuilding teams, Christian dance clubs, Christian amusement parks, and I even read about a Christian nudist colony.

Where did Christians ever get the idea we could win the world by imitating it? Is there a shred of biblical justification for that kind of thinking? Many church marketing specialists affirm that there is, and they have convinced a myriad of pastors. Ironically, they usually cite the apostle Paul as someone who advocated adapting the gospel to the tastes of the audience. One has written, "Paul provided what I feel is perhaps the single most insightful perspective on marketing communications, the principle we call *contextualization* (1 Corinthians 9:19-23). Paul . . . was willing to shape his communications according to their needs in order to receive the response he sought."[4] "The first marketeer was Paul," another echoes.[5]

After all, the apostle *did* write, "I have become all things to all men, that I may by all means save some. And I do all things for the sake of the gospel, that I may become a fellow partaker of it" (1 Cor. 9:22, 23). Is that a mandate for pragmatism in ministry? Was the apostle Paul suggesting that the gospel message can be made to appeal to people by accommodating their relish for certain amusements or by pampering their pet vices? How far do you suppose he would have been willing to go with the principle of "contextualization"?

THE GREAT NON-NEGOTIABLE

This much is very clear: the apostle Paul was no people-pleaser. He wrote, "Am I now seeking the favor of men, or of God? Or am I striving to please men? If I were still trying to please men, I would not be a bond-servant of Christ" (Gal. 1:10). Paul did not amend or abridge his message to make people happy. He was utterly unwilling to try to remove the offense from

---

[4]George Barna, *Marketing the Church* (Colorado Springs, Colo.: NavPress, 1988), 33.
[5]Cited in Mike McIntyre, "Marketing the Maker," *The San Diego Union* (6 November 1988), D8.

the gospel (Gal. 5:11). He did not use methodology that catered to the lusts of his listeners. He certainly did not follow the pragmatic philosophy of modern market-driven ministers.

What made Paul effective was not marketing savvy, but a stubborn devotion to the truth. He was Christ's ambassador, not His press secretary. Truth was something to be declared, not negotiated. Paul was not ashamed of the gospel (Rom. 1:16). He willingly suffered for the truth's sake (2 Cor. 11:23-28). He did not back down in the face of opposition or rejection. He did not compromise with unbelievers or make friends with the enemies of God.

Paul's message was *always* non-negotiable. In the same chapter where he spoke of becoming all things to all men, Paul wrote, "I am under compulsion; for woe is me if I do not preach the gospel" (1 Cor. 9:16). His ministry was in response to a divine mandate. God had called him and commissioned him. Paul preached the gospel exactly as he had received it directly from the Lord, and he always delivered that message "as of first importance" (1 Cor. 15:3). He was not a salesman or marketer, but a divine emissary. He certainly was *not* "willing to shape his communications" to accommodate his listeners or produce a desirable response. The fact that he was stoned and left for dead (Acts 14:19), beaten, imprisoned, and finally killed for the truth's sake ought to demonstrate that he didn't adapt the message to make it pleasing to his hearers! And the personal suffering he bore because of his ministry did *not* indicate that something was wrong with his approach, but that everything had been right!

So what did Paul mean when he wrote, "I have become all things to all men, that I may by all means save some. And I do all things for the sake of the gospel"? As always, the context makes his meaning clear.

GIVING UP TO GAIN

Look again at what Paul is actually saying in these verses:

> For though I am free from all men, I have made myself a slave to all, that I might win the more. And to the Jews I became as a Jew, that I might win Jews; to those who are under the Law, as under the Law, though not being myself under the Law, that I might win those who are under the Law; to those who are without law, as without law, though not being without the law of God but under the law of Christ, that I might win those who are without law. To the weak I became weak, that I might win the weak; I have become all things to all men,

that I may by all means save some. And I do all things for the sake of the gospel, that I may become a fellow partaker of it (1 Cor. 9:19-23).

The first sentence in that brief excerpt shows clearly what Paul was talking about. He was describing not his willingness to sacrifice the message, but his willingness to sacrifice himself to preach the message. He would give up everything—even become "a slave to all"—if that would promote the spread of the unadulterated gospel. His desire to win souls is the heart of this text, and he repeats it several times: "that I might win the more"; "that I might win Jews"; "that I might win those who are under the Law"; "that I might win those who are without law"; "that I might win the weak"; and "that I may by all means save some." So winning people to Christ was his one objective. In order to do that, Paul was willing to give up all his rights and privileges, his position, his rank, his livelihood, his freedom— ultimately even his life. If it would further the spread of the gospel, Paul would claim no rights, make no demands, insist on no privileges.

And that is precisely how Paul lived and ministered. Not that he would modify the message to suit the world, but that he would behave so that he personally would never be an obstacle to anyone's hearing and understanding the message of Christ. He was describing an attitude of personal sacrifice, not compromise. He would never alter the clear and confrontive call to repentance and faith.

Paul was making the point that Christian liberty must be circumscribed by love. That is the whole theme of the eighth through the tenth chapters of 1 Corinthians. It is the context in which these verses are found. The Corinthians were evidently debating about the nature and extent of Christian freedom. Some wanted to use their liberty to do whatever they desired. Others leaned toward legalism, begrudging those who enjoyed their liberty in Christ. Paul was reminding both groups that Christian freedom is to be used to glorify God and serve others, not for selfish reasons.

Here's an example of how that principle applies. Some of the Corinthians apparently had asked Paul whether they were free to eat meat offered to idols (8:1). Such meat often was collected from the pagan temples and sold in the marketplace at bargain prices. Paul told them it is not inherently wrong to eat such food, but if doing so places a stumbling block in someone else's way, such an offense against another person is wrong. Paul summarized his reply with these words: "Whether, then, you eat or drink or whatever you do, do all to the glory of God. Give no offense either to Jews or to Greeks or to the church of God; just as I also please all men in all things, not seeking my own profit, but the profit of the many, that they may be saved" (10:31-33).

How did Paul use his own liberty in Christ? "Though I am free from all men, I have made myself a slave to all, that I might win the more" (9:19). He saw his personal liberty and human rights as something to be used for God's glory, not his own enjoyment. If he could trade his own liberty for an opportunity to proclaim the gospel and thus liberate others, he would do it gladly.

LIBERTY IN CHRIST

It is crucial that we understand the nature of Christian liberty. We are not under law, but under grace (Rom. 6:14). Freedom from the law certainly does not mean that the principles of righteousness revealed in the Old Testament law are now nullified. It does not mean that the Ten Commandments have no application to our present lives. It does not mean that we can subjugate God's holy standards to personal preference. It obviously does not mean we are free from any moral requirements.

What does it mean? It means that Christians are not bound to observe Old Testament ritual. We don't have to sacrifice animals, observe the laws of ceremonial cleanness, and celebrate all the new moons and feasts and sacrifices. We don't have to follow the dietary laws given to Israel through Moses. We are free from all that.

Likewise, obviously, we are free from all Gentile religious ceremony and superstition. Whatever our religious background or heritage, in Christ we are free from all the trappings of it. We now live by God's grace, which has the principle of true righteousness built in.

In other words, our spiritual lives are governed not merely by an external code, but by God's grace, which operates in us to fulfill the righteous requirements of the law (Rom. 8:4). Grace teaches us to deny ungodliness and worldly desires, and to live sensibly, righteously, and godly (Titus 2:12). And grace empowers us to live holy lives.

This tremendous liberty is one of the most remarkable aspects of the Christian life. We have no need to yield to custom or ceremony or human opinion. There are no earthly priests to intercede between us and God: "There is one God, and one mediator also between God and men, the man Christ Jesus" (1 Tim. 2:5). We don't need to make a pilgrimage to a temple somewhere to worship; our very bodies are temples of the Holy Spirit (1 Cor. 6:19). We can worship God in spirit and in truth anytime, anyplace (John 4:23, 24). Whatever we ask in Jesus' name He will do (John 14:13, 14). The Holy Spirit is given to us as our advocate and comforter (vv. 16, 26). All things belong to us, and we are Christ's, and Christ is God's (1 Cor. 3:21-23).

SERVANTS OF A NEW COVENANT

Yet there is a paradox that balances that truth. Though free, all Christians are slaves. It is a new kind of bondage: we are "servants of a new covenant, not of the letter, but of the Spirit; for the letter kills, but the Spirit gives life" (2 Cor. 3:6). As willing slaves, we must voluntarily restrict our own liberty for others' sakes. Isn't that what Jesus Himself taught? "If anyone wants to be first, he shall be last of all, and servant of all" (Mark 9:35). Paul applied the principle of voluntary servitude to evangelism. He made himself a slave to all—including the roughest, most contemptible, loathsome pagan. Being free, he nevertheless joyfully entered into slavery for the gospel's sake.

This principle of voluntary slavery was pictured graphically in the Old Testament law. Exodus 21:5, 6 describes the process by which one could choose to make himself another's servant: "If the slave plainly says, 'I love my master, my wife and my children; I will not go out as a free man,' then his master shall bring him to God, then he shall bring him to the door or the doorpost. And his master shall pierce his ear with an awl; and he shall serve him permanently." The Israelites were permitted to keep fellow Jews as slaves only for six years. On the seventh year they were to be set free. But if one voluntarily chose to continue serving as a slave, his master would literally put his ear against the doorpost, take an awl, and drive it through the ear. The hole in the slave's ear was a sign to all that he was serving out of love, not because he had to. Paul was saying he had voluntarily relinquished his freedom in order to serve all men. In a spiritual sense, Paul had perforated his ear on behalf of the unsaved. "Though I am free from all men, I have made myself a slave to all, that I might win the more" (1 Cor. 9:19).

The word translated "made . . . a slave" is the Greek verb *douloō*, "to enslave." This is a strong expression. It is the same word used in 1 Corinthians 7:15 in relation to the marriage bond. And the same word is used in Romans 6:18, 22 to speak of our union with Christ. It describes an exceedingly secure bond. Paul had denied himself in the truest sense by placing himself under such a bond to everyone else.

The phrase "that I might win the more" is not talking about winning earthly or heavenly rewards. Paul was speaking of winning the lost to Christ. Such was Paul's concern for lost souls that, though he was free in Christ, he was willing to enslave himself to people if it would give him an opportunity to proclaim the gospel. He expressed a similar commitment in 2 Timothy 2:10: "I endure all things for the sake of those who are chosen, that they also may obtain the salvation which is in Christ Jesus and with it eternal glory."

Consider all that Paul suffered for the gospel's sake. He became a prisoner. He went to jail. He was beaten, whipped, shipwrecked, and stoned. He continually set his own life aside. Ultimately he was killed for the testimony of the gospel. He would have gone even further if it were possible. To the church at Rome Paul wrote these shocking words: "I have great sorrow and unceasing grief in my heart. For I could wish that I myself were accursed, separated from Christ for the sake of my brethren, my kinsmen according to the flesh" (9:23, 24). In other words, he felt as if he would have given up his own salvation if he could, so that his Jewish brethren could be saved.

In contrast, the Corinthians were demanding their rights. They were misusing their freedom at others' expense. Weaker brothers were stumbling, and it is very likely that unbelievers were repelled by the selfishness and strife that dominated the Corinthian fellowship, so carefully chronicled in Paul's first letter to them.

Instead Paul wanted them to follow his example. "Be imitators of me, just as I also am of Christ" (1 Cor. 11:1). And what was his example? Go back one verse, to the end of 1 Corinthians 10: "Just as I also please all men in all things, not seeking my own profit, but the profit of the many, that they may be saved." So the only sense in which we as believers are to be men-pleasers is in looking "not only to [our] own interests, but also to the interests of others" (Phil. 2:4, NIV).

That's the point Paul was making here. He was not advocating a marketing plan. He was not making a plea for "contextualization." He was not suggesting that the message be made more acceptable, or that the role of preaching be replaced by psychology, skits, and worldly entertainment. He was calling for self-denial and sacrifice for the sake of proclaiming the unadulterated truth to those who do not know Christ.

FOR THE JEWS I BECOME JEWISH

How did Paul apply this principle? In 1 Corinthians 9:20 he describes the practical outworking of self-denial: "To the Jews I became as a Jew . . . to those who are under the Law, as under the Law." This describes a self-less sacrifice of Paul's personal liberty: "though not being . . . under the Law," Paul willingly subjected himself to the law's ritual requirements in order to win those who were under the law. In other words, he adopted their customs. Whatever their ceremonial law dictated, he was willing to do. If it was important to them to abstain from eating pork, he abstained. If their sensibilities demanded that a certain feast be observed, he observed it. Why? Not to appease their pride or affirm their religion, but in order to open a door of opportunity for him to preach the uncompromised truth, so that he might win them to Jesus Christ.

John Calvin understood this passage:

[Paul] adopted the Jewish way of life in the company of Jews, but not before all of them; for many of them were obstinate, and under the influence of Pharisaism, pride, or ill-will they would have liked to see Christian freedom suppressed altogether. *Paul would never have deferred to the same extent to people like that, for Christ does not want us to trouble ourselves about them.* Our Lord says "Let them alone, they are blind, and leaders of the blind" (Matt. 15.14). Therefore we must adapt ourselves to the weak, but not to the stubborn. *His purpose was to bring them to Christ, not to further his own interests, or to retain their goodwill.*

. . . Those people are in the wrong, whose main concern is to keep their lives free from trouble, and who, for that reason, take care not to give offence to people, to the wicked that is, rather than to the weak. Moreover, those who do not distinguish between things which are neutral, and things which are forbidden, are doubly in the wrong. Because they do not make that distinction they have no hesitation about undertaking things, which God has forbidden, in order to please men. *But their crowning sin is their making wrong use of this sentence of Paul's, in order to make excuses for their own wicked hypocrisy.*[6]

Paul would stoop to no compromise of the truth. He simply sacrificed personal freedoms and preferences, removing any unnecessary diversion or excuse that would thwart the opportunity to declare the powerful, saving gospel plainly to them.

Paul was not suggesting that the gospel can be made more powerful by adapting it to a certain cultural context. He was not speaking about

---

[6]John W. Fraser, trans., *The First Epistle of Paul to the Corinthians* (Grand Rapids, Mich.: Eerdmans, 1960), 196, emphasis added.

accommodating the *message*. He was simply saying he would not jeopardize his ability to preach the message by unnecessarily offending people. If the message was an offense, so be it: "We preach Christ crucified, to Jews a stumbling block, and to Gentiles foolishness" (1 Cor. 1:23). But Paul would not make *himself* a stumbling block to unbelievers: "Give no offense either to Jews or to Greeks or to the church of God" (10:32).

Several illustrations of this may be adduced from the New Testament. In the fifteenth chapter of Acts the Jerusalem Council, the first church council, met to determine how they should assimilate the Gentile converts. Many of the Jewish believers were so steeped in Jewish tradition that they were skeptical about the Gentiles who were turning to Christ. Then some men came down from Judea and began teaching the Christians, "Unless you are circumcised according to the custom of Moses, you cannot be saved" (15:1). In other words, they were claiming the Gentiles couldn't become Christians unless they became Jewish first. The church was thrown into confusion.

The Jerusalem Council was assembled to discuss the issue. Scripture says there was much debate (v. 7). At one point Peter testified that he had been present when Gentiles first received the Holy Spirit, and all the evidence demonstrated that God was in it (vv. 7-12). Finally, James, the leader, handed down this ruling: "It is my judgment that we do not trouble those who are turning to God from among the Gentiles" (v. 19).

That settled the question. The church would accept Gentiles as they were, without placing them under the Jewish ceremonial law.

But then notice the next verse. James went on to add this: "We [will] write to them that they abstain from things contaminated by idols and from fornication and from what is strangled and from blood." He listed four things the Gentiles were to stay away from. First, "things contaminated by idols" meant food offered to idols. That was precisely the issue that troubled the Corinthians. Eating food offered to pagan idols was grossly offensive to Jewish people. They despised pagan idolatry. But as Paul suggested, there is nothing inherently wrong with eating food that had been offered to idols. What is an idol, anyway? "We know that there is no such thing as an idol in the world, and that there is no God but one" (1 Cor. 8:4). Nevertheless, the Jerusalem Council added this warning to stay away from things contaminated by idols, so as not to needlessly offend the Jews.

Second, the Gentiles were to stay away from fornication. This does not mean simply that they were not to *commit* fornication. That is obvious. It is not a gray area. There was much in the apostolic teaching that prohibited every form of fornication, or sexual sin. So "abstain . . . from fornication" is much more than a command against acts of fornication. Since the Gentile religions revolved around sex rites, temple prostitutes, and orgiastic ritual, James was saying the Gentile believers should have nothing to do with their former ways of worship. They should not attend any ceremonies where these things were going on. They were to sever the tie completely with pagan styles of worship so repulsive to Jews.

Third, they were to abstain from the meat of strangled animals; and fourth, they were to stay away from blood. Strangled meat retains a lot of blood. Jewish law demanded that any animals to be eaten must have the blood completely drained from them. To the Jews, the eating of blood was one of the most offensive of all Gentile practices. And some pagan religious rites involved the drinking of pure animal blood. The Jerusalem Council therefore commanded Gentile believers to abstain from all such practices.

Understand the significance of this. The Jerusalem Council's decision was an explicit condemnation of legalism. The Council refused to put the Gentiles under the Mosaic law. So why did they lay these four prohibitions on them? The reason is made clear in Acts 15:21: "For Moses from ancient generations has in every city those who preach him, since he is read in the synagogues every Sabbath."

In other words, they were to abstain from those four things so they would not offend the Jewish unbelievers. If Christians practiced these most offensive of all Gentile rituals, unbelieving Jews might turn away from the gospel before hearing it.

Acts chapter sixteen includes a similar illustration. It is the first time in Scripture we meet Timothy. Luke records that he was "the son of a Jewish woman who was a believer, but his father was a Greek" (v. 1). Jews would have considered him a Gentile, because his father was a Gentile. Moreover, Timothy's mother would have been considered a virtual traitor for marrying a Gentile.

Yet Timothy "was well spoken of by the brethren who were in Lystra and Iconium. Paul wanted this man to go with him; and he took him and circumcised him" (vv. 2, 3).

Wait a minute. Why did he do that? Paul certainly didn't believe Gentiles needed be circumcised to be saved. In fact, Paul refused to have Titus circumcised when the Jerusalem legalists demanded it (Gal. 2:1-5). Furthermore, Paul once opposed Peter to his face because Peter had compromised with the legalists (Gal. 2:11-14). He asked Peter, "If you, being a

Jew, live like the Gentiles and not like the Jews, how is it that you compel the Gentiles to live like Jews?" (v. 14). So why did Paul have Timothy circumcised? Was he compromising the issue, demonstrating inconsistency?

No. Timothy wasn't doing it for salvation. He obviously had *not* undergone circumcision when he was saved. And he wasn't doing it to make hardened legalists happy or to tone down the offense of the gospel. He simply wanted to identify with the Jews so he might have an entrance to preach the gospel to them. Paul and Timothy were not hoping to pacify pseudo-Christian legalists, act the part of hypocrites, or mitigate the gospel in any way. They simply wanted to keep open lines of communication to the Jews they were going to preach to. This was not an act of compromise or men-pleasing. It was loving—and physically very painful—self-sacrifice for the sake of the lost.

Wherever he could acknowledge the strong religious tradition of a people and not offend their sensitivities, Paul was glad to do so—when it did not violate God's Word or impinge on the gospel. But the apostle never adapted his ministry to pander to worldly lusts or sinful selfishness.

FOR THE GENTILES I BECOME A GENTILE

Going back to the ninth chapter of 1 Corinthians, we read in verse 21, "To those who are without law, [I become] as without law, though not being without the law of God but under the law of Christ, that I might win those who are without law." "Those who are without law" are the Gentiles. Note the qualifier Paul inserted. He specifically stated that he is "*not . . . without the law of God but under the law of Christ.*" He clearly was not saying he became morally lawless to please despisers of true righteousness.

Though he became as "without law" in the ritual or ceremonial sense, he was not living licentiously or behaving unrighteously. He would have no sympathy with *antinomians*—people who believe all law is abolished for Christians. "Without law" is not a reference to the moral law. Paul is not implying that he lived it up just to make the Gentiles admire him. He did not encourage people to think they could become Christians and hang on to a worldly lifestyle. Again, he was talking about the Old Testament ceremonial law. When he ministered to Gentiles, he dropped all his non-moral Jewish traditions. When Paul was with the Gentiles he followed Gentile customs and culture insofar as it did not conflict with the law of Christ. He avoided needlessly offending the Gentiles.

When Paul was in Jerusalem, for example, he followed Jewish religious customs. He observed the feasts and Sabbaths, and he followed Jewish dietary laws. When he went to Antioch, however, he ate with the Gentiles, even though that violated his own tradition and upbringing. Peter came to Antioch and also ate with the Gentiles, until some Judaizers showed up. Then Peter and some others withdrew and held themselves aloof (Gal. 2:12). Paul says, "Even Barnabas was carried away by their hypocrisy" (v. 13). That was when Paul rebuked Peter to his face in front of others.

Notice why Paul confronted Peter: "I saw that they were not straightforward about the truth of the gospel" (v. 14). Paul's reason for becoming all things to all men was not so he could slip the gospel in covertly. On the contrary, it was so he could without hindrance proclaim the truth of the gospel more straightforwardly than ever. He wanted to remove any personal offense, so the offense of the gospel would be the only one. Paul saw Peter's compromise as something that undermined the clarity and the force of the gospel, and that is why he confronted him.

FOR THE WEAK I BECOME WEAK

Returning to 1 Corinthians 9, we again note that Paul mentions a third group: "To the weak I became weak, that I might win the weak" (v. 22). Who are the weak? In Pauline theology this expression refers to over-scrupulous Christians—immature believers who don't understand their liberty. In the Jewish community, for example, some new Christians still wanted to observe the Sabbaths, attend the synagogues, follow the dietary laws, and maintain all the feasts and ceremonies of the Old Testament law. Some in the Christian community had weak consciences and still felt such things were obligatory. They were just emerging out of Judaism and still holding on, feeling the pangs of conscience to do those things that had become habit and were associated with the true God and the Old Testament Scriptures.

Among the Gentiles, on the other hand, there were those saved out of idolatry who now feared having anything to do with meat offered to idols. Perhaps some clung to old superstitions and feared demonic idols or simply wanted nothing to do with anything reminiscent of the former lifestyle.

Paul, of course, was free from such fears and superstitions. And he was free from the ceremonial law of the Old Testament. The law of Christ governed him. Although he felt free to do things that other people's consciences wouldn't allow them to do, when Paul was with weaker brethren he was careful not to violate their sensibilities. He adapted his behavior so as not to offend them. He yielded in love rather than offend a weaker brother.

How did he do that? At one point he took a Nazirite vow to quell a false rumor among the believing Jews in Jerusalem that he was preaching against Moses and urging Jewish people not to circumcise their children (Acts 21:17-26). Ironically, it was the carrying out of that vow that ultimately led to his arrest and imprisonment. The unbelieving Jews hated the message of the gospel, so they undertook to destroy the messenger. But they had no legitimate complaint against Paul personally, for he had gone out of his way to be a Jew for the Jews, a Gentile for the Gentiles, and a weak brother for the weak brethren.

Again the question comes, why did Paul subject himself to all that? First Corinthians 9:22, 23 says: "That I may by all means save some. And I do all things for the sake of the gospel." "By all means" may sound at first like an echo of pragmatism, but don't forget, Paul is speaking here of condescension, not compromise. What is the difference? To condescend is to remove needless offenses to people's religious consciences by setting aside some personal, optional liberty. To compromise is to set aside an essential truth and thereby alter or weaken the gospel message.

Paul set himself in contrast with the compromisers and marketeers in 2 Corinthians 2:17: "We are not like many, peddling the word of God, but as from sincerity, but as from God, we speak in Christ in the sight of God." The compromiser sells a cheap gospel and tries to make it appealing by stripping away the offense of Christ. Paul simply wanted to keep himself from being an obstacle or a stumbling block to people's consciences so that the unadulterated message could penetrate hearts and do its work. If people were offended by the message, Paul did not try to remove the offense of the gospel or abolish the stumbling block of the cross, and he would not tolerate those who tried (cf Gal. 5:11). But he was willing to practice self-denial and deference if that opened opportunities for him to preach.

"CONTEXTUALIZATION" AND THE CORRUPTION OF THE CHURCH

It should be clear that modern church marketers cannot look to the apostle Paul for approval of their methodology or claim him as the father of their philosophy. Although Paul ministered to the vilest pagans throughout the Roman world, he never adapted the church to secular society's tastes. He would not think of altering either the message or the nature of the church. Each of the churches he founded had its own unique personality and set of problems, but Paul's teaching, his strategy, and above all his message remained the same throughout his ministry. His means of ministry, as we shall note in the next chapter, was always preaching—the straightforward proclamation of biblical truth.

By contrast, the "contextualization" of the gospel today has infected the church with the spirit of the age. It has opened the church's doors wide for worldliness, shallowness, and in some cases a crass, party atmosphere. The world now sets the agenda for the church.

This is demonstrated clearly in a book by James Davison Hunter, a sociology professor at the University of Virginia. Hunter surveyed students in evangelical colleges and seminaries, and concluded that evangelical Christianity has changed dramatically in the past three decades. He found that young evangelicals have become significantly more tolerant of activities once viewed as worldly or immoral—including smoking, using marijuana, attending R-rated movies, and premarital sex. Hunter wrote,

> The symbolic boundaries which previously defined moral propriety for conservative Protestantism have lost a measure of clarity. Many of the distinctions separating Christian conduct from "worldly conduct" have been challenged if not altogether undermined. Even the words *worldly* and *worldliness* have, within a generation, lost most of their traditional meaning. . . . The traditional meaning of worldliness has indeed lost its relevance for the coming generation of Evangelicals.[7]

What Hunter noted among evangelical students is a reflection of what has happened to the entire evangelical church. Many professing Christians appear to care far more about the world's opinion than about God's. Churches are so engrossed in trying to please non-Christians that many have forgotten their first duty is to please God (2 Cor. 5:9). The church has been so over-contextualized that it has become corrupted by the world.

BY ALL MEANS SAVE SOME

Paul's one aim in making himself the slave of all was so that they might be saved. He was not trying to win a popularity contest. He was not seek-

---

[7] *Evangelicalism: The Coming Generation* (Chicago: University of Chicago, 1987), 63.

ing to make himself or the gospel appealing to them. His whole purpose was evangelistic. C. H. Spurgeon, preaching on this passage, said,

> I fear there are some who preach with the view of *amusing* men, and as long as people can be gathered in crowds, and their ears can be tickled, and they can retire pleased with what they have heard, the orator is content, and folds his hands, and goes back self-satisfied. But Paul did not lay himself out to please the public and collect the crowd. If he did not save them he felt that it was of no avail to interest them. Unless the truth had pierced their hearts, affected their lives, and made new men of them, Paul would have gone home crying, "Who hath believed our report, and to whom is the arm of the Lord revealed?" . . .
>
> Now observe, brethren, if I, or you, or any of us, or all of us, shall have spent our lives merely in amusing men, or educating men, or moralizing men, when we shall come to give our account at the last great day we shall be in a very sorry condition, and we shall have but a very sorry record to render; for of what avail will it be to a man to be educated when he comes to be damned? Of what service will it be to him to have been amused when the trumpet sounds, and heaven and earth are shaking, and the pit opens wide her jaws of fire and swallows up the soul unsaved? Of what avail even to have moralized a man if still he is on the left hand of the judge, and if still, "Depart, ye cursed," shall be his portion?[8]

That is precisely my concern about today's pragmatic church-growth strategies. The design is to attract the unchurched. For what? To entertain them? To get them to attend church meetings regularly? Merely "churching" the unchurched accomplishes nothing of eternal value. Too often, however, that is where the strategy stalls. Or else it is combined with a watered-down gospel that wrongly assures sinners a positive "decision" for Christ is as good as true conversion. Multitudes who are not authentic Christians now identify themselves with the church. The church has thus been invaded with the world's values, the world's interests, and the world's citizens.

By all means we are to seek the salvation of the lost. We must be servants to all, deferential to every kind of person. For Jews we should

---

[8]"Soul Saving Our One Business," *The Metropolitan Tabernacle Pulpit*, Vol. 25 (London: Passmore and Alabaster, 1879), 674-76.

become Jewish; for Gentiles we should be like Gentiles; for children we should be childlike; and so on for every facet of humanity. But the primary means of evangelism we dare not overlook: the straightforward, Christ-centered proclamation of the unadulterated Word of God. Those who trade the Word for amusements or gimmicks will find they have no effective means to reach people with the truth of Christ.

5

The Foolishness of God

Pray without ceasing, and preach the faithful Word in clearer terms than ever. Such a course of conduct may seem to some to be a sort of standing still and doing nothing, but in very truth it is bringing God into the battle; and when HE comes to avenge the quarrel of his covenant he will make short work of it. "Arise, O Lord, plead thine own cause!"

CHARLES HADDON SPURGEON[1]

DOWN-GRADE tendencies have been continuous, not intermittent, throughout church history. There has never been a time when biblical Christianity was not threatened with worldliness and false doctrine. Twentieth-century evangelicalism provides a particularly poignant example of this. The history of the evangelical movement worldwide in the past century has been one long and frustrating struggle against the influences of liberal theology and worldly compromise. Beginning more than a hundred years ago with Spurgeon and the Down-Grade Controversy, evangelicalism has been torn and disrupted again and again by the very same issues that troubled Spurgeon.

Spurgeon's early warnings against modernism and the down-grade went largely unheeded. But by the first decade of this century, it was evident that orthodox Protestantism was losing the battle against liberalism. Beginning in 1909, an international group of Christian leaders committed to biblical truth began to write and publish a series of articles known as *The Fundamentals*. A. C. Dixon, pastor of Moody Memorial Church, Chicago, was chief editor of the series, assisted by R. A. Torrey and Louis Meyer. In 1911 Dixon was called to pastor The Metropolitan Tabernacle,

---

[1]"Restoration of Truth and Revival," *The Sword and the Trowel* (December 1887), 607.

London—Spurgeon's famous church. So the headquarters in the battle against the down-grade at last moved back to where it had begun.

The Fundamentals articles were compiled into twelve books and the series was completed by 1915. Financed by two Christian businessmen from California, nearly three million copies of the books were supplied free of charge to Christian workers around the world. They provided a sound biblical defense for every one of the essential doctrines then under attack by theological liberals. The articles condemned "higher criticism" (which imposed humanistic assumptions on biblical scholarship and often resulted in rank unbelief). They defended biblical inerrancy and authority, the historicity of Scripture, verbal inspiration, the deity of Christ, the doctrine of substitutionary atonement, and several other crucial biblical distinctives. Well-known contributors to the series included B. B. Warfield, J. C. Ryle, G. Campbell Morgan, C. I. Scofield, James M. Gray (president of Moody Bible Institute), A. T. Pierson (another of Spurgeon's successors at the Tabernacle), and Thomas Spurgeon, Charles's son.

Those books gave rise to the movement known as *fundamentalism.* By 1919, the movement was a force to be reckoned with. In May of that year The World Conference on Christian Fundamentals was held in Philadelphia, attended by more than six thousand Christians from a variety of denominational backgrounds. Fundamentalism seemed to have a bright future. But the Philadelphia gathering proved to be the high-water mark of the fundamentalist movement. Before the end of the century "fundamentalist" would become a derogatory word, applied more often to ruthless Islamic Ayatollahs than to true men of God. The fundamentalist movement is now fragmented and subdivided into tiny factions. And as we have seen, a new kind of modernism is pushing Christians onto the down-grade.

What happened? Why is it that biblical Christianity in modern times has been so vulnerable to doctrinal compromise and worldly influence?

A fascinating historical account of the fundamentalist/evangelical movement in microcosm is found in *Reforming Fundamentalism: Fuller Seminary and the New Evangelicalism,* by George Marsden.[2] Tracing the history of one influential institution, Marsden recounts in detail how Fuller Seminary compromised and ultimately abandoned its commitment to biblical inerrancy. The school was originally founded to provide a conserva-

---

[2]Grand Rapids, Mich.: Eerdmans, 1987.

tive, biblical training ground after denominational seminaries had embraced liberalism or otherwise abandoned the faith. But within a few decades, Fuller Seminary itself capitulated on the issue of biblical inerrancy. Why? Marsden's account reveals that many of Fuller's founders and early faculty were obsessed with the notion of intellectual and academic respectability. They wanted Fuller Seminary to be viewed in the elite academic community with the same esteem as the liberal denominational schools. Unfortunately, the intellectual climate of the age was almost unanimously sympathetic to skepticism, liberalism, humanism, and sub-Christian rationalism. The very community from which the Fuller men sought to win acceptance was at war with the theology Fuller Seminary was founded to uphold. In order to gain the stature they sought, the Fuller men were willing to compromise. The history of the school therefore often reads like a sad chronicle of controversy and doctrinal decline.

WHEN FOOLISHNESS IS WISE

Is intellectual and academic respectability a worthy goal? Not if the world sets the standards that determine what is acceptable and what is not. "Let no man deceive himself. If any man among you thinks that he is wise in this age, let him become foolish that he may become wise. *For the wisdom of this world is foolishness before God*" (1 Cor. 3:18, 19, emphasis added). It is folly to seek the approval of human wisdom; the goal itself is incompatible with biblical integrity.

The apostle Paul addressed this very issue at length in his first epistle to the Corinthians. Realizing that biblical truth is often viewed by the world as utter foolishness, Paul wrote, "The foolishness of God is wiser than men, and the weakness of God is stronger than men" (1 Cor. 1:25). Even to speak of "the foolishness of God" is shocking, but Paul was using the expression to bring into clear focus the conflict between human philosophy and biblical truth. Divine wisdom may not always *appear* wise under human evaluation. In a pragmatic age like ours, what is true may be at odds with what works. And what is right may be profoundly different from what is acceptable in the world's judgment. In fact, this is often the case. But that does not demonstrate any defect in the gospel. Rather, it underscores the deficiency of human wisdom.

Paul defended the gospel against the charge that it is inferior to this world's wisdom. He did not attempt to argue that the message of Christ is intellectually erudite, nor did he seek appreciation and esteem from the world's so-called scholars. Instead, he conceded that the gospel is utter foolishness in the eyes of human wisdom. He wrote:

> For Christ did not send me to baptize, but to preach the gospel, not in cleverness of speech, that the cross of Christ should not be made void. For the word of the cross is to those who are perishing foolishness, but to us who are being saved it is the power of God. For it is written, "I will destroy the wisdom of the wise, and the cleverness of the clever I will set aside." Where is the wise man? Where is the scribe? Where is the debater of this age? Has not God made foolish the wisdom of the world? For since in the wisdom of God the world through its wisdom did not come to know God, God was well-pleased through the foolishness of the message preached to save those who believe. For indeed Jews ask for signs, and Greeks search for wisdom; but we preach Christ crucified, to Jews a stumbling block, and to Gentiles foolishness, but to those who are the called, both Jews and Greeks, Christ the power of God and the wisdom of God. Because the foolishness of God is wiser than men, and the weakness of God is stronger than men.
>
> For consider your calling, brethren, that there were not many wise according to the flesh, not many mighty, not many noble; but God has chosen the foolish things of the world to shame the wise, and God has chosen the weak things of the world to shame the things which are strong, and the base things of the world and the despised, God has chosen, the things that are not, that He might nullify the things that are, that no man should boast before God. But by His doing you are in Christ Jesus, who became to us wisdom from God, and righteousness and sanctification, and redemption, that, just as it is written, "Let him who boasts, boast in the Lord."
>
> And when I came to you, brethren, I did not come with superiority of speech or of wisdom, proclaiming to you the testimony of God. For I determined to know nothing among you except Jesus Christ, and Him crucified. And I was with you in weakness and in fear and in much trembling. And my message and my preaching were not in persuasive words of wisdom, but in demonstration of the Spirit and of power, that your faith should not rest on the wisdom of men, but on the power of God (1 Cor. 1:17—2:5).

THE INFERIORITY OF HUMAN WISDOM

Remember that Paul was ministering in a civilization that had been brought to the pinnacle of glory under the Greek empire and was now enjoying a revival of high culture under Roman government. The ancient Greeks viewed philosophy as the highest of human attainments, and they built their whole society around it. Educated Greeks took their philosophy very seriously. There were at least four dozen distinct philosophical systems that competed with each other for influence and acceptance. Many of them were overtly religious, explaining human origin, morality, social relationships, and human destiny in terms of a pantheon of pagan gods. These Greek philosophies were very sophisticated and were the basis of all social, economic, political, and educational relations. Most if not all of them were totally at odds with the revealed truth of Scripture.

In short, Greek society worshiped human wisdom. The very word *philosophy* means "love of wisdom." Unfortunately, some of the Corinthian converts held on to their love of human wisdom and tried to import it into the church. Evidently they thought human wisdom could enhance divine revelation or add to what they had in Christ. Paul set out in the above passage to correct them.

Paul included a similar admonition in his epistle to the Colossians: "See to it that no one takes you captive through philosophy and empty deception, according to the tradition of men, according to the elementary principles of the world, rather than according to Christ" (2:8). His point was that Christians have no business pursuing human wisdom. It does no good spiritually for the unsaved, and it can add nothing to the believer. In fact, human wisdom has nothing to offer but confusion and division.

It is important to note that Paul's argument was not against natural facts or rational truth. He was not taking a mindless, anti-intellectual stance. On the contrary, Paul himself usually appealed to the *minds* of his disciples: "Be transformed by the renewing of your *mind* (Rom. 12:2); "Be renewed in the spirit of your *mind*" (Eph. 4:23); "Set your *mind* on the things above" (Col. 3:2); "Be filled with the *knowledge* of His will in all *spiritual wisdom* and *understanding*" (Col. 1:9, emphasis added). He was no anti-intellectual. For Paul, all truth was objective, fixed, revealed infallibly by God through His Word. Knowing the truth required study, diligence (2 Tim. 2:15). It was a matter of understanding, not feeling (1 Cor. 14:14-20). Truth, he emphasized, is something to be understood rationally, not discerned by mystical intuition (cf Job 38:36; Luke 24:45). Don't get the idea Paul depreciated the importance of the mind.

Nor was Paul on the offensive against technology and science. Medicine, architecture, engineering, mathematics, and other sciences had made great advances in Paul's day, just as they have in ours. Paul was not condemning any of these fields of knowledge per se. He was not opposed to learning and applying the God-given benefits of the scientific disciplines. Nor would he have objected to new areas of learning such as electronics or automotives. Christians can and should thank God for the blessings we enjoy from these sciences. As long as they are used properly—that is, as long as they don't become a basis for speculation about God, right and wrong, good and evil, or the spiritual meaning of life—the true sciences pose no threat to the truth of the gospel.

What Paul opposed was the human wisdom behind worldly philosophy: "Has not God made foolish the wisdom of the world?" (1 Cor. 1:20). In another place Paul wrote, "Our proud confidence is this, the testimony of our conscience, that in holiness and godly sincerity, *not in fleshly wisdom but in the grace of God*, we have conducted ourselves in the world, and especially toward you" (2 Cor. 1:12, emphasis added).

In contrast to Paul, contemporary evangelicalism has elevated human opinion and worldly, fleshly wisdom to an undue level. For most of the past century, evangelical theology has bowed at the shrine of academia, attempting to assimilate secular theology, philosophy, politics, psychology, moral relativism, evolutionary theory, and every other academic fad. Finding those things incompatible with the Bible and the simplicity of the gospel, Christians have too often been willing to twist and shape divine truth to try to make it fit. Multitudes have thus been drawn away from singular devotion to biblical doctrine to embrace human wisdom.

The desire for intellectual acceptability has undoubtedly steered more Christian leaders and institutions onto the down-grade than any other single force. In pursuit of that misguided goal, the worldly church has dutifully stayed one or two steps behind the world in its fashions and thinking. Bible-believing evangelicals have therefore had to wage a continual war against current human opinion.

The will to carry on that battle may be waning as more and more churches conform to the world. It is now standard practice among core evangelicals to borrow psychology and methodology from the world. Some think they can simply add human insights to Scripture and thus baptize worldly wisdom to make it "Christian."

Paul, on the other hand, was completely unwilling to incorporate human wisdom into the church. Instead he attacked it head on as a despised enemy: "For Christ [sent me] to preach the gospel, not in cleverness of speech, that the cross of Christ should not be made void" (1 Cor.

1:17). "Cleverness of speech" is from the Greek expression *sophia logou*—literally "wisdom of words." Paul's task was to preach God's Word, not man's wisdom.

It might be fair at this point to ask if it is *always* wrong to appeal to human wisdom, even in evangelistic contexts. After all, if our task is to reach the world with the gospel, why not try to express it in ways that appeal to the human mind? Paul answers that question by saying such an approach makes the cross of Christ void. There are two reasons why this is so. First of all, the message of the cross "is to those who are perishing foolishness" (v. 18). There is no way to make it otherwise and be faithful to the message. And second, it is impossible to elevate human wisdom without lowering God's truth. Human wisdom caters to self-will, intellectual and social pride, fleshly lusts, and the desire for independence from God. Human wisdom and the gospel are therefore constitutionally incompatible. Try to combine the two, and Paul says you render the gospel null and void.

The very reason people love sophisticated religion and highbrow morality is that those things appeal to the human ego. At the same time, worldly wisdom scoffs at the gospel precisely because it confronts human conceit. The gospel demands that people acknowledge their sin and spiritual impotence. It humiliates them, convicts them, and calls them sinners. Moreover, it offers salvation as a gracious work of God—not something people can accomplish on their own. In every way the cross crushes human pride.

THE SUPERIORITY OF GOD'S WISDOM

Human wisdom dismisses the truth of God as "foolishness" (v. 18). Those who are wise according to this world often employ epithets like "simplistic," "irrelevant," "naive," "unsophisticated," and even "foolish" to describe the gospel—and so it seems to them. After all, how could Jesus' being nailed to a piece of lumber on a remote hill in a barren part of the world ages ago have any possible relevance to modern humanity or eternal destiny? Is there really no place for personal accomplishment, human goodness, natural benevolence, or religious merit? Is God really so harsh that He would punish sinners? Are we really such vile sinners after all? Thus reasons the fallen mind.

And so the word of the cross is foolishness to those who are perishing. When Paul speaks of "the word of the cross," he has in mind, of

111

course, the gospel message. The cross is central to all we believe and proclaim. Remember that before people began to fashion crosses into pieces of jewelry and wear them as ornaments, the cross was a despised tool of execution. It was a place where the lowest of criminals were tortured and killed. What could be more contemptible than that? But the gist of Paul's argument embraces not just the part of the message that deals with the cross, but all of God's saving truth. The cross, being at the heart of God's revelation, is the central target of human contempt, but divinely revealed truth as a whole is deemed "foolishness" by the world and subject to the scorn of this world's wisdom.

Paul had confronted human wisdom on Mars' Hill in Athens just before he arrived in Corinth (Acts 17:18-21)—see Chapter 7. The Athenian intellectuals sneered at him over the resurrection (v. 32). He knew he would face more of the same in Corinth, a city known for its devotion to worldly philosophy, earthly pleasure, and fleshly appetites. A marketing expert might have suggested to Paul that he change his approach, adapt the message, soft-pedal the bits that he knew would offend people, speak to them about things that seemed more immediately relevant to their lives and interests. But Paul "determined to know nothing among [them] except Jesus Christ, and Him crucified" (1 Cor. 2:2). He was not going to change his message to suit the Corinthians. They had enough human opinion and earthly philosophy without Paul's adding his own. What they needed was the profoundly simple yet simply profound message of the cross.

HUMAN WISDOM v. THE FOOLISHNESS OF GOD

Although the natural mind finds the cross offensive and foolish, "to us who are being saved it is the power of God" (v. 18). The cross is the apex of divine wisdom and the demonstration of its superiority. God's wisdom overthrows human wisdom in several ways.

HUMAN WISDOM IS TEMPORARY; DIVINE WISDOM IS ETERNAL

"I will destroy the wisdom of the wise, and the cleverness of the clever I will set aside" (v. 19) is a quotation from Isaiah 29:14. In 1 Corinthians Paul then fires off a series of questions that mock human wisdom: "Where is the wise man? Where is the scribe? Where is the debater of this age? Has not God made foolish the wisdom of the world?" (v. 20). In essence, he is asking, "Where are the people who have refined human wisdom to such a degree that they can claim superiority over God?" Has human wisdom eliminated war, or hunger, or crime, or poverty, or immorality? Where have all the clever arguments and impressive rhetoric brought humanity? Are people better off because of them—or simply more self-satisfied and complacent? Human wisdom has changed nothing. Life is filled with the same problems and the same dilemmas that have always troubled the human race.

Human opinions are often contradictory, always changing, sometimes falling out of vogue only to appear again in another generation. Having rejected divine authority, this world's recycled wisdom has no anchor to hold it steady.

HUMAN WISDOM IS IMPOTENT; DIVINE WISDOM IS POWERFUL

Paul points out in verses 21-25 that worldly wisdom is spiritually ineffective. It cannot improve human nature or bring people closer to God.

The contemporary church desperately needs to see this truth. All the philosophers, intellectuals, sociologists, anthropologists, psychologists, politicians, and other wise people put together have never found any solution to the problem of sin or brought humanity one step closer to God. In fact, our species is spiritually worse off today than ever before, with higher suicide rates, the threat of nuclear war, and epidemic levels of frustration, confusion, depression, and debauchery. Human wisdom in our age is as bankrupt as all the philosophies in ancient Corinth—maybe more so.

The truth is, human wisdom and human philosophy tend to make the state of humanity worse, not better. Contemporary problems such as war, racism, drunkenness, crime, divorce, drug abuse, and poverty all attest to this. Those things are universally diagnosed as evil, but they continually grow more widespread and more serious as no cure is found. And the more the world depends on human wisdom, the worse these problems will become.

Is there a solution? There certainly is: "God was well-pleased through the foolishness of the message preached to save those who believe" (v. 21). "Message preached" is one word in the Greek text: *kērugma*. It emphasizes both the *message* and the *method* through which God chose to be the primary means of saving people: plainly proclaiming the gospel. The King James Version says, "It pleased God by the foolishness of preaching to save them that believe." Those who want to replace preaching with drama, music, and subtler means would do well to consider this: God *purposefully* chose a message and a methodology that the world's wisdom counts as foolishness. The Greek word for "foolishness" is *mōria*, from which we get the word *moronic*. God's means of salvation is literally moronic in the eyes of human wisdom. But it is God's only strategy for getting the message out.

"To us who are being saved it is the power of God" (v. 18). Those who give up human wisdom for divine foolishness receive eternal life. This "foolishness" is every person's only hope. The simple gospel thus provides everything complex human wisdom has ever sought. "If any man among you thinks that he is wise in this age, let him become foolish that he may become wise" (3:18).

Note that God does not *expect* people to come to a knowledge of the truth through human ingenuity. *He* chose the foolishness of preaching. People cannot reason their way to God or be led there by manipulation. But God is "well-pleased through the foolishness of the message preached to save those who believe" (v. 21). That is His plan, ordained "in the wisdom of God."

Paul was not advocating foolish preaching. He was simply pointing out that preaching the gospel is foolish *according to worldly wisdom*. Those who promote marketing principles in church ministry suggest that if people don't want preaching, we should give them what they want. What was Paul's perspective on that?

Paul was unequivocal: "Indeed Jews ask for signs, and Greeks search for wisdom; *but we preach Christ crucified*, to Jews a stumbling block, and to Gentiles foolishness" (vv. 22, 23, emphasis added). The Jews want a sign; why not give them one? The Greeks love philosophy; why not frame the message in a philosophical dialogue? After all, isn't this the same apostle who said, "I have become all things to all men"? But here again we see that although Paul was willing to become a servant to all, he was *not* willing to modify the gospel or alter God's design for preaching it. He would not cater to the preferences of human wisdom, performing signs on demand for those who wanted something sensational, or fashioning the message in philosophical terms for those whose tastes were more cerebral. Instead Paul preached Christ crucified, a stumbling block to unbelieving Jews, and foolishness to the philosophical Greeks.

The Jews wanted to see power; the Greeks wanted to hear wisdom. Only those who responded to the foolishness of the preached message found both: "To those who are the called, both Jews and Greeks, Christ the *power* of God and the *wisdom* of God" (v. 24, emphasis added). Ironically—and tragically—the very thing human wisdom deems foolish and weak is the clearest possible expression of God's power and wisdom. "The [so-called] foolishness of God is wiser than men, and the [supposed] weakness of God is stronger than men" (v. 25).

HUMAN WISDOM IS FOR THE ELITE; DIVINE WISDOM IS FOR ALL

Paul knew very well the members of the Corinthian church. And so he reminded them that very few of them had attained stature in the world: "Consider your calling, brethren, that there were not many wise according to the flesh, not many mighty, not many noble; but God has chosen the foolish things of the world to shame the wise, and God has chosen the weak things of the world to shame the things which are strong" (vv. 26, 27). Carrying on with the dual contrast of foolish/wise and weak/strong, Paul pointed out that very few Christians in Corinth were highly educated, powerful, rich, or famous. And of course those who were would have lost much of their status when they became Christians.

God's strength is made perfect in human weakness (2 Cor. 12:9). His wisdom appears foolish by human standards. Yet He uses the foolishness of this world to shame those who are wise; the weak things to shame those who are powerful; the lowly things to shame those who are proud; the despised things to shame those who are eminent (1 Cor. 1:27, 28). We tend to think God must use intellectuals to win other intellectuals. But the fact is, no one is won to Christ by intellectual prowess or cleverness. Those seeking to be impressed intellectually will find the message foolish. On the other hand, those who have plumbed the depths of worldly wisdom and found it empty do not need an impressive argument to convince them of the gospel. I know doctors and college professors who were won to Christ by janitors and day laborers. The Lord designed the gospel that way so "that no man should boast before God" (v. 29).

HUMAN WISDOM EXALTS MAN; DIVINE WISDOM GLORIFIES GOD

"By His doing you are in Christ Jesus, who became to us wisdom from God, and righteousness and sanctification, and redemption, that, just as it is written, 'Let him who boasts, boast in the Lord'" (1:30, 31). Salvation is entirely God's doing. "For by grace you have been saved through faith; and that not of yourselves; it is the gift of God; not as a result of works, that no one should boast. For we are His workmanship" (Eph. 2:8-10). "Where then is boasting? It is excluded. By what kind of law? Of works? No, but by a law of faith. For we maintain that a man is justified by faith apart from works of the Law" (Rom. 3:27, 28). "But he who boasts, let him boast in the Lord" (2 Cor. 10:17).

Human wisdom wants to devise a way of salvation where people get the credit. If they can't have all the credit, they will settle for some of it. But in God's design no one who is saved has anything to boast about. That's because God accomplishes everything on behalf of those He saves. They contribute nothing. He chooses them, calls them, draws them, and enables them to believe. His sovereign will—not human resolve or a human decision—even determines *who* will be saved. Everything is "by *His* doing." No aspect of salvation hinges on anything good in the believer. But "Christ Jesus [becomes] to us wisdom from God, and righteousness and sanctification, and redemption" (1 Cor. 1:30).

We will examine more closely in Chapter 8 God's sovereign role in salvation. Note here, however, that the essence of God's saving work is seen in our union with Christ. God doesn't simply *give* us wisdom, righteousness, sanctification, and redemption. Rather, He places us "*in* Christ Jesus, who *became to us* wisdom . . . , righteousness and sanctification, and redemption" (v. 30). God sovereignly unites us with Christ, so that all that He is becomes ours.

Note the perfect sufficiency of God's saving work. Wisdom, righteousness, sanctification, and redemption—is there more that we need beyond what is given to us in Christ? Certainly not. In fact, any attempt to augment what God has done on our behalf only nullifies His grace (cf Gal. 2:21). Any effort to add to His perfect gift only diminishes it (James 1:17). Any bid to amplify divine wisdom with earthly insights only defaces its utter perfection. How could we ever improve on Christ and His Word?

Unlike human wisdom, which exalts the sinner, divine wisdom glorifies God. "Just as it is written, 'Let him who boasts, boast in the Lord'" (1 Cor. 1:31). Elsewhere Paul wrote, "May it never be that I should boast, except in the cross of our Lord Jesus Christ, through which the world has been crucified to me, and I to the world" (Gal. 6:14).

No wonder Paul was determined to know nothing except Jesus Christ crucified (1 Cor. 2:2). Why should he discuss philosophy or human insight? Those things have nothing to offer. But Jesus Christ—the crucified, risen, and redeeming Savior—offers the only true hope for the world. The faithful preacher—indeed, every true disciple—must uphold Jesus Christ to an unbelieving world as the only way, the only truth, and the only true life (cf John 14:6). If we try to win them with entertainment, or clever arguments, or scholastic credentials, or worldly wisdom, we will fail, and we will ultimately mislead them.

Paul told the Corinthians, "My message and my preaching were not in persuasive words of wisdom, but in demonstration of the Spirit and of power, that your faith should not rest on the wisdom of men, but on the power of God" (1 Cor. 2:4, 5). If he had won them through erudition, or clever language, or a dynamic speech, their confidence would have been misplaced.

Remember, Paul came to Corinth after being beaten and imprisoned in Philippi, run out of Thessalonica and Berea, and sneered at in Athens (Acts 16:22-24; 17:10, 13, 14, 32). He knew that Corinth was a morally corrupt city—a center of loose living and prostitution. The city epitomized the pagan lifestyle. Paul might have been tempted to be less confrontive, perhaps packaged his ministry differently, maybe softened the offense of the cross. But he explicitly says that he consciously determined not to do any of those things. His "message and . . . preaching were not in persuasive words of wisdom" (1 Cor. 2:4). He was not interested in changing people's minds; he wanted God to change their lives. He did not have a message of his own to preach; he was called to proclaim the gospel. And that was what made his ministry so powerful.

In an 1871 sermon, Charles Spurgeon said,

> Jesus Christ is made of God unto us wisdom. We look no more for wisdom from the thoughts that spring of human mind, but to Christ himself; we do not expect wisdom to come to us through the culture that is of man, but we expect to be made wise through sitting at our Master's feet and accepting him as wisdom from God himself.

He then added this wry observation, which foreshadowed his stance years later in the Down-Grade Controversy:

> Now, as it was in the apostle's day, so is it very much at this present. There are those who will have it that the gospel—the simple gospel— such as might have been preached by John Bunyan or Whitefield, or Wesley, and others, was very well for the many, and for the dark times in which they lived—the great mass of mankind would be helped and improved by it; but there is wanted, according to the wiseacres of this intensely luminous century, a more progressive theology, far in advance of the Evangelism now so generally ridiculed. Men of mind, gentlemen of profound thought, are to teach us doctrines that were

unknown to our fathers; we are to go on improving in our knowledge of divine truth till we leave Peter and Paul, and those other old dogmatists far behind. Nobody knows how wise we are to become.

Brethren, our thoughts loathe this; we hate this cant about progress and deep thought; we only wish we could know as much of Christ as the olden preachers did. We are afraid that instead of getting into greater light through the thinkings of men, the speculations and contemplations of the scribes, ancient and modern, and the discoveries of the intellectual and eclectic, have made darkness worse, and have quenched some of the light that was in the world. Again has it been fulfilled: "I will destroy the wisdom of the wise, and will bring to nothing the understanding of the prudent. Where is the wise? Where is the scribe? Where is the disputer of this world? Hath not God made foolish the wisdom of this world?"[3]

God has again and again made foolish the wisdom of the world. Yet the church has again and again been romanced by the notion that worldly wisdom has something of value, or something useful, that we must master in order to minister effectively. Paul knew otherwise. Men of God throughout the ages have always known otherwise. Our faith cannot rest on the wisdom of men, but on the power of God (1 Cor. 2:5).

---

[3]"The Fourfold Treasure," *The Metropolitan Tabernacle Pulpit*, Vol. 17 (London: Passmore and Alabaster, 1871), 281.

6

The Power of God
Unto Salvation

Where the gospel is fully and powerfully preached, with the Holy Ghost sent down from heaven, our churches do not only hold their own, but win converts; but when that which constitutes their strength is gone— we mean when the gospel is concealed, and the life of prayer is slighted—the whole thing becomes a mere form and fiction. For this thing our heart is sore grieved.

CHARLES HADDON SPURGEON[1]

A RECENT BOOK in the "user-friendly" genre includes a section entitled, "Different Times Require Different Messages." That title caught my eye, so I began reading. This author—who pastors a large, user-friendly church—says modern times have ravaged people's self-esteem so badly that people today actually need to hear a different message from what was appropriate a hundred years ago. He writes,

> In times past the human spirit was far more sturdy than it is now. Modernity has taken a high toll of the human spirit, as has the high cost of the American dream. The stress of modern life has had a greatly negative impact on the self-esteem of modern man.
>
> Consequently, there is a high level of fragility in the modern human ego. [Baby] boomers particularly have been fragmented and shattered by the fast pace of modern-day development. That's why our baby boomers today are in a very fragile state.

---

[1]"Another Word Concerning the Down-Grade," *The Sword and the Trowel* (August 1887), 398-99.

Have you ever taken the time to read messages by some of the great nineteenth-century preachers . . . ? If you have, you will probably have noted that [men of that era] addressed quite a different crowd than we do today and they addressed them in a very different manner. And because of those differences, I disagree with those who say that such messages are appropriate for our time.

You see, people in our culture are truly broken and deeply wounded. They need desperately to be healed and put back together. But the process of healing, I believe, is different for every era and every generation, including this one.

Yes, different times do require different messages.[2]

That author is unusually frank in stating his perspective. He candidly admits he believes preaching should accommodate the spirit of the age. (His book also carries unqualified endorsements from several of the top names in the user-friendly, church-marketing, and church-growth movements.) How does this pastor think we should determine what is the appropriate message for our time? He gives this list of suggestions for preachers:

1. Visit those how-to sections in your local bookstores.

2. Regularly have a small group submit a list of their greatest challenges at home and on the job.

3. Similarly, acquire inventories of needs from several secular people in your community.

4. Periodically, examine issues of *Time, Newsweek* and *USA Today*, as these publications tend to be on the cutting edge of the felt needs and fears that people are facing.

5. Apply practical aims to every study, message or program in your church.

6. Practice composing practical, catchy titles for your messages (sermons) from various biblical texts.

7. Limit your preaching to roughly 20 minutes, because boomers don't have too much time to spare. And don't forget to keep your messages light and informal, liberally sprinkling them with humor and personal anecdotes.[3]

---

[2]Doug Murren, *The Baby Boomerang* (Ventura, Calif.: Regal, 1990), 217-18.
[3]*Ibid.*, 102-3.

That list is a recipe for weak and insipid preaching. It is also diametrically opposed to biblical ministry.

In a superb critique of the church-marketing movement, Douglas D. Webster compares biblical preaching to user-friendly methods:

> Biblical preaching was God-centered, sin-exposing, self-convicting and life-challenging—the direct opposite of today's light, informal sermons that Christianize self-help and entertain better than they convict.
>
> There are so many illustrations in today's market-sensitive sermons that the hearer forgets the biblical truth that is being illustrated; so many personal anecdotes that the hearer knows the pastor better than she knows Christ; so many human-interest stories that listening to the sermon is easier than reading the Sunday paper; so practical that there is hardly anything to practice.
>
> No wonder nominal Christians leave church feeling upbeat. Their self-esteem is safely intact. Their minds and hearts have been sparked and soothed with sound-bite theology, Christian maxims and a few practical pointers dealing with self-esteem, kids or work. But the question remains: has the Word of God been effectively and faithfully proclaimed, penetrating comfort zones and the veneer of self-satisfaction with the truth of Jesus Christ?[4]

The simple reality is that one *cannot* follow a market-driven strategy and remain faithful to Scripture. Preachers who concern themselves with user-friendliness cannot fearlessly proclaim the whole counsel of God. Those who aspire to preach a timely message will find themselves at odds with the timeless truth of the Bible. Ministers who take their cues from *USA Today* rather than from God's Word will quickly discover the message that seemed so relevant last week is now yesterday's news. Preaching that conceals the unchanging gospel behind the fleeting issues of our time cloaks the very force that makes good preaching truly powerful. After all, it is not our anecdotes, applications, how-tos, jokes, catchy titles, clever outlines, or other contrivances—but the *gospel* that is "the power of God for salvation" (Rom. 1:16).

I AM SET APART FOR THE GOSPEL

Paul's epistle to the Romans is an exposition of the gospel in almost point-by-point fashion. In the first verse of the epistle, Paul

---

[4]*Selling Jesus: What's Wrong with Marketing the Church* (Downers Grove, Ill.: InterVarsity, 1992), 83-84.

describes himself as one "set apart for the *gospel*." The gospel was the foundation of Paul's ministry, and in Romans he gives a clear and thorough presentation of it. He writes about God's wrath and human sin (chapters 1-3), justification and imputed righteousness (3-5), sanctification and practical righteousness (6-8), election and Israel's rejection of Christ (9-11), and then makes practical applications of various gospel truths in chapters twelve through the end of the epistle. The gospel is his theme throughout, and one of Paul's reasons for writing Romans seems to be to demonstrate the centrality of the gospel to all Christian life and ministry.

When we speak of "the gospel" we tend to think of an evangelistic message—and surely the gospel is that. But it is not only a four- or five-point outline of salvation truths. The *gospel*—in the sense Paul and the apostles employed the word—includes all the revealed truth about Christ (cf Rom. 1:1-6; 1 Cor. 15:3-11). It does not stop at the point of conversion and justification by faith, but embraces every other aspect of salvation, from sanctification to glorification. The gospel's significance therefore does not end the moment the new birth occurs; it applies to the entire Christian experience. And when Paul and the other New Testament writers spoke of "preaching the gospel," they were not talking about preaching only to unbelievers (cf v. 15).

All ministry in the early church revolved around the gospel. No one would have suggested a debate about secular politics, a weight-loss program, a comedy act, a stage show, a seminar on potty training for young children, or a class on time management for businessmen as a means to boost church attendance. The church and all its ministries were single-mindedly committed to the one task of strengthening believers for furthering the gospel in the world.

Paul's personal commitment to the gospel as the heart of all ministry is seen clearly in the opening chapter of Romans, where he expresses his desire to come to Rome and minister to the saints there. He desperately wanted to get to Rome. He wanted to get there not to renew old personal relationships, though he had many good friends who were part of the church there. Nor was he interested in ministering in one of his own churches, for Paul did not plant the church at Rome. And it was not to escape persecution elsewhere, for he was certain to become a target in a city that was militantly opposed to Christianity. But Paul's passion was to preach the gospel, and he couldn't wait to do it in Rome, the center of the civilized world.

I SERVE GOD BY PREACHING THE GOSPEL

Paul writes, "I thank my God through Jesus Christ for you all, because your faith is being proclaimed throughout the whole world. For God, whom I serve in my spirit in the preaching of the gospel of His Son, is my witness as to how unceasingly I make mention of you, always in my prayers making request, if perhaps now at last by the will of God I may succeed in coming to you" (Rom. 1:8-10). There's a wealth of spiritual truth about biblical ministry in those brief verses, and I have commented on them in depth elsewhere.[5] Here I want to begin by focusing on one brief phrase in verse 9: "I serve [God] in my spirit in the preaching of the gospel of His Son."

For Paul, preaching the gospel was an act of spiritual worship. The Greek word translated "serve" is *latreuō*, the same word translated "worship" in Philippians 3:3: "We are the true circumcision, who worship in the Spirit of God and glory in Christ Jesus and put no confidence in the flesh." Paul "served" (worshiped) God in his spirit by preaching the gospel. In other words, Paul viewed his ministry like that of a priest before God rendering high and holy duty: "If I preach the gospel, I have nothing to boast of, for I am under compulsion; for woe is me if I do not preach the gospel" (1 Cor. 9:16). Yet it was not only a duty; it was an immense privilege as well. "I am eager to preach the gospel to you" (Rom. 1:15).

Paul's eagerness to serve God poured out from his spirit from the moment of his salvation. His first question as a Christian was, "What shall I do, Lord?" (Acts 22:10). His heart and energies were fixed on preaching, and he did it with his whole soul.

Notice that Paul's concern was for the *spiritual* welfare of those to whom he ministered: "I long to see you in order that I may impart some spiritual gift to you" (Rom. 1:11). He was not wanting to visit Rome as a tourist. He was not interested in merely entertaining the Roman believers or seeing how many unbelievers he could draw to their meetings. He wasn't thinking of his own rewards or reputation or remuneration. He wanted to give of himself for their spiritual benefit.

What "spiritual gift" did Paul want to impart to the Romans? He was not, of course, speaking about spiritual gifts such as those listed in 1 Corinthians 12 and Romans 12. Those gifts are imparted by the Holy Spirit to every believer (1 Cor. 12:7-11), not handed out from person to

---

[5] *Romans 1-8* (Chicago: Moody Press, 1991).

person. Paul was speaking of a gift of spiritual value, something that would help them "be established." What he had in mind involved preaching to them (cf Rom. 1:15). He wanted to encourage them with the full riches of gospel truth and be encouraged in return by their faith in that truth: "That is, that I may be encouraged together with you while among you, each of us by the other's faith, both yours and mine" (v. 12).

So Paul's burden for the church at Rome was bound up in his desire to serve them through the preaching and ministry of the gospel. Ultimately Paul did make it to Rome, but at a very dear price. He was brought there in chains, bound to Roman guards. But even had he known when he wrote this epistle what it would finally cost him to get to Rome, Paul's desire to preach the gospel in Rome would not have been diminished in the least. After all, he went to Jerusalem even though he knew he would be imprisoned there (cf Acts 21:10-15). When the brethren tried desperately to talk him out of going to Jerusalem, he replied, "What are you doing, weeping and breaking my heart? For I am ready not only to be bound, but even to die at Jerusalem for the name of the Lord Jesus" (Acts 21:13). Paul would have willingly gone to Rome under the same circumstances—and ultimately he did. He wrote to the Philippians from Rome, "All the saints greet you, especially those of Caesar's household" (Phil. 4:22). Paul was under house arrest when he wrote that, waiting for the verdict of the imperial court. Even under those trying circumstances Paul was faithfully preaching the gospel. Evidently he had even been used to lead people from Caesar's own household to a saving knowledge of Christ.

Obviously, proclaiming the gospel was a compulsion for Paul. That's why he spoke of himself as "set apart for the gospel" (1:1). He knew of no other kind of ministry.

I AM DEBTOR TO ALL THE LOST

Paul wrote, "I am under obligation both to Greeks and to barbarians, both to the wise and to the foolish" (Rom. 1:14). The King James Version renders that verse, "*I am debtor* both to the Greeks, and to the Barbarians; both to the wise, and to the unwise" (emphasis added). Paul did not preach the gospel only for personal reasons or because the calling seemed attractive. He considered himself under obligation.

At the time of Paul's conversion, he was the church's most determined opponent. He hated Christ and all Christians. When Stephen, the first martyr, was killed, Paul was there, "in hearty agreement with putting him to death" (Acts 8:1). After his salvation, Paul's zeal for Christ was even greater than his zeal to persecute Christians had been before. This verse gives us an insight as to why. Paul's perspective was that since God had chosen and called an enemy like him, "foremost of all sinners" (1 Tim. 1:15), Paul was then obligated to other sinners to preach the gospel to them. He knew he had been sovereignly appointed to this role, and he was obliged to carry it out.

All of us who have believed the gospel are under the same kind of obligation. First, as we noted earlier, Christ Himself commands us to preach the gospel (Mark 16:15). And second, we who know the way of eternal life are obligated to unbelievers in the same sense we would be responsible to warn someone whose house is on fire, or morally constrained to give water to someone dying of thirst.

Paul was equally obligated to Jews and Gentiles, educated people and barbarians. He didn't target the young, upwardly mobile, cultured people and ignore the slaves and dregs of society. He preached the gospel to them all, because he was obligated to them all. "There is no partiality with God" (Rom. 2:11); so Paul was no respecter of persons.

In contrast, "target marketing" is a key concept in the user-friendly church movement. George Barna has written,

> To successfully market your product, you have to identify its prospective market. The key to market identification—sometimes referred to as "target marketing"—is to be as specific as possible in selecting the audience to whom you will market the product. By matching the appeal of your product to the interests and needs of specific population segments, you can concentrate on getting your product to your best prospects without wasting resources on people who have no need or interest in your product. . . . By knowing the product's market, the product itself can be developed to address the special needs of that segment, and the entire marketing effort can be designed with maximum efficiency.[6]

In other words, decide who you're going to minister to, fashion the "product" to suit that audience, and don't "waste resources" on people outside that targeted group.

---

[6]*Marketing the Church* (Colorado Springs, Colo.: NavPress, 1988), 42-43.

Why do you suppose nearly all the user-friendly churches identify their "target market" as young suburban professionals and other moneyed groups? Why are so few of these churches targeting poor and inner-city congregations or mixtures of all classes and types of people? The answer may be obvious. One leading pastor in the movement says, "A pastor can define his appropriate target audience by determining with whom he would like to spend a vacation or an afternoon of recreation." It would be hard to imagine a ministry philosophy more at odds with the Word of God than that. Doesn't Scripture say, "My brethren, do not hold your faith in our glorious Lord Jesus Christ with an attitude of personal favoritism" (James 2:1)? And, "Did not God choose the poor of this world to be rich in faith and heirs of the kingdom which He promised to those who love Him?" (v. 5). "But if you show partiality, you are committing sin and are convicted by the law as transgressors" (v. 9).

Those who narrow their ministry to a select "target audience" certainly are not ministering in the spirit of Paul, who considered himself debtor to all and ministered to all alike.

I AM EAGER TO PREACH THE GOSPEL

By saying he was "under obligation" to preach the gospel, Paul was in no way implying that he was a grudging witness for Christ. He makes this clear to the Romans: "For my part, I am eager to preach the gospel to you also who are in Rome" (Rom. 1:15). He was not only willing but also eager, even *determined* to preach the gospel.

The King James Version translates verse 15, "So, as much as in me is, I am ready to preach the gospel." That captures even more of Paul's eagerness. With every fiber of his being, he desired to preach the gospel at Rome. Paul would not have been able to understand preachers who, given the privilege of preaching the gospel, choose instead to entertain people, tell anecdotes, or give speeches on self-esteem. He was ready to suffer persecution, be beaten, go to prison, or even be killed for the privilege of preaching the gospel.

C. H. Spurgeon said,

> The apostle was ready to go anywhere with the gospel, but he was not ready to preach another gospel; no one could make him ready to do that. He was not ready to hide the gospel, he was not ready to tone it down, he was not ready to abridge it or to extend it. He said, "I am not ashamed of the gospel of Christ: for it is the power of God unto

126

salvation to everyone that believeth; to the Jew first, and also to the Greek." As to the matter of preaching the gospel, Paul was always ready for that; he kept not back any one of its truths, nor any part of its teaching. Even if it should bring upon him ridicule and contempt, though it should be to the Jews a stumbling block, and to the Greeks foolishness, Paul would say, "As much as in me is, I am ready to preach the gospel" to them all. He did not always feel alike fit for the work; he did not always find the same openings, or the same freedom in speech; but he was always ready to preach wherever the Lord gave him the opportunity.[7]

At the end of his life, Paul was able to say, "I have fought the good fight, I have finished the course, I have kept the faith" (2 Tim. 4:7). That's because he never allowed himself to be deterred from his calling. He never gave in to the temptation to seek popularity. He never compromised with the enemies of the gospel. He never allowed his ministry to be conformed to the world. He never tickled the ears of the crowds.

Externally, it may have seemed to the world that Paul was a failure. He was arrested, imprisoned for years, and finally killed by the Roman officials. Yet even in those dark hours Paul kept preaching. When he couldn't preach to crowds, he witnessed to the soldiers assigned to guard him. When he couldn't minister in the churches, he ministered in the prisons. He was always ready to give the gospel—but never to compromise.

I AM NOT ASHAMED OF THE GOSPEL

Paul's next statement could be called the thesis statement of the epistle: "I am not ashamed of the gospel, for it is the power of God for salvation to everyone who believes" (Rom. 1:16). That is one of the most potent, penetrating statements in all the New Testament. Paul equates the gospel itself with God's almighty power! No wonder he says he is not ashamed of the gospel.

The rest of the epistle is an exposition of this one statement, unfolding in brilliant detail the truth of the gospel and showing why it is so powerful. That's why Romans takes such a prominent place among the Pauline epistles. Paul was so committed to the gospel that occasionally

---

[7]"Paul the Ready," *The Metropolitan Tabernacle Pulpit*, Vol. 38 (London: Passmore and Alabaster, 1892), 578.

he referred to it as "my gospel" (Rom. 2:16; 16:25; 2 Tim. 2:8). Far from being ashamed of it, he spoke of it as if it were his own prized possession!

But as Paul well knew, the cost of standing up for the gospel could be great. Consequently, too many Christians *did* behave as if they were ashamed of the gospel.

Mockery was a key weapon used by the earliest enemies of Christianity. The Romans especially tended to look upon Christianity as a crude and uncultured religion. Rumors circulated among Roman society that Christians were cannibals, because they partook of the Lord's Supper. Christians were accused of sedition, murder, and other treacherous crimes. Some enemies of the gospel claimed the Christians were having orgies. Pagans even attacked believers as atheists because they rejected all the mythological gods. The price for following Christ could be extremely high.

As we have noted repeatedly, the gospel itself is disagreeable, unattractive, repulsive, and alarming to the world. It exposes sin, condemns pride, convicts the unbelieving heart, and shows human righteousness—even the best, most appealing aspects of human nature—to be worthless, defiled, filthy rags (cf Isa. 64:6). It affirms that the real problems in life are not because of anyone but ourselves. We are fallen sinners, with deceitful hearts, evil motives, pervasive pride. We cannot blame anyone else for our failure and misery. That is not a popular view, particularly in today's psychological climate. It comes as bad news to those who love sin, and many who hear it for the first time react with disdain against the messenger.

It is not easy to take a bold stand for the gospel and be unashamed. Most of us must confess that we have a lot in common with the weakness of Peter, who on the night of Jesus' crucifixion denied the Lord three times, cowering in fear before a servant girl who recognized him as a follower of Christ (Luke 22:56-62).

There is no record of any incident like that in Paul's life, however. From the moment of his conversion, Paul was a man with a mission, and he never wavered from his one purpose: to preach the gospel. He knew the gospel's remarkable power to transform lives, and he longed to be the herald to proclaim it. How could he ever be ashamed of the gospel? Having received the gospel directly from the risen Lord Himself (Acts 20:24; 1 Cor. 11:23; 15:23), Paul was eager to proclaim it to everyone, without fear or shame.

THE GOSPEL IS THE POWER OF GOD

It is hard to imagine that anyone who truly understands the power of the gospel can possibly be ashamed to proclaim it. "It is the power of God" (1:16). *Dunamis* is the Greek word translated "power." We derive the word *dynamite* from the same Greek word, and *dynamite* is not too strong a word to express what Paul is saying here.

Inherent in the gospel message is the power of an omnipotent God. That power alone is sufficient to save the vilest sinner and transform the hardest heart—apart from any human arguments, illustrations, or ingenuity.

The prophet Jeremiah wrote, "Can the Ethiopian change his skin or the leopard his spots? Then you also can do good who are accustomed to do evil" (Jer. 13:23). The truth is, people are utterly powerless to overcome their own sin. Sin is part of our nature, like a leopard's spots. We cannot change ourselves. Self-help techniques and recovery programs might temporarily help people feel better about themselves, but they have no power to remove sin or change the human heart.

Only the gospel can do that. It is the power of God unto salvation. In other words, the objective truth of the gospel is inherently powerful for transforming lives when divinely applied. Peter spoke of the Word of God as the seed that generates new life and a new birth: "You have been born again not of seed which is perishable but imperishable, that is, through the living and abiding word of God" (1 Peter 1:23). Both apostles were saying essentially the same thing: God's Word—the message of the gospel—is the vehicle through which God's transforming power invades a life and brings about the new birth.

We noted in a previous chapter Paul's similar words to the Corinthian believers: "The word of the cross is to those who are perishing foolishness, but *to us who are being saved it is the power of God*" (1 Cor. 1:18, emphasis added). And, "We preach Christ crucified, to Jews a stumbling block, and to Gentiles foolishness, but to those who are the called, both Jews and Greeks, Christ *the power of God and the wisdom of God*" (vv. 23, 24). The gospel is the *only* message God uses for salvation. There is a place for persuasion, graphic illustration, and relevant application. Certainly every worthy preacher or evangelist will seek ways to stimulate people's interest—but only to capture a hearing for the gospel. If the plain truth of the gospel doesn't penetrate the heart, no amount of cajoling or salesmanship on the part of the evangelist is going to bring a person to salvation.

Note that the gospel "is the power of God for salvation *to everyone who believes*" (Rom. 1:16, emphasis added). Some people remain unaffected by the gospel. As powerful as the message is, it has no positive effect on those who turn away disbelieving. Paul, of course, experienced much rejection and mocking from those who rejected the gospel. Nevertheless he refused to change his methods or adapt the message to their tastes. He did not assume unbelievers' rejection was due to any lack of power in the gospel. He knew too well the unrivaled power of the gospel to transform "everyone who believes."

In referring to the gospel as "the power of God for salvation," Paul was also affirming that the gospel reveals the *only way* of salvation. Jesus said, "I am the way, and the truth, and the life; no one comes to the Father, but through Me" (John 14:6). Acts 4:12 says, "There is salvation in no one else; for there is no other name under heaven that has been given among men, by which we must be saved." Biblical preaching means preaching Jesus Christ (2 Cor. 4:5)—His person and work. Perhaps the most serious indictment of contemporary market-conscious preaching is the absence of Christ. His name or some fact about Him may be thrown in at the end, but our Lord is rarely central in the trendy preaching of today.

THE GOSPEL REVEALS GOD'S RIGHTEOUSNESS

The term "the gospel" is much abused these days. Elsewhere I have addressed in detail some of the contemporary fallacies regarding the gospel.[8] Here it is sufficient to note that many evangelicals have redefined the gospel in human-centered terms. Instead of declaring Christ crucified and focusing on God's righteousness, they talk about human needs. But the gospel is first of all a message about God's righteousness: "For in it the righteousness of God is revealed from faith to faith; as it is written, 'But the righteous man shall live by faith'" (Rom. 1:17).

The word *righteousness* and its derivatives appear at least thirty-five times in Romans. Divine righteousness is the starting point and the theme of the gospel message. God's righteousness, rejected by sinning humanity, was perfectly fulfilled by Christ incarnate. It is imputed to the sinner who repents and believes in the Lord Jesus, and will be manifested in practical ways in the life of the Christian. That is a summary of the gospel as Paul unfolds it in Romans.

"The righteousness of God" carries two connotations. In one sense

---

[8]*The Gospel According to Jesus*, second ed. (Grand Rapids, Mich.: Zondervan, 1994); *Faith Works: The Gospel According to the Apostles* (Dallas, Tex.: Word, 1993).

it speaks of God's holy hatred of sin. In the early 1500s, Martin Luther sat in the tower of the Black Cloister, Wittenberg, reading this verse. "That expression 'righteousness of God' was like a thunderbolt in my heart," Luther said years later. "I hated Paul with all my heart when I read that the righteousness of God is revealed in the gospel."[9] Luther saw God's righteousness as an unassailable obstacle to eternal life. Luther was deeply aware of his own sinfulness, and he knew because of it he was unacceptable to a righteous God. Therefore, as he read this verse he was seized with despair.

But there is a second connotation of righteousness in verse 17: "As it is written, 'But the righteous man shall live by faith.'" This speaks of Christ's perfect righteousness, which is imputed to the account of the believing sinner (Rom. 4:24). When Luther finally understood this sense of the word *righteousness*, he knew the true meaning of the gospel, and that discovery resulted in the Protestant Reformation.

The doctrine is known as *justification*. It means that God freely reckons all of Christ's perfect righteousness to the assets side of the believer's ledger, and He cancels out all the sin on the debit side. When God looks at the believing one, he sees that person as if he or she were as fully righteous as Christ Himself. That's how God "justifies the ungodly" (Rom. 4:5). Because Christ made full atonement for sin by His death and resurrection, God can justify sinners without compromising His own righteousness—"that He might be just and the justifier of the one who has faith in Jesus" (Rom. 3:26). This is the very heart of the gospel. It is why the message is *good news*.

THE GOSPEL REVEALS GOD'S WRATH

But the gospel is not *all* good news. In fact, it is not good news at all for those who turn away from Christ. Note that the starting point for Paul's gospel is God's wrath against sin: "For the wrath of God is revealed from heaven against all ungodliness and unrighteousness of men" (v. 18). Paul then spends more than two full chapters systematically proving that all humanity is sinful and under the wrath of God.

God's wrath is almost entirely missing from modern presentations of the gospel. It is not fashionable to speak of God's wrath against sin or to tell people they should fear God. The typical presentation today starts

---

[9]*Table Talk*, Theodore G. Tappert, ed. in Helmut T. Lehmann, gen. ed., *Luther's Works*, 55 vols. (Philadelphia: Fortress, 1967), 54: 308-9.

exactly opposite where Paul started. He wrote of "the wrath of God . . . against all ungodliness and unrighteousness of men." But modern evangelism begins with, "God loves you and wants to make you happy."

Read the literature of the user-friendly movement and you'll notice a preoccupation with conveying every message in a positive tone. One leading pastor in the movement writes,

> Though unchurched [baby] boomers may privately acknowledge they are flawed—and maybe even sinful—they are hardly going to sit in a public place and listen to themselves being described as worms, wretches, fallen creatures and other totally depraved types. . . .
>
> As a pastor to boomers, I'm convinced that they need to hear even negative messages presented in positive terms. It's the grid through which we filter things. So if we can't be positive—even when talking about negative topics—boomers will probably not listen.
>
> We need to be very careful, therefore, about the tone we take in our services. . . . I've made a deliberate practice of making sure that the messages I direct to my age-group always strike a positive note.[10]

Comments like that in recent church-growth writings almost always come with disclaimers assuring readers that what the author has in mind is not compromise—and this one is no exception. That author goes on to say, "Now, I'm not backing down on the biblical premise that we are all fallen sinners and desperately need to be saved. Admittedly, we are depraved; yet the gospel also presents the premise that because we were created in God's image, God considered us of high enough value to send His Son to redeem us."[11] He goes on to say again that those who want to minister effectively in this generation must remember to keep their tone "optimistic."

Let me say first of all that I minister to a rather large group from the baby-boom generation, and I disagree with that writer's unwarranted generalization that they automatically tune out negative truth. The ones truly being saved certainly must and will accept the negative as motivation to repent. Furthermore, it is one thing to say "that we are all fallen sinners and desperately need to be saved," and quite another to say, as Paul does, that "the wrath of God is revealed from heaven against all ungodliness and unrighteousness of men." Both statements are true, of

---

[10]Murren, 215-17.
[11]*Ibid.*

course. The gospel is not complete without both sides, however. It is Paul's starting point—the wrath of God, not a statement about human need—that is frequently left out by preachers today.

As we noted in an earlier chapter, there is no way to synthesize the truth about God's wrath with a positive-only presentation of the gospel. There is no way to declare the truth about God's wrath to an unbelieving sinner in an "optimistic" tone. As a result, the gospel preached in these churches is often truncated—and the point that is most deliberately censored is the very place Paul began his gospel presentation—the reality of divine wrath!

Those who feel they must be forever optimistic are forced to ignore crucial sections of Scripture, including most of Romans 1, Luke 16, all the Hebrews warning passages, much of the core of Old Testament truth, and about half of Jesus' teaching. And so the philosophy shapes the message.

Don't get the impression I am in favor of preaching that is dour, always negative, oppressive, and grim. Of course I am not. But as we have noted repeatedly, there must be a biblical balance of negative *and* positive, or we're not ministering according to the will of God. And the strategy currently in fashion is to try to style the gospel so that it is entirely positive. That can't be the biblical message. It certainly is not the gospel that is the power of God unto salvation.

For Paul, the threat of God's eternal wrath was the *first* point to be taken up. He was determined that people understand the awful reality of God's holy wrath and the desperate heinousness of human depravity. It was not an upbeat way to introduce the subject. But that is how Paul, under the inspiration of the Holy Spirit, dealt with it.

God's wrath is crucial to who He is. All His attributes are balanced in divine perfection. If He had no righteous anger, He would not be God. Apart from His wrath, the concept of His love is rendered meaningless: "Thou hast loved righteousness, and hated wickedness" (Ps. 45:7). Furthermore, God hates sin just as perfectly and as thoroughly as He loves fallen sinners. One side without the other is utterly hollow.

Often the twin emphases of wrath and mercy are side by side. "He who believes in the Son has eternal life; but he who does not obey the Son shall not see life, but the wrath of God abides on him" (John 3:36). That verse appears in the same chapter as the more familiar words of John 3:16. Without an understanding of the severity of God's wrath against sin, even the phrase "shall not perish" in John 3:16 loses its significance.

God's wrath is not a secondary theme in Scripture. It is emphasized throughout both the Old and New Testaments. Psalm 7:11, 12 says, "God is a righteous judge, and a God who has indignation every day. If a man does not repent, He will sharpen His sword; He has bent His bow and made it ready." The phrase "the anger of the Lord burned against Israel" is found repeatedly in the Old Testament (e.g., Judg. 2:14, 20; 3:8; 10:7; 2 Sam. 6:7; 24:1; 2 Kings 13:3; Ps. 106:40). The New Testament also is replete with warnings about God's wrath (e.g., Rom. 2:5; 3:5; 9:22; Eph. 5:6; Col. 3:6; Rev. 14:10). The writer to the Hebrews says simply, "Our God is a consuming fire" (Heb. 12:29; cf Deut. 4:24; 9:3).

Those truths are not *supposed* to make us feel comfortable or self-confident. They are supposed to fill us with severe fear and dread. After all, "The fear of the Lord is the beginning of wisdom" (Prov. 9:10). Only when the gospel provokes a holy terror of God can it be appreciated for the truly good news it is. "In the fear of the Lord there is strong confidence" (Prov. 14:26); "The fear of the Lord is a fountain of life" (14:27); "The fear of the Lord is the instruction for wisdom" (15:33); and "The fear of the Lord leads to life, so that one may sleep satisfied, untouched by evil" (19:23).

A DIFFERENT MESSAGE FOR A DIFFERENT TIME?

The gospel that should be preached today is the same message Paul committed his life to preach. He solemnly warned the church not to tamper with that gospel or alter it in any way (Gal. 1:6-9). Church history is strewn with examples of those who thought they could mold the message for their own time—but ended up corrupting the truth and damning themselves. Most of those seeking to make the church "user-friendly" have no intention of perverting the gospel in such a way. But they need to recognize that their desire for a pleasing, attractive message is utterly incompatible with the true gospel. As their movement gathers momentum, it is becoming more and more clear that they are heading down the same road traveled by the modernists a hundred years ago.

If church history teaches us anything, it is that different times and different societies do *not* require different messages. Those who preach anything other than the unadulterated gospel forfeit the power of God in their ministries.

Charles Spurgeon said the modernists of his day were trying to devise "a faith fashioned for the present century—perhaps we ought rather to say, for the present month."[12] He wrote,

> The idea of a progressive gospel seems to have fascinated many. To us that notion is a sort of cross-breed between nonsense and blasphemy. After the gospel has been found effectual in the eternal salvation of untold multitudes, it seems rather late in the day to alter it; and, since it is the revelation of the all-wise and unchanging God, it appears somewhat audacious to attempt its improvement. When we call up before our mind's eye the gentlemen who have set themselves this presumptuous task, we feel half inclined to laugh; the case is so much like the proposal of moles to improve the light of the sun. . . .
>
> Do men really believe that there is a gospel for each century? Or a religion for each fifty years?[13]

Spurgeon clearly understood that those who desired to be embraced as "relevant" by a changing world could not and would not long remain faithful to the unchanging Word of God. He quoted approvingly from a letter written by Henry Varley to the editor of a periodical titled *Word and Work*. Varley wrote, "Revelation, which is unchanging, is not fast enough for an age of which it may be said, 'Change is its fashion.' All the more necessary, therefore, does it become to 'hold fast the form of sound words,' and contend earnestly . . . 'for the faith once for all delivered to the saints.'"[14]

If change was the fashion of the nineteenth century, how much more true is that today? More than any preceding generation of Christians we must be careful to guard the treasure that has been entrusted to us (2 Tim. 1:14). Let's not exchange it for the fads and fancies of a vacillating world.

The gospel is to be preached persuasively, earnestly, and clearly. There certainly is a crucial need for preachers and witnesses for Christ with unique intellectual and creative gifts to apply their communication

---

[12]"Attempts at the Impossible," *The Sword and the Trowel* (December 1888), 619.

[13]"Progressive Theology," *The Sword and the Trowel* (April 1888), 157-58.

[14]Quoted in "Notes," *The Sword and the Trowel* (August 1888), 445. Years before, Varley, a butcher turned lay evangelist, had been one of the key men responsible for encouraging D. L. Moody on his first visit to England. Varley and Spurgeon were from widely differing traditions, Varley being a Plymouth Brethren. Over the years Spurgeon had been outspoken in his criticism of the Plymouth Brethren and their exclusivist tendencies. But Varley's defense of Spurgeon in this lengthy and eloquent letter to the editor was one of the high points of the Down-Grade Controversy.

skills to the careful presentation of the gospel. It is by no means wrong to want to be fresh, resourceful, persuasive, and interesting. Any preacher who is truly excited about and committed to the gospel will naturally display those attributes. But keep the focus on the message, not the style. We must make the gospel our one message to the world. After all, it is the gospel—not human inventiveness, not "user-friendliness," not clever techniques or modern methodology—that is the power of God unto salvation to all who believe.

$$\overline{7}$$

Paul on Mars' Hill

In days gone by, [preachers on the down-grade] aimed at being thought respectable, judicious, moderate, and learned, and, in consequence, they abandoned the Puritanic teaching with which they started, and toned down their doctrines. The spiritual life which had been the impelling cause of their dissent declined almost to death's door. . . . Alas! Many are returning to the poisoned cups which drugged that declining generation.

CHARLES HADDON SPURGEON[1]

THOSE WHO believe "cultural relevance" is the secret to powerful preaching often point to Paul's ministry in Athens as a prime example of how Paul accommodated his message and his methodology to the culture in which he ministered. They suggest that Paul's sermon on Mars' Hill is a paradigm for market-driven ministry.

And at first sight, it may seem that they have a case. Paul was preaching among the city's intellectual elite. He spoke to them in their own language, quoted extemporaneously from their own poets and philosophers, and used their method of discourse—public debate—as the vehicle through which he communicated to them. Is this not a fitting prototype for "contextualization" and market-driven methodology?

Acts 17:16-33 thus becomes a key text in addressing the contemporary church-marketing movement:

Now while Paul was waiting for [Silas and Timothy] at Athens, his spirit was being provoked within him as he was beholding the city full of idols. So he was reasoning in the synagogue with the Jews and the

---

[1]"Another Word Concerning the Down-Grade," *The Sword and the Trowel* (August 1887), 398.

God-fearing Gentiles, and in the market place every day with those who happened to be present. And also some of the Epicurean and Stoic philosophers were conversing with him. And some were saying, "What would this idle babbler wish to say?" Others, "He seems to be a proclaimer of strange deities,"—because he was preaching Jesus and the resurrection. And they took him and brought him to the Areopagus, saying, "May we know what this new teaching is which you are proclaiming? For you are bringing some strange things to our ears; we want to know therefore what these things mean." (Now all the Athenians and the strangers visiting there used to spend their time in nothing other than telling or hearing something new.) And Paul stood in the midst of the Areopagus and said, "Men of Athens, I observe that you are very religious in all respects. For while I was passing through and examining the objects of your worship, I also found an altar with this inscription, 'TO AN UNKNOWN GOD.' What therefore you worship in ignorance, this I proclaim to you. The God who made the world and all things in it, since He is Lord of heaven and earth, does not dwell in temples made with hands; neither is He served by human hands, as though He needed anything, since He Himself gives to all life and breath and all things; and He made from one, every nation of mankind to live on all the face of the earth, having determined their appointed times, and the boundaries of their habitation, that they should seek God, if perhaps they might grope for Him and find Him, though He is not far from each one of us; for in Him we live and move and exist, as even some of your own poets have said, 'For we also are His offspring.' Being then the offspring of God, we ought not to think that the Divine Nature is like gold or silver or stone, an image formed by the art and thought of man. Therefore having overlooked the times of ignorance, God is now declaring to men that all everywhere should repent, because He has fixed a day in which He will judge the world in righteousness through a Man whom He has appointed, having furnished proof to all men by raising Him from the dead."

Now when they heard of the resurrection of the dead, some began to sneer, but others said, "We shall hear you again concerning this." So Paul went out of their midst.

The early part of Acts 17 describes how Paul had been run out of Thessalonica and Berea. Some of the Christians at Berea had smuggled Paul out of the city by sea, and they took him as far as Athens (v. 15). Silas and Timothy had been left in Berea, and Paul sent word for them to join him at Athens.

So Paul was in Athens alone, waiting for Timothy and Silas. This could very well have been a low point for Paul. He had felt the sense of aloneness at other times in his life as well (cf 2 Tim. 4:9-22). The ministry that had brought him to this point was one long chronicle of persecution and rejection. Now he was by himself in a vast, highly cultured but extremely pagan city.

Scripture says nothing about Paul's feelings at this point, but don't get the idea he was spiritually discouraged. His epistles give wonderful insight into how he handled situations like this. He wrote to the Corinthians, "We are afflicted in every way, but not crushed; perplexed, but not despairing; persecuted, but not forsaken; struck down, but not destroyed" (2 Cor. 4:8, 9). In the same epistle, he wrote, "Therefore I am well content with weaknesses, with insults, with distresses, with persecutions, with difficulties, for Christ's sake; for when I am weak, then I am strong" (12:10). Paul, from a position of weakness, was about to be a channel for the power of God to be unleashed in Athens.

ONE MAN AGAINST A CITY

Remember that Paul was brought up under the strictest Pharisaical discipline. "A Jew, born in Tarsus of Cilicia, but brought up in this city, educated under Gamaliel, strictly according to the law of our fathers, being zealous for God" (Acts 22:3); "circumcised the eighth day, of the nation of Israel, of the tribe of Benjamin, a Hebrew of Hebrews; as to the Law, a Pharisee . . . as to the righteousness which is in the Law, found blameless" (Phil. 3:5, 6). He was also a Roman citizen, with knowledge of military and political matters. Tarsus, where Paul grew up and was trained, was very cosmopolitan, so Paul's rich education equipped him and acclimated him for almost any culture in the Roman Empire. Even Athens, for several centuries the very heart of the intellectual and art world, was no exception. Paul was thoroughly familiar with Greek culture, manners, religion, art, and philosophy. He was a scholar, well-read and well-traveled. By God's design Paul's entire life had equipped him for situations precisely like this one.

In the fourth and fifth centuries B. C. Athens was considered by many the greatest city in the world. Some aspects of Athenian culture have never been equaled. Athens reached the pinnacle in art, literature, architecture, and philosophy. Never in history has any one city achieved the height of glory in those fields that was seen in Athens during the golden age of the Greek empire. Athens was in the province of Achaia, where Corinth, not far away, was the capital city. But Athens was still the center of the cultural and intellectual world, just as Rome was the political center. Athens was sometimes referred to as the university of the world. All the great minds of the world congregated there.

Athens also offered a home to the pantheon of gods in Greek mythology. Every civic building in Athens was a shrine to a god. The place where public records were kept, for example, was dedicated to the Mother of the Gods. The centerpiece of the city council building was an idol of Apollo. A popular saying was, "It is easier to find a god in Athens than a man." The city was pagan to the core; although they had gods for everything, they did not know the one true God.

It is interesting to note how Athens affected Paul. You might think that with his cultural and educational background, Paul would have been fascinated to see Athens. The city was filled with ancient temples, glorious artwork, magnificent buildings, sublime sculptures, engaging orators, ingenious philosophers, and spectacular sights to interest a scholar like Paul. And in Paul's day the marble and gold still glittered.

What *was* Paul's response to Athens? "His spirit was being provoked within him as he was beholding the city full of idols" (Acts 17:16). Instead of being awed by all the marvelous sites, Paul saw only a city full of idols, and it grieved him greatly.

A nineteenth-century Bible dictionary says,

> Paul had at his feet the Theseion [a spectacular marble temple near the marketplace], and on his right hand the Akropolis, with its splendid temples intact. Such surroundings would fill with enthusiasm every cultured Christian of to-day. Wherever St. Paul turned, his glance must have fallen on the severe and lovely works of art which still adorned the decadent city. Thus a table was spread before him of which nineteenth century humanists are laboriously but thankfully gathering up the scattered crumbs. To St. Paul's Semitic imagination nothing of all this appealed. It was to him just gold or silver or stone, graven by art and man's device, the work of a period of ignorance at which God had mercifully winked.[2]

---

[2]F. C. Conybeare, "Areopagus," *A Dictionary of the Bible*, James Hastings, ed. (New York: Scribner's, 1898), 1: 144.

One writer who lived in Paul's time visited Athens and wrote six volumes describing the glories of the city. If Paul had been writing a travelogue, he would have said simply, "It's full of idols." Period. Obviously Paul was not obtuse or insensible. It wasn't that he lacked the knowledge to appreciate Athenian culture; on the contrary, here was a man who was ideally suited for such a city. But he had a higher calling and more serious business than tourism, or curiosity, or even academic research. He saw deeper than the city's glittering facade or the well-dressed, well-bred Athenian intellectuals. And what he saw were people doomed to a Christless eternity.

Athens stirred Paul's emotions. The phrase "his spirit was being provoked within him" employs a Greek word, *paroxunō* ("provoked"), which speaks of intense agitation. Our word *paroxysm* comes from this root. Paul was saddened, grieved, indignant, and outraged at the widespread idolatry he saw. He knew these people were giving stone idols glory, which rightfully belongs to God alone.

PAUL IN THE MARKETPLACE

Paul's response was to do what he had done in virtually every city where he had ever ministered. He went to the synagogue and the marketplace and preached Christ. Verse 17 says, "So he was reasoning in the synagogue with the Jews and the God-fearing Gentiles, and in the market place every day with those who happened to be present." His approach was direct, confrontive evangelism. He did not do a community survey. He did not conduct any special research. He did not try to put together an evangelization committee. He just went to the synagogue and the marketplace and preached to whoever was there.

"God-fearing Gentiles" refers to Gentiles who were associated with the synagogue—people who knew about Jehovah and believed enough about Him to fear Him. So Paul was ministering to Jews, God-fearing Gentiles, and rank pagans. There was no marketing focus or target group. Paul proclaimed the truth everywhere, just as he had done all over Asia Minor.

The marketplace in Athens was called the Agora. It was the hub of all activity for Athens. Situated at the southern edge of the ancient city, it stood in the shadow of the hill called Areopagus. Looming to the southeast was the great Acropolis, the geographical high point of Athens, where the most spectacular temples were situated—including the massive Parthenon, a magnificent marble structure that was already five hundred years old by the time Paul saw it.

The Agora was a large courtyard in the midst of all the civic buildings. There, under a large colonnade, people would set up little shops and booths. Vendors would peddle their wares. Farmers brought produce and cattle to sell. Tradesmen would be there to ply their services. It was always a busy place. A modern equivalent might be a town square or the central area of a city mall. In the middle of the marketplace, philosophers would congregate and vie with one another for people's attention. Peripatetic teachers in the tradition of Aristotle, specialists in the healing arts, magicians, hucksters, and street performers of all kinds had a forum where they could work the crowds.

Paul saw it as an ideal place to preach. Scripture says he reasoned there "every day with those who happened to be present." What form did his discourse take? Verse 18 says he preached the gospel. He was preaching about "Jesus and the resurrection"—classic Pauline ministry.

How could one man hope to have an effect on a city like Athens? From a human perspective Paul stood literally alone against centuries of traditional paganism—and intellectual paganism at that. What could he hope to accomplish by standing in the marketplace and preaching about Jesus and the resurrection?

Those are questions a marketing specialist might have asked, but not Paul. He didn't see himself as one man alone against a city. He saw himself as a voice through which the power of God—the gospel—could be turned loose on the largest and most influential metropolis in that part of the world. He believed that by standing there in the Agora proclaiming Christ he was unleashing God's own power on the city of Athens. The impact of it was in God's hands.

THE APOSTLE V. THE PHILOSOPHERS

It didn't take Paul long to be noticed. "Some of the Epicurean and Stoic philosophers were conversing with him." Far from being impressed with his speaking savvy and relevance, some were saying, "What would this idle babbler wish to say?" (v. 18). The word translated "idle babbler" is the Greek word *spermologos*, literally meaning "seed-picker." It referred to the birds that picked seeds out of the gutter. It was a mockery of Paul and his message. Clearly, the Athenian intellectuals were not swept away by Paul's erudition or cleverness!

Nonetheless, Paul had attracted the attention and piqued the interest of these two groups of philosophers. The Epicureans dated back four centuries to their founder, Epicurus. They believed that everything happens by chance. They had no god in their system who was sovereign. Therefore they believed the outcome of everything is questionable. They also believed death is the end of human existence. And so they taught that pleasure is the natural aim and highest good in life (though they emphasized that true pleasure is found only in right living, so they were highly moral). A corrupted form of Epicureanism is echoed in the beer ads once popular on television: "You only go around once, so grab all the gusto you can get." Modern existentialism is often nothing more than a dissipated variety of Epicureanism.

The other group that took notice of Paul were the Stoics. Their philosophy was in many ways antithetical to the Epicureans. They were pantheistic fatalists. They believed everything is god, and everything happens because god wills it. In contrast to the Epicureans, they were strongly humanitarian. Because of their extreme pantheism, they treated everyone as a god. Their philosophy was therefore very altruistic, charitable, and magnanimous. We use the word *stoic*, of course, to refer to someone who is able to bear suffering unemotionally. That's because the Stoics' fatalism caused them to be resigned to the notion that whatever happened was the will of god.

As we noted, some of these pagan philosophers were overtly mocking Paul, calling him a seed-picker. But others were intrigued by his message: "'He seems to be a proclaimer of strange deities,'—because he was preaching Jesus and the resurrection" (v. 18). It is certainly curious that they used the plural "deities," but it seems they may have misunderstood the word for "resurrection," *anastasis*. They were so used to personifying everything as a deity, perhaps they thought he was speaking of a goddess named Anastasia. They had gods of piety, mercy and modesty, for example—why not a goddess of resurrection? Perhaps they mistakenly thought that was what Paul was saying.

Whatever their assumption, they wanted to hear more.

THE PREACHER AND THE SCHOLARS

"They took him and brought him to the Areopagus, saying, 'May we know what this new teaching is which you are proclaiming? For you are bringing some strange things to our ears; we want to know therefore what these things mean'" (vv. 19, 20). It was not at all that they were under conviction. To them, Paul was a philosophical oddity, someone with something novel to say. This was but a pastime with them: "All the Athenians and the strangers visiting there used to spend their time in nothing other than telling or hearing something new" (v. 21). Something about Paul caught their fancy, so they took him off to the Areopagus.

The Areopagus was the Athenian court of philosophers. The Greek word *areopagus* means "hill of Ares." The Roman name for Ares was Mars, so the Latinized name of the place where this court met is Mars' Hill. So when Scripture says Paul "stood in the midst of the Areopagus" (v. 22), it has reference primarily to the court of philosophers, not the hill. But this meeting probably took place either on the hill or in the very near vicinity. The Areopagus court included at least thirty men who were the supreme judges of Athens. They ruled on criminal and civil cases, just like a court of appeals. But more than that, they were the guardians of Athenian philosophy. They listened to new teachings to determine if they should be outlawed as blasphemy. Evidently the philosophers wanted the judges to hear Paul's teaching and try to decide whether the "strange deities" he was proclaiming could be added to all the ones already in the pantheon.

What an opportunity! These men actually hauled Paul before the highest court in the city and asked him to explain what he was preaching about! This was the kind of situation Paul lived for, and he made the most of it.

This, of course, was by no means Paul's only sermon in Athens, nor was it the first. The text does not say how many days he had been preaching in the synagogue and marketplace. Nor are any of those sermons recorded for us in Scripture. But this message before the Areopagus is a fascinating insight into the way Paul preached. Several remarkable features make it a unique model of gospel preaching.

PAUL WAS POLITE BUT CONFRONTIVE

"Paul stood in the midst of the Areopagus and said, 'Men of Athens, I observe that you are very religious in all respects'" (v. 22). The King James Version translates that last phrase, "I perceive that in all things ye are too superstitious." About that translation, Spurgeon said,

> He did not say, " Too superstitious," as our version has it, that would have needlessly provoked them at the outset. He went on to say,

". . . What, therefore, ye worship without knowing it, that I announce unto you." He did not say, "Whom ye ignorantly worship." He was far too prudent to use such an expression. They were a collection of thoughtful men, of cultured minds, and he aimed at winning them by courteously declaring to them the gospel.[3]

As we have noted, there *is* a legitimate sense in which the apostle matched his style to the people he was trying to win. To the Jews he became Jewish. In Athens he became Greek. He spoke to these men with great respect for their position. He addressed them as deferentially as if he were a citizen of the city they presided over.

"While I was passing through and examining the objects of your worship, I also found an altar with this inscription, 'TO AN UNKNOWN GOD.' What therefore you worship in ignorance, this I proclaim to you" (v. 23). Note the tact with which Paul confronts them. Having noticed the altar to an unknown god, Paul used that to make the very powerful point that their religion was unable to give them certain knowledge of *any* god, much less the true God. He gently implied that the existence of such an altar was a plain admission that they did not know the truth about God at all. He clearly regarded the inscription on the altar as their own testimony of spiritual ignorance.

Paul framed his message in terminology that was diplomatic, courteous, and friendly ("I observe that you are very religious in all respects")— yet he got right to the point ("What therefore you worship in ignorance, this I proclaim to you"). Boldly, he immediately established that he was going to declare the truth about the God they did not know. No careful posturing, no guarded rhetoric—he just came out with it. That dogmatic approach was no more typical in the Areopagus court than it is today. In fact, it may have been something of a shock to these men who represented the most elite minds of Athens. But Paul did not ease off, lose confidence, or try to soften the authority of the gospel. He spoke with as much boldness as he would have anywhere.

What was this altar to an unknown god? Actually, there were many of these in Athens. Six hundred years before Paul's time, Athens had been stricken with a terrible plague. Hundreds were ill and dying, and the city grew desperate. A famous poet from Crete named Epimenides devised a

---

[3]"By All Means Save Some," *The Metropolitan Tabernacle Pulpit*, Vol. 20 (London: Passmore and Alabaster, 1874), 248.

plan to pacify whatever gods were causing the plague. He went to the Areopagus and turned loose a flock of sheep. The plan was to let the sheep roam the city freely. When the sheep lay down, they were to be sacrificed to the god of the nearest temple. The assumption was that the angry gods would draw the sheep to themselves. When the sheep were turned loose, however, many of them lay down in places with no temples nearby. Epimenides decided to sacrifice the sheep anyway and erect altars wherever they lay down, just to make sure no unfamiliar deities were overlooked. Since these were nameless gods, the people simply erected altars and shrines "TO AN UNKNOWN GOD." It was undoubtedly one of these altars Paul spotted.

Paul boldly said, "I know this unknown God. Let me tell you who He is." He then began with great authority to tell them very clearly and very thoroughly who God is.

HE RELATED TO THEM WITHOUT COMPROMISING THE MESSAGE

Paul launched right into his message, beginning with creation: "The God who made the world and all things in it, since He is Lord of heaven and earth, does not dwell in temples made with hands; neither is He served by human hands, as though He needed anything, since He Himself gives to all life and breath and all things" (vv. 24, 25). There's a wealth of truth about God in those words, and it directly contradicted Greek religious belief. Paul was not stepping around their sensitivities or trying to avoid truth they might not want to hear.

All their gods dwelt in man-made temples, and they were manlike entities, not at all like the transcendent Supreme Being Paul was describing. These men were well-educated, and undoubtedly familiar with the Hebrew God. They knew about His exclusivity ("The Lord is our God, the Lord is one! And you shall love the Lord your God with all your heart and with all your soul and with all your might"—Deut. 6:4, 5). They knew His first commandment was, "You shall have no other gods before Me" (Ex. 20:3; Deut. 5:7). Surely as soon as Paul began speaking these men understood that he was declaring the same God the Hebrews worshiped, and they would have understood the ramifications of that.

Paul identified God as the *Creator*: He "made the world and all things in it" (Acts 17:24). He is the *sustainer* of all life: "He Himself gives to all life and breath and all things" (v. 25). He is *sovereign*: "He is Lord of heaven and earth" (v. 24); "He made from one, every nation of mankind to live on all the face of the earth, having determined their appointed times, and the boundaries of their habitation" (v. 26). And He is *omnipresent*: "He is not far from each one of us" (v. 27).

Moreover, Paul told them, God desires that people "should seek God, if perhaps they might grope for Him and find Him" (v. 27). Paul was telling these philosophers that seeking God is a moral obligation. If He is indeed the sovereign, omnipotent Creator, who desires that we seek Him, then *not* to seek Him is a sin. That truth would not have escaped these philosophers. They knew that Paul was laying before them a clear imperative that they seek and worship the one true God he represented. In other words, Paul said, the God I declare to you is supreme over every other being, and He is worthy of your exclusive loyalty and worship. You had better seek Him until you find Him. This struck a blow directly at their syncretism and polytheism. There could have been no question in their minds about *adding* Paul's God to their own pantheon. Paul was urging them to abandon their religion and worship the eternal Creator of all things, the God who made all other gods petty and obsolete.

Notice the unusual way Paul buttresses his defense of the true God: he quotes Greek poetry. "In Him we live and move and exist, as even some of your own poets have said, 'For we also are His offspring'" (v. 28). Both the first and the closing phrases of that verse are quotations from Greek poets. Epimenides—the *same* poet who erected the altars to the unknown god—said, "In him we live and move and have our being." And it was probably the poet Aradus who said, "We are his offspring."

Oddly enough, when Epimenides said, "In him we live and move and have our being," he was talking about Zeus. Why would Paul quote this paean for an idol and apply it to God? Because he was making a defense of the faith. His point may be paraphrased like this: "Your own poets, with no knowledge of the true God whatsoever, nevertheless gave testimony to the inescapable fact that there had to be a sovereign, life-giving, all-powerful creator. Zeus does not fit that description. But the God I declare to you, whom you don't know yet, is that Almighty One." Paul's use of ancient poets simply underscored the truth of Romans 1:19, 20: "That which is known about God is evident within them; for God made it evident to them. For since the creation of the world His invisible attributes, His eternal power and divine nature, have been clearly seen, being understood through what has been made." The rational mind demands an eternal cause for the effect of creation. Therefore many attributes of God are so obvious that even pagan poets understand them—although they attach them to the wrong god.

It was a powerful point. Paul was making the most of the situation, declaring that the true God whom they didn't know is Creator, sustainer, and sovereign of the universe, then quoting their own poets as proof that such a sovereign Creator must exist. Spurgeon said, "It was most adroit on his part to refer to that inscription upon the altar, and equally so to quote from one of their own poets. If he had been addressing Jews, he would neither have quoted from a Greek poet nor referred to a heathen altar: his intense love for his hearers taught him to merge his own peculiarities in order to secure their attention."[4]

But Paul was not content with *merely* securing their attention. He was not trying to impress them with his intellect or obtain their approval of him personally. He was not trying to win the world's respect or to gain acceptance as a philosopher. His sole aim was to convert these people to Christ, and he was just coming to the heart of his message.

HE WAS BOTH BOLD AND DIRECT

Paul's next words were a fatal shot at Athenian paganism. "Being then the offspring of God, we ought not to think that the Divine Nature is like gold or silver or stone, an image formed by the art and thought of man" (Acts 17:29). In other words, if God made us (as your own poets have indicated), God Himself must be greater than any man-made image. This is a very important point. It was as if Paul took one enormous philosophical sledgehammer and smashed all their idols. If God is really the sovereign, infinite being even the poets acknowledged He must be, we can't know Him by means of an idol, a shrine, or any other graven image.

Paul goes directly to the heart of the matter: "Therefore having overlooked the times of ignorance, God is now declaring to men that all everywhere should repent, because He has fixed a day in which He will judge the world in righteousness through a Man whom He has appointed, having furnished proof to all men by raising Him from the dead" (vv. 30, 31). Note that Paul preached repentance, as always. He didn't try to accommodate the Epicureans by promising them a wonderful and pleasure-filled life. And he didn't attempt to win the Stoics by trying to make the gospel sound as much like their philosophy as possible. He called both groups to repentance, referring to the golden age of Greek philosophy as "times of ignorance."

---

[4]*Ibid.*

The word "ignorance" comes from the same Greek root as "unknown" in verse twenty-three. And the word "overlooked" comes from a word that means "to not interfere." It doesn't mean God disregarded or was indifferent to sinful idolatry. It means He chose not to intervene in judgment by wiping Athens off the face of the earth.

As Paul told them, however, God has appointed a day in which He *will* judge the world—including Athens—in righteousness. The agent of that judgment will be a Man whom He has ordained and given testimony to by raising Him from the dead. We know who that Man is, of course. It is Jesus Christ, to whom God has given all judgment (John 5:22).

But at this point Paul was interrupted, and he evidently never even got to name the name of Christ. "When they heard of the resurrection of the dead, some began to sneer, but others said, 'We shall hear you again concerning this.' So Paul went out of their midst" (Acts 17:32, 33). The Epicureans did not believe in a resurrection at all, while the Stoics believed in a spiritual resurrection but not the resurrection of the body. Perhaps stung by his call for repentance, they responded collectively by mocking Paul. In fact, as soon as he mentioned the resurrection, the skeptics began to scoff. Evidently some had heard enough to reject Paul's message without even hearing him out. Others said they would hear more later. So Paul simply went out of their midst.

Not everyone doubted or delayed, however. "Some men joined him and believed, among whom also were Dionysius the Areopagite and a woman named Damaris and others with them" (v. 34). Enough of the truth had penetrated their hearts so that these people followed Paul to find out more. Obviously, Paul continued his sermon for those who wanted to hear, and some of them were converted. One of the converts was Dionysius, a member of the Areopagus court. Another was a woman named Damaris. Since she is given no title, we can assume she was a common woman. So this sermon reached people at both ends of the social spectrum—philosophers and housewives, men and women, intellectuals and ordinary people. This little band of converts joined Paul and became the first Christians in Athens.

THE CHRISTIAN IN SECULAR SOCIETY

It may seem to some that Paul did not have much impact on Athens. That handful of converts in Athens somehow looks less spectacular than the revivals Paul saw in Antioch or Thessalonica. But Paul had a dramatic effect on the city at the top level. He exposed its highest court to the knowledge of the true God. This event planted a church in Athens and launched Paul's ministry in nearby Corinth. Paul also opened up more opportunities to preach ("We shall hear you again concerning this"). Although the response of the Areopagus court may not have been as sensational as Paul's preaching had provoked elsewhere, we can be certain that God's purposes were accomplished and the Word did not return void. The threefold response of that day—contempt, curiosity, and conversion—is typical whenever the gospel is faithfully preached.

It was immediately after the Areopagus incident that Paul went to Corinth. Years later, he wrote, "When I came to you, brethren, I did not come with superiority of speech or of wisdom, proclaiming to you the testimony of God. For I determined to know nothing among you except Jesus Christ, and Him crucified" (1 Cor. 2:1, 2). Some interpreters believe Paul was renouncing the approach he had employed at the Areopagus. That view undoubtedly reads too much into the second chapter of 1 Corinthians. Paul nowhere indicates he viewed his Athens ministry as a failure. I reject the notion that his sermon at the Areopagus miscarried. From all we are told in Scripture, it was totally consistent with Paul's approach to ministry everywhere else. Nevertheless, this much is clear from 1 Corinthians 2, as well as the rest of Paul's pastoral epistles: Paul did not believe the secret to his powerful ministry lay in his ability to quote Greek poets. You don't see him counseling Timothy or Titus to bone up on secular culture, learn to quote the classics, or study philosophy so they could engage in debates with the intellectual elite. He simply commanded them to preach the Word, in season and out of season—and to be prepared to face the world's hostility if they were faithful in that task.

Acts chapter 17 proves that while Paul adjusted his style in speaking, he never adapted his message. Most significantly, he never adopted the spirit of his age. A few years ago Francis Schaeffer wrote, "To accommodate to the world spirit about us in our age is the most gross form of worldliness in the proper definition of the word."[5] That is precisely what many

---

[5] *The Great Evangelical Disaster* (Westchester, Ill.: Crossway, 1984), 142. Schaeffer added, "Unhappily, today we must say that in general the evangelical establishment has been accommodating to the forms of the world spirit as it finds expression in our day. I would say this with tears—and we must not in any way give up hoping and praying. We must with regret remember that many of those with whom we have a basic disagreement over these issues of accommodation are brothers and sisters in Christ. But in the most basic sense, the evangelical establishment has become deeply worldly" (*ibid*).

today are doing—but what Paul would not do. He never conformed himself—and more importantly he never tried to conform the God he declared—to the tastes and expectations of his audience. He was content—as we must be—to allow the power of the gospel to speak for itself.

8

The Sovereignty of God
in Salvation

Children of God, whatever you have not got, you have a God in whom you may greatly glory. Having God you have more than all things, for all things come of him; and if all things were blotted out, he could restore all things simply by his will. He speaketh, and it is done; he commandeth, and it stands fast. Blessed is the man that hath the God of Jacob for his trust, and whose hope Jehovah is. In the Lord Jehovah we have righteousness and strength; let us trust in him for ever. Let the times roll on, they cannot affect our God.

CHARLES HADDON SPURGEON[1]

ONE OF the most ridiculous ideas I have seen in a long time is a "Jesus action figure" doll for children. The plastic character comes dressed in a robe and sandals. It is just one of a whole line of "Bible Greats Action Figures" manufactured by a Michigan-based company. Others in the series include John the Baptist, Peter, David and Goliath, and Daniel and the lions. For girls, the alternatives include Mary, Ruth, and Esther. Or, resourceful parents may simply buy biblical costumes from the company and turn their child's Barbie doll into a "woman of faith."

Not to be outdone, a Florida doll-maker offers "Jesus The Doll," a $29.95 rag doll that is fully machine washable. Designed primarily to "help children discover Jesus," the floppy toy supposedly also "can provide solace for the elderly and the infirm, for those in recovery programs, and those under emotional duress. In other words, everybody." What kind

---

[1] "A Sermon for the Time Present," *The Metropolitan Tabernacle Pulpit*, Vol. 33 (London: Passmore and Alabaster, 1887), 605-6. This sermon was preached 30 October 1887.

of "solace" can a rag-doll Jesus provide that the real Jesus can't? According to the doll-maker, the actual Jesus isn't tangible enough: "It's hard to hug air."

More rag dolls are planned to complete the line, which the manufacturer calls "Firstfruits." The next two will be Mary and God. Asked what a rag-doll god might look like, the doll-maker brought out a prototype. It is two feet tall, white-haired and white-bearded, with a long, rainbow-colored robe—completely machine washable, of course.

When I first read about Jesus The Doll and the Jesus action figure, they struck me as fitting metaphors of the way some professing Christians imagine our Lord. Too many think of Him as someone who can be manipulated any way they please, rather than the utterly sovereign Jehovah of the Bible. The truth is, the average person would actually prefer a benign, utterly passive, white-bearded rag-doll image to the Almighty God revealed in Scripture.

GOD'S ABSOLUTE SOVEREIGNTY

No doctrine is more despised by the natural mind than the truth that God is absolutely sovereign. Human pride loathes the suggestion that God orders everything, controls everything, rules over everything. The carnal mind, burning with enmity against God, abhors the biblical teaching that nothing comes to pass except according to His eternal decrees. Most of all, the flesh hates the notion that salvation is entirely God's work. If God chose who would be saved, and if His choice was settled before the foundation of the world, then believers deserve no credit for any aspect of their salvation.

But that is, after all, precisely what Scripture teaches. Even faith is God's gracious gift to His elect. Jesus said, "No one can come to Me, unless it has been granted him from the Father" (John 6:65). "Nor does anyone know the Father, except the Son, and anyone to whom the Son wills to reveal Him" (Matt. 11:27). Therefore no one who is saved has anything to boast about (cf Eph. 2:8, 9). "Salvation is from the Lord" (Jonah 2:9).

The doctrine of divine election is explicitly taught throughout Scripture. For example, in the New Testament epistles alone, we learn that all believers are "chosen of God" (Titus 1:1). We were "predestined according to His purpose *who works all things after the counsel of His will*" (Eph. 1:11, emphasis added). "He chose us in Him before the foundation of the world. . . . He predestined us to adoption as sons through Jesus Christ to Himself, according to the kind intention of His will" (vv. 4, 5). We "are called according to His purpose. For whom He foreknew, He also predestined to become conformed to the image of His Son . . . and whom He predestined, these He also called; and whom He called, these He also justified; and whom He justified, these He also glorified" (Rom. 8:28-30).

When Peter wrote that we are "chosen according to the foreknowledge of God the Father" (1 Peter 1:1, 2), he was not using the word "foreknowledge" to mean that God was aware beforehand who would believe and therefore chose them because of their foreseen faith. Rather, Peter meant that God determined before time began to know and love and save them; and He chose them without regard to anything good or bad they might do. We'll return to this point again, but for now, note that those verses explicitly state that God's sovereign choice is made "according to the kind intention of His will" and "according to His purpose who works all things after the counsel of His will"—that is, not for any reason external to Himself. Certainly He did not choose certain sinners to be saved because of something praiseworthy in them, or because He foresaw that they would choose Him. He chose them solely because it pleased Him to do so. God declares "the end from the beginning . . . saying, 'My purpose will be established, and I will accomplish all My good pleasure'" (Isa. 46:10). He is not subject to others' decisions. His purposes for choosing some and rejecting others are hidden in the secret counsels of His own will.

Moreover, everything that exists in the universe exists because God allowed it, decreed it, and called it into existence. "Our God is in the heavens; He does whatever He pleases" (Ps. 115:3). "Whatever the Lord pleases, He does, in heaven and in earth, in the seas and in all deeps" (Ps. 135:6). He "works all things after the counsel of His will" (Eph. 1:11). "From Him and through Him and to Him are all things" (Rom. 11:36). "For us there is but one God, the Father, from whom are all things, and we exist for Him; and one Lord, Jesus Christ, by whom are all things, and we exist through Him" (1 Cor. 8:6).

What about sin? God is not the author of sin, but He certainly allowed it; it is integral to His eternal decree. God has a purpose for allowing it. He cannot be blamed for evil or tainted by its existence (1 Sam. 2:2: "There is no one holy like the Lord"). But He certainly wasn't caught off-guard or standing helpless to stop it when sin entered the universe. We do not know His purposes for allowing sin. If nothing else, He permitted it in order to destroy evil forever. And God sometimes uses evil to accomplish good (Gen. 45:7, 8; 50:20; Rom. 8:28). How can these things be? Scripture does not answer all the questions for us. But we know from His Word that God is utterly sovereign, He is perfectly holy, and He is absolutely just.

Admittedly, those truths are hard for the human mind to embrace, but Scripture is unequivocal. God controls all things, right down to choosing who will be saved. Paul states the doctrine in inescapable terms in the ninth chapter of Romans, by showing that God chose Jacob and rejected his twin brother Esau "though the twins were not yet born, and had not done anything good or bad, in order that God's purpose according to His choice might stand, not because of works, but because of Him who calls" (v. 11). A few verses later, Paul adds this: "He says to Moses, 'I will have mercy on whom I have mercy, and I will have compassion on whom I have compassion.' So then it does not depend on the man who wills or the man who runs, but on God who has mercy" (vv. 15, 16).

Paul anticipated the argument against divine sovereignty: "You will say to me then, 'Why does He still find fault? For who resists His will?'" (v. 19). In other words, doesn't God's sovereignty cancel out human responsibility? But rather than offering a philosophical answer or a deep metaphysical argument, Paul simply reprimanded the skeptic: "On the contrary, who are you, O man, who answers back to God? The thing molded will not say to the molder, 'Why did you make me like this,' will it? Or does not the potter have a right over the clay, to make from the same lump one vessel for honorable use, and another for common use?" (vv. 20, 21).

Scripture affirms both divine sovereignty and human responsibility. We must accept both sides of the truth, though we may not understand how they correspond to one another. People are responsible for what they do with the gospel—or with whatever light they have (Rom. 2:19, 20), so that punishment is just if they reject the light. And those who reject do so voluntarily. Jesus lamented, "You are unwilling to come to Me, that you may have life" (John 5:40). He told unbelievers, "Unless you believe that I am [God], you shall die in your sins" (John 8:24). In John chapter 6, our Lord combined both divine sovereignty and human responsibility when He said, "All that the Father gives Me shall come to Me, and the one who comes to Me I will certainly not cast out" (v. 37); "For this is the will of My Father, that everyone who beholds the Son and believes in Him, may have eternal life" (v. 40); "No one can come to Me, unless the Father who sent Me draws him" (v. 44); "Truly, truly, I say to you, he who believes has eternal life" (v. 47); and, "No one can come to Me, unless it has been granted him from the Father" (v. 65). How both of those two realities can be true simultaneously cannot be understood by the human mind—only by God.

Above all, we must not conclude that God is unjust because He chooses to bestow grace on some but not to everyone. God is never to be measured by what seems fair to human judgment. Are we so foolish as to assume that we who are fallen, sinful creatures have a higher standard of what is right than an unfallen and infinitely, eternally holy God? What kind of pride is that? In Psalm 50:21 God says, "You thought that I was just like you." But God is *not* like us, nor can He be held to human standards. "'My thoughts are not your thoughts, neither are your ways My ways,' declares the Lord. 'For as the heavens are higher than the earth, so are My ways higher than your ways, and My thoughts than your thoughts'" (Isa. 55:8, 9).

We step out of bounds when we conclude that anything God does isn't fair. In Romans 11:33 the apostle writes, "Oh, the depth of the riches both of the wisdom and knowledge of God! How unsearchable are His judgments and unfathomable His ways! For who has known the mind of the Lord, or who became His counselor?" (Rom. 11:33, 34).

DIVINE SOVEREIGNTY v. PRAGMATISM

What does God's sovereignty have to do with the subject of this book? Everything. The very reason many contemporary churches embrace pragmatic methodology is that they lack any understanding of God's sovereignty in the salvation of the elect. They lose confidence in the power of God to use the preached gospel to reach hardened unbelievers. That's why they approach evangelism as a marketing problem. Their methodology is shaped accordingly.

More than thirty years ago, J. I. Packer wrote,

> If we forget that it is God's prerogative to give results when the gospel is preached, we shall start to think that it is our responsibility to secure them. And if we forget that only God can give faith, we shall start to think that the making of converts depends, in the last analysis, not on God, but on us, and that the decisive factor is the way in which we evangelize. And this line of thought, consistently followed through, will lead us far astray.

157

Let us work this out. If we regarded it as our job, not simply to present Christ, but actually to produce converts—to evangelize, not only faithfully, but also successfully—our approach to evangelism would become pragmatic and calculating. We should conclude that our basic equipment, both for personal dealing and for public preaching, must be twofold. We must have, not merely a clear grasp of the meaning and application of the gospel, but also an irresistible technique for inducing a response. We should, therefore, make it our business to try and develop such a technique. And we should evaluate all evangelism, our own and other people's, by the criterion, not only of the message preached, but also of visible results. If our own efforts were not bearing fruit, we should conclude that our technique still needed improving. If they were bearing fruit, we should conclude that this justified the technique we had been using. We should regard evangelism as an activity involving a battle of wills between ourselves and those to whom we go, a battle in which victory depends on our firing off a heavy enough barrage of calculated effects.[2]

What Packer was warning against is exactly the kind of thinking that has given rise to the user-friendly church and its market-driven, pragmatic philosophy.

Actually, the pragmatic approach to ministry is nothing new. It has roots deep in American church history. The main contribution was not made by Harry Emerson Fosdick, Norman Vincent Peale, Robert Schuller, or any other contemporary advocate of pragmatism. They, along with others, have followed the influence of another man—early nineteenth-century evangelist Charles G. Finney.

Charles Finney got off on the wrong foot when he dismissed the orthodox view of divine election as "an exercise of arbitrary sovereignty."[3] He rejected the doctrine that conversion is wholly a work of God. He taught instead that faith is fundamentally a human decision and that salvation is secured by the sinner's own movement toward God.

Although Finney's fundamental theological error was his rejection of God's sovereignty, that led inevitably to other errors in his teaching. He concluded that people are sinners by *choice*, not by nature. He believed the purpose of evangelism should therefore be to convince people to

[2]*Evangelism and the Sovereignty of God* (Downers Grove, Ill.: InterVarsity, 1961), 27-28.
[3]Charles G. Finney, *Systematic Theology* (Whittier, Calif.: Colporter Kemp, 1944 reprint), 489.

choose differently—or as many would say today, "make a decision for Christ." The sinner's choice—not God's—therefore became the determinative issue in conversion. The means of moving out of darkness into light was in Finney's opinion nothing more than a simple act of the human will. The preacher's task was to secure a decision of faith, applying whatever means proved useful. Finney introduced "new measures" (unconventional methodology) into his ministry, often using techniques whose sole design was to shock and intrigue apathetic churchgoers. He was willing to implement virtually any means that would elicit the desired response from his audiences.

Charles Finney's approach to ministry thus foreshadowed and laid the foundation for modern pragmatism. His teaching and his methods have colored much of American evangelism for the past century and a half. He could rightly be called the father of evangelical pragmatism. The modern market-driven ministry is simply a culmination of the movement Finney began (see Appendix 2). We would expect those who reject the biblical doctrine of God's sovereignty to follow Finney, but not those who say they affirm it. Their pragmatism becomes a denial of their theology—a kind of spiritual schizophrenia.

SALVATION IS OF THE LORD

Spurgeon fought the Down-Grade Controversy several years after Finney's heyday. But Finney's influence was still being felt—even in London.[4] Reformation theology was in serious decline. Pragmatic methodology was all the rage. Spurgeon was often a lone voice, particularly on the doctrine of God's sovereignty. One of Spurgeon's contemporaries, R. W. Dale, wrote in 1881 that "Mr. Spurgeon stands alone among the modern leaders of Evangelical Nonconformity in his fidelity to the older Calvinistic creed."[5] Virtually all the other influential evangelicals in England had abandoned their confidence in divine sovereignty.

Spurgeon saw very clearly how that disastrous loss of confidence could put churches on the down-grade. He was in full agreement with a

---

[4]Finney held an extensive campaign in London in 1849-1851, and returned to minister throughout the British Isles in 1859-60. He left a lasting mark on certain segments of English evangelicalism. His *Systematic Theology* was published in England in 1851. Editions of the book were still being printed in England as late as 1878—less than ten years before the Down-Grade Controversy erupted.

[5]Cited in Iain Murray, *The Forgotten Spurgeon* (Edinburgh: Banner of Truth, 1966), 176.

published letter to the editor of *The Christian Age* written by Dr. David Brown, principal of the Free Church College, Aberdeen: "All our churches are honeycombed with the mischievous tendency to minimize all those features of the gospel which the natural man cannot receive. And no wonder, for their object seems to be to attract the natural mind. Wherever this is the case, the spirituality of the pulpit is done away, and the Spirit himself is not there."[6]

Spurgeon regarded divine sovereignty as "the clue to the truth of God."[7] He saw this doctrine at the heart of the gospel itself: "I have my own private opinion that there is no such thing as preaching Christ and Him crucified, unless we preach what nowadays is called Calvinism. . . . I do not believe we can preach the gospel, if we do not preach justification by faith, without works; nor unless we preach the sovereignty of God in His dispensation of grace."[8]

Spurgeon quoted Jonah 2:9, "Salvation is of the Lord," and then commented,

That is just an epitome of Calvinism; it is the sum and substance of it. If anyone should ask me what I mean by a Calvinist, I should reply, "He is one who says, *Salvation is of the Lord*." I cannot find in Scripture any other doctrine than this. It is the essence of the Bible. "He *only* is my rock and my salvation." Tell me anything contrary to this truth, and it will be a heresy; tell me a heresy, and I shall find its essence here, that it has departed from this great, this fundamental, this rock-truth, "God is my rock and my salvation." What is the heresy of Rome, but the addition of something to the perfect merits of Jesus Christ— the bringing in of the works of the flesh, to assist in our justification? And what is the heresy of Arminianism but the addition of something to the work of the Redeemer? Every heresy, if brought to the touchstone, will discover itself here.[9]

SCRIPTURE AND THE SOVEREIGNTY OF GOD

Is salvation wholly the Lord's work? Or has He already done all He can do, and now awaits the sinner's decision? Scripture is clear. If salvation

---

[6]Cited by Spurgeon in "The Case Proved," *The Sword and the Trowel* (October 1887), 512.

[7]*C. H. Spurgeon's Autobiography*, 4 vols. (London: Passmore and Alabaster, 1897), 1: 167.

[8]*Ibid.*, 1: 172.

[9]*Ibid.*

were dependent on the sinner's initiative, no one would ever be saved. "There is none who understands, there is none who seeks for God" (Rom. 3:11). "No one can come to Me, unless the Father who sent Me draws him" (John 6:44). God Himself prompts faith in those whom He has appointed to eternal life (Acts 13:48). After this prompting, the seeking begins, as in Isaiah 55:6, 7: "Seek the Lord while He may be found; call upon Him while He is near. Let the wicked forsake his way, and the unrighteous man his thoughts; and let him return to the Lord, and He will have compassion on him; and to our God, for He will abundantly pardon." That text is followed by an affirmation of God's sovereignty in the classic words of verse 11: "So shall My word be which goes forth from My mouth; it shall not return to Me empty, without accomplishing what I desire, and without succeeding in the matter for which I sent it." And if such a paradox is confusing, verses 8, 9 help explain it: "'My thoughts are not your thoughts, neither are your ways My ways,' declares the Lord. 'For as the heavens are higher than the earth, so are My ways higher than your ways, and My thoughts than your thoughts.'"

God commands all to repent (Acts 17:30)—but ultimately it is He himself who must grant repentance (Acts 5:31; 11:18; 2 Tim. 2:25). And although God demands the response of faith, *He* must graciously prompt and empower that response in the hearts of the elect (Acts 18:27). The human heart is so depraved that left to ourselves, none of us would ever believe. If we could generate faith on our own, we would certainly have something to boast about. But Scripture says "By grace you have been saved through faith; and that not of yourselves, it is the gift of God; not as a result of works, that no one should boast. For we are His workmanship, created in Christ Jesus for good works, which God prepared beforehand, that we should walk in them" (Eph. 2:8-10).

These truths are not hidden in isolated passages of Scripture, but as Spurgeon suggested, they are "the essence of the Bible," affirmed throughout the sacred text. I want to focus, however, on one brief passage that is particularly clear regarding God's sovereignty in salvation, 1 Peter 1:1-5:

Peter, an apostle of Jesus Christ, to those who reside as aliens, scattered throughout Pontus, Galatia, Cappadocia, Asia, and Bithynia, who are chosen according to the foreknowledge of God the Father, by the sanctifying work of the Spirit, that you may obey Jesus Christ and be sprinkled with His blood: May grace and peace be yours in fullest

161

measure. Blessed be the God and Father of our Lord Jesus Christ, who according to His great mercy has caused us to be born again to a living hope through the resurrection of Jesus Christ from the dead, to obtain an inheritance which is imperishable and undefiled and will not fade away, reserved in heaven for you, who are protected by the power of God through faith for a salvation ready to be revealed in the last time.

CHOSEN BY GOD

This, of course, is only the salutation of Peter's letter. He thus takes a theological plunge of profound proportions at the very outset. Many preachers—even some who would affirm the doctrine—avoid any mention of election in their public teaching, because the subject is so often misunderstood and abused. But Peter began his first epistle with a clear affirmation of the doctrine. He gets into the thick of the issue before he is finished with the first sentence.

Remember, Peter was writing to persecuted believers at all levels of maturity, scattered throughout Asia Minor. In the midst of their persecution—when they might be questioning God's sovereignty or His care for them—Peter was eager to remind them that they were the chosen of God. The Greek word translated "chosen" is *eklektos*, from the verb *kaleo*, "to call," and the preposition *ek*, "out." Literally, it means "the called-out ones." The term is often used in the New Testament as a synonym for Christians (e.g., Col. 3:12; 2 Tim. 2:10; Titus 1:1).

The expression "called-out ones" emphasizes that we who are saved are redeemed because of God's choice, not our own. Jesus told His disciples, "You did not choose Me, but I chose you" (John 15:16). In other words, if you are a Christian, it is ultimately because you were chosen by God Himself, not because of anything you did to get yourself into the Kingdom of God. As Spurgeon wrote,

> When I was coming to Christ, I thought I was doing it all myself, and though I sought the Lord earnestly, I had no idea the Lord was seeking me. . . . [Then] the thought struck me, *How did you come to be a Christian?* I sought the Lord. *But how did you come to seek the Lord?* The truth flashed across my mind in a moment—I should not have sought Him unless there had been some previous influence on my mind to *make me* seek Him. . . . I saw that God was at the bottom of it all, and that He was the Author of my faith, and so the whole doctrine of grace

opened up to me. . . . I desire to make this constant confession, "I ascribe my change wholly to God."[10]

In 1 Peter 2:9, Peter restates the theme of God's sovereign election in these terms: "You are a chosen race, a royal priesthood, a holy nation, a people for God's own possession, that you may proclaim the excellencies of Him who has called you out of darkness into His marvelous light." Is God attempting to save the whole world? No, He is calling out a people for His name (cf Acts 15:14). In John 17:9, Jesus is praying for the elect: "I ask on their behalf; I do not ask on behalf of the world, but of those whom Thou hast given Me."

Before the world began, in the timelessness of eternity past, the Father chose a people for His name. Ephesians 1:4, 5 says, "He chose us in Him before the foundation of the world, that we should be holy and blameless before Him. In love He predestined us to adoption as sons through Jesus Christ to Himself, according to the kind intention of His will." We who are saved were in His mind before the beginning of time. Before the world began, we were chosen. We have always been chosen. That is an unfathomable yet intensely thrilling thought.

He "saved us, and called us with a holy calling, not according to our works, but according to His own purpose and grace which was granted us in Christ Jesus *from all eternity*" (2 Tim. 1:9, emphasis added). That's how our names can be "written from the foundation of the world in the book of life of the Lamb who has been slain" (Rev. 13:8). The apostle Paul clearly stated that he preached as "an apostle of Jesus Christ for the faith of those chosen of God" (Titus 1:1). He knew when he preached the gospel that God would save the elect through the truth he preached (cf Acts 18:9-11). His task was to preach saving truth so God's Spirit could use it to activate the faith of the elect.

If you struggle with these truths, you're not alone. They are difficult to receive, impossible to comprehend, even repugnant to our human sensibilities. The fallen human mind tends to think it is unjust for God to choose some but not everyone—as if we had a right to demand His grace. *That's not fair!* is the typical response. But it's not supposed to be fair. We wouldn't want it to be fair. "Fair" would mean everyone is eternally condemned. God graciously saves many who deserve only His wrath. If He

---

[10] *Ibid.,* 1:168-69.

chooses to display His wrath on others, that in no way taints His righteousness (Rom. 9:21-23).

Nevertheless, it is not unusual for people to respond to the sovereignty of God by becoming angry. The fourth chapter of Luke describes an incident when Jesus touched on the doctrine of election, and the crowd became hostile. He was teaching in the synagogue at Nazareth, just after He commenced His public ministry. At first, "All were speaking well of Him, and wondering at the gracious words which were falling from His lips" (4:22). They had heard of His great miracles done in Capernaum and wanted to see some similar miracles in Nazareth. They were astonished— and obviously a bit skeptical—that one from their own community would have the power to display such signs and wonders.

But it was not God's sovereign plan for Him to work miracles in Nazareth. Anticipating what the people wanted, Jesus told them,

> "No doubt you will quote this proverb to Me, 'Physician, heal yourself! Whatever we heard was done at Capernaum, do here in your home town as well.'" And He said, "Truly I say to you, no prophet is welcome in his home town. But I say to you in truth, there were many widows in Israel in the days of Elijah, when the sky was shut up for three years and six months, when a great famine came over all the land; and yet Elijah was sent to none of them, but only to Zarephath, in the land of Sidon, to a woman who was a widow. And there were many lepers in Israel in the time of Elisha the prophet; and none of them was cleansed, but only Naaman the Syrian" (vv. 23-28).

In other words, God is sovereign as to how, when, and where He displays His grace. Jesus would not perform a show of miracles on demand.

What was the crowd's response? These people who had seemed so appreciative moments before "were filled with rage as they heard these things; and they rose up and cast Him out of the city, and led Him to the brow of the hill on which their city had been built, in order to throw Him down the cliff" (Luke 4:28, 29). They didn't want to hear the truth. They hated it. And they vented their hatred against Him. "But passing through their midst, He went His way" (v. 30). The miracle they wanted to see happened without their realizing it: He simply walked through their midst and supernaturally escaped the mob.

Sovereign choice is one of those truths that proves the Bible is the inspired Word of God. It is not a truth human reason would or could invent. The only reason anyone believes it is that it is so clearly revealed in the Word of God. We cannot comprehend it with our limited facilities; we must simply receive it by faith. But receive it we must. Otherwise we are not giving God the glory He is due as the sovereign, all-wise, perfectly righteous Lord who chose us. And otherwise, we will ultimately take credit ourselves for what is really God's work in us.

RESIDING AS ALIENS

Notice another phrase in 1 Peter 1:1 that Peter uses to describe his audience: "those who reside as aliens." Peter was writing to Jewish believers who had been dispersed throughout Asia Minor in a series of terrible persecutions. But he had in mind far more than their alien status in an earthly nation. He was reminding them that as God's chosen ones they were "strangers and exiles on the earth" (Heb. 11:13)—aliens in this world.

As Christians, we belong to the kingdom of heaven, not to this world. We are not to love the world (1 John 2:15). We are not to be friends of the world (James 4:4). We are here as ambassadors of Christ (2 Cor. 5:20). We are alien people who live by a higher standard. We are *in* the world, but not *of* the world (cf John 17:11, 14, 16).

Peter wanted those scattered, persecuted believers to understand that although the world had rejected them, God Himself had chosen them. He knew it would encourage them and strengthen them to know that while they were foreigners and outcasts in this world, they were chosen citizens of the kingdom of God.

FOREKNOWN FROM ETERNITY

Let's examine the phrase "according to the foreknowledge of God the Father" (1 Peter 1:2). That is similar to the language Paul used in Romans 8:29: "Whom He foreknew, He also predestined. . . ." God chose us according to His foreknowledge. As we noted earlier, this does not mean that God sat back in eternity and looked across time to see what we would do, then elected those who He foresaw would choose to believe. That would make people sovereign and God subject to their choice. After all, the very point Peter is making is that God chose us, not that we chose Him.

The word "foreknowledge" is from the Greek word *prognōsis*. Peter uses a different form of the same word later in this chapter. Verse 20 says that Christ Himself "was foreknown before the foundation of the world." Could "foreknown" in that verse possibly refer simply to God's omniscient foresight? Obviously not. God did not look into the future to see what Christ would do. In this context it clearly means God the Father knew Christ Himself intimately and personally before the foundation of the world.

Peter also used the word "foreknowledge" in his Pentecost sermon. In Acts 2:23, speaking of Jesus, he says, "This Man, delivered up by the predetermined plan and foreknowledge of God, you nailed to a cross by the hands of godless men and put Him to death." Peter was not suggesting that God foresaw the crucifixion and decided to make the best of it. No, this was His "predetermined plan." He knew it ahead of time because He decreed it. He planned it. He predetermined it. The crucifixion was the focus of His eternal design for redemption. Here "foreknowledge" clearly carries the idea of deliberate foreordination.

(Notice, by the way, the corresponding truth: "*You* nailed to a cross by the hands of godless men and put Him to death." These people who had cried, "Crucify Him" were not absolved of their horrible responsibility just because their actions were part of God's eternal plan. *You* did it, Peter told them. They were guilty. They were responsible for their actions, even though those actions accorded perfectly with God's eternal plan. Divine sovereignty does not negate human responsibility. The fact that God predetermined and foreknew Christ's death did not absolve those who actually murdered Him, nor did it spare them from damning guilt.)

How, then, are we to understand the term *foreknowledge*? We have seen that it can mean personal, intimate knowledge. And it can signify deliberate choice. Combine those two ideas and you have the sense of it.

This kind of foreknowledge was a familiar concept to Peter's Jewish readers. Similar expressions were employed in the Old Testament to speak of God's eternal love for His elect. For example, God told Jeremiah, "Before I formed you in the womb I knew you, and before you were born I consecrated you" (Jer. 1:5). In Amos 3:2 (KJV), God says to Israel, "You only have I known of all the families of the earth." He told Moses, "You have found favor in My sight, and I have known you by name" (Ex. 33:17). All those passages speak of an intimate relationship. The Hebrew word *yada* ("to know") carried this connotation so strongly that it was often employed as a euphemism for sexual relations: "Adam *knew* Eve his wife; and she conceived" (Gen. 4:1, KJV, emphasis added).

The New Testament also uses the word *know* to describe our Lord's close personal relationship with His elect. Jesus said, "My sheep hear My voice, and I know them" (John 10:27). Those who lack that relationship are damned. To them He will say in the judgment, "I never *knew* you; depart from Me" (Matt. 7:23, emphasis added).

When Scripture says God's election is according to His foreknowledge, it means He knew His chosen ones intimately from before the foundation of the earth. He predetermined in His eternal plan to set His love upon certain people, and those were the ones He chose. In other words, He established His loving relationship with them even before time began, and it is in that sense that He eternally foreknew them. The writer of Hebrews thus calls the plan "the eternal covenant" (13:20). Paul told Titus that this entire saving plan was promised by God "long ages ago"—a phrase meaning before time (1:2).

APPOINTED TO SANCTIFICATION

Election is not the same thing as salvation. Believers are *chosen* from eternity past. But at a specific point in time they pass from death unto life. All who are elect will certainly be saved, but God does not save them apart from the means He has chosen: the Word of God, conviction of sin, repentance, faith, and sanctification. God's chosen ones must believe to be saved. That is how the divine and eternal decree becomes a fact of history.

Peter stresses this truth by the phrase "elect . . . through sanctification of the Spirit" (1 Peter 1:2, KJV). Here he uses the term *sanctification* not in the technical, doctrinal sense, but as a broad term to include every experiential aspect of salvation—repentance, faith, regeneration, obedience, sanctification, and all that the Holy Spirit produces in the elect.

Note that it is the "sanctification of the *Spirit*." This is the Spirit's work, to set us apart from sin, consecrate us, make us holy. He is conforming us to the image of Christ. In 2 Thessalonians 2:13, the apostle Paul uses similar language: "God has chosen you from the beginning for salvation through sanctification by the Spirit and faith in the truth." In other words, all three members of the Trinity are involved in the process. God planned our salvation. Christ purchased our salvation. The Holy Spirit effects our salvation.

Sanctification does not mean perfection. It means separation. It speaks of being set apart from sin and set apart unto God. Every Christian is sanctified. That's why Paul could write even to the troubled Corinthian church and say, "You were washed . . . you were sanctified . . . you were justified in the name of the Lord Jesus Christ, and in the Spirit of our God" (1 Cor. 6:11). Separation from sin is now the *direction* of our lives, and someday it will be the *perfection* of our lives.

Sanctification is both an event and a lifelong process. We have been and yet are constantly *being* separated from sin and conformed to Christ's likeness. We will not reach ultimate sanctification or perfection until death or the Second Coming brings us face to face with Him: "When He appears, we shall be like Him, because we shall see Him just as He is" (1 John 3:2). And no one falls out of that process (cf John 6:39, 40 and Rom. 8:30-39).

As Peter's language suggests, sanctification is so closely related to election that the two are inseparable. Thus he affirms that no one who is truly chosen of God can skirt the sanctification process. We are "predestined to become conformed to the image of His Son" (Rom. 8:29). It would be a contradiction to say that God chose a person to be in Christ but did not begin to make that person holy. Yet thousands today believe they are Christians but have never seen any change in their lives. Such people had better "be all the more diligent to make certain about His calling and choosing [them]" (2 Pet. 1:10).

God's sovereign election encompasses every aspect of our salvation from beginning to end. He is the author and the perfecter of our faith (Heb. 12:2). Saving us is all *His* work, including foreknowledge and election, regeneration (James 1:18), repentance (Acts 11:18), faith (John 6:44; Rom. 12:3), justification (Rom. 3:24), sanctification (Heb. 2:11)— everything from our predestination to our final glorification (Rom. 8:30). Those who are elect are chosen by God not for heaven only, but for every phase of His saving work. We dare not view sanctification as something optional. "Without [holiness] no man shall see the Lord" (Heb. 12:14, KJV).

ORDAINED TO OBEDIENCE

Peter carries this thought a step further. You are chosen, he says, "[in order] that you may obey Jesus Christ." Again we return to Ephesians 2:10, which says, "We are His workmanship, created in Christ Jesus for good works, which God prepared beforehand, that we should walk in them." So even our good works were foreordained by a sovereign God.

Jesus said, "You did not choose Me, but I chose you, and appointed you, *that you should go and bear fruit*" (John 15:16, emphasis added).

Good works are certainly not the *cause* of our election. They are not *grounds* for justification. They are not in any sense the *basis* for our salvation. But they are the inevitable *evidence* of it. If we are truly "His workmanship," if He chose us and sovereignly prepared good works that we should walk in them—then there is no way God's elect can live an earthly life devoid of obedience to Jesus Christ. To suppose such a possibility is to attack the sovereignty and omnipotence of the One who chose us so that we might obey Jesus Christ.

SPRINKLED WITH HIS BLOOD

Peter continues, "[You are chosen] that you may obey Jesus Christ *and be sprinkled with His blood*" (v. 2, emphasis added). What does this refer to?

In the Old Testament, blood from the sacrifices was often sprinkled on inanimate objects. At the Passover, it was sprinkled on the doorposts and lintel. In connection with some of the sin offerings it was sprinkled on the altar and around the Tabernacle. Hebrews 9:22 says, "According to the Law . . . all things are cleansed with blood."

But rarely in the Old Testament were *people* sprinkled with blood. In fact, blood was applied directly to people in only two cases of the Levitical law. One was in the symbolic cleansing of a leper (Lev. 14:7, 14). The other was when the Levites were consecrated to the priesthood (Ex. 29:20, 21; Lev. 8:24, 30).

First Peter 2 is not talking about cleansing lepers or consecrating priests, however. So we turn to the only other incident in Scripture where people were sprinkled with blood. This was a one-time occurrence, in which Moses sprinkled the Israelites (Ex. 24:8).

The blood Moses sprinkled on the Israelites was called "the blood of the covenant." After Moses had proclaimed to the people God's Word, they responded several times with a promise to obey it. That was the covenant. Blood sprinkled symbolized their obedience. It was the outward sign of their promise to obey. Moses built an altar and made a sacrifice of two oxen. Half of the blood of those sacrifices he sprinkled on the altar, symbolizing God's promise to save and bless. The rest he sprinkled on the people, saying, "Behold, the blood of the covenant which the Lord has made with you in accordance with all these words" (Ex. 24:8), symbolizing the people's promise to obey. The blood was required to seal

169

the covenant: "Therefore even the first covenant was not inaugurated without blood. For when every commandment had been spoken by Moses to all the people according to the Law, he took the blood of the calves and the goats, with water and scarlet wool and hyssop, and sprinkled both the book itself and all the people" (Heb. 9:18, 19).

It is this symbolic sprinkling of the blood of Jesus Christ upon believers that Peter has in mind in 1 Peter 1:1, 2. "Chosen . . . that you may obey Jesus Christ and be sprinkled with His blood" means that the elect upon their salvation pledged obedience to the Lord who had already provided salvation and blessing for them. Peter is saying God brought us into this covenant when He chose us—before the foundation of the world.

Do you see how comprehensively God's sovereignty covers our salvation? *He* chose us before time began. *He* loved us with an everlasting love (Jer. 31:3). *He* saved us. *He* appointed us to sanctification. *He* ordained us to obedience. *He* established His covenant with us. We are truly *His* workmanship (Eph. 2:10).

APPLYING THE DOCTRINE OF DIVINE SOVEREIGNTY

The doctrine of God's sovereignty is often abused, misunderstood, and misapplied. Many Christians decide it is too deep, too confusing, too hard to understand, or too offensive. But we should not run from it; we should run *to* it. We should not be afraid of it; we should rejoice in it. This doctrine crushes human pride, exalts God, and strengthens the believer's faith. What could be more encouraging than to know that God is sovereignly in control of all His creation? The universe is not subject to chance. There is no possibility that God's plans will fail. "We *know* that God causes all things to work together for good . . . to those who are called according to His purpose" (Rom. 8:28). That's the best-known and best-loved promise in all of Scripture, and it hinges on the doctrine of God's sovereignty.

Moreover, the doctrine of God's sovereignty should be a motivation for evangelism. We know when we witness or preach that God has His chosen ones who *will* respond positively, and that should encourage us to be faithful. Election is not an excuse for inactivity. Those who think they can remain idle and leave it to God to save the elect through some mystical means do not understand the Scriptures. The elect are not saved apart from evangelism. "How . . . shall they call upon Him in whom they have not believed? And how shall they believe in Him whom they have not heard? And how shall they hear without a preacher?" (Rom. 10:14).

That's why we are to proclaim the gospel to every person (Mark 16:15; Luke 24:47). And we can do it with the confidence that "*whoever* believes in Him should not perish, but have eternal life" (John 3:16).

Central to the theme of this book, our confidence in God's sovereignty will lead us in determining *how* we should preach. Our methods of ministry will be revolutionized if we are willing to examine them in light of God's sovereignty. In J. I. Packer's wonderful book *Evangelism and the Sovereignty of God,* he discusses these very issues with much insight and wisdom. Packer includes a valuable section entitled "By What Means and Methods Should Evangelism Be Practised?" In it he writes,

> There is only one *method* of evangelism: namely, the faithful explanation and application of the gospel message. From which it follows— and this is the key principle which we are seeking—that the test for any proposed strategy, or technique, or style, of evangelistic action must be this: will it in fact serve the word? Is it calculated to be a means of explaining the gospel truly and fully and applying it deeply and exactly? To the extent to which it is so calculated, it is lawful and right; to the extent to which it tends to overlay and obscure the realities of the message, and to blunt the edge of their application, it is ungodly and wrong.[11]

Packer suggests a number of questions we should ask about every new form of ministry: "Is this way of presenting Christ calculated to impress on people that the gospel is a *word from God?*" "Does this way of presenting Christ savour of human cleverness and showmanship? Does it tend thereby to exalt man?" "Is this way of presenting Christ calculated to promote, or impede, the work of the word in men's *minds*? Is it going to clarify the meaning of the message, or to leave it enigmatic and obscure?" "Is this way of presenting Christ calculated to convey to people the *doctrine* of the gospel, and not just part of it?" "Is this way of presenting Christ calculated to convey to people the *application* of the gospel? . . . Will it, for instance, leave people unaware that they have any immediate obligation to respond to Christ at all?" "Is this way of presenting Christ calculated to convey gospel truth in a manner that is

---

[11]Packer, *Evangelism and the Sovereignty of God*, 86.

appropriately *serious?* Is it calculated to make people feel that they are indeed facing a matter of life and death?. . . Will it help them to realize that it is a fearful thing to fall into His hands? Or is this way of presenting Christ so light and casual and cosy and jolly as to make it hard for the hearers to feel that the gospel is a matter of any consequence . . . ?"[12]

Faith in God's absolute sovereignty would deliver the church from the down-grade of pragmatism and worldliness. It would drive us back to biblical preaching. If preachers only had confidence in God's power and God's Word, they would not feel it necessary to trim and adjust and tone down the message. They would not feel they could use artificial means and thereby induce more people to be saved. They would not view evangelism as a marketing problem, but they would see it for what it is—the proclamation of divine revelation as the only means by which God calls the elect to Himself. They would rely more on the gospel, "the power of God unto salvation." And they would abandon the worldly gimmicks that are propelling the church faster and further along the downhill slope.

Listen to the God-breathed Word:

> *You have been born again* not of seed which is perishable but imperishable, that is, *through the living and abiding word of God.* For, "All flesh is like grass, and all its glory like the flower of grass. The grass withers, and the flower falls off, but the word of the Lord abides forever. *And this is the word which was preached to you*" (1 Peter 1:23-25, emphasis added).

---

[12] *Ibid.*, 87-90.

9

I Will Build My Church

Let no man dream that a sudden crotchet has entered our head, and that we have written in hot haste: we have waited long, perhaps too long, and have been slow to speak. Neither let any one suppose that we build up our statements upon a few isolated facts. . . . We have had no motive but the general progress of the cause of truth, and the glory of God.

CHARLES HADDON SPURGEON[1]

SEVERAL YEARS ago a journalist writing a feature on large churches came to interview me about Grace Community Church. At one point near the end of our conversation he asked, "Have you always been driven by a desire to build a large church?"

It was an unexpected question, but I answered immediately, "I have no desire to build the church. None."

He looked at me quizzically and said, "I don't understand that."

I said, "Jesus Christ said *He* would build His church, and I don't want to be in competition with Him."

I wasn't being funny. That is precisely my perspective on the church. Frequently at pastor's conferences and leadership seminars I am asked the secret to growing a large church. I have to confess that if one desires to be faithful to Christ and His Word, there is no technique or system that will guarantee a large church. Growth in the spiritual realm is like growth in the physical realm. It can be nourished and encouraged. We can do things to insure *healthy* growth. But we cannot *engineer* true growth. Nothing can make a miniature shrub grow as large as a giant redwood. If some genetic technology could be found to make

---

[1]"Our Reply to Sundry Critics and Enquirers," *The Sword and the Trowel* (September 1887), 463.

it happen, the result would be a monstrosity. The same is true in the spiritual realm. "Unless the Lord builds the house, they labor in vain who build it" (Ps. 127:1).

I must ascribe our church's numerical and spiritual growth to the will of our sovereign God. There are no marketing techniques or modern methods that can explain it. Nor would we rely on such tactics. We don't want growth that is manufactured by human formulas, programs, and gimmicks. We are content to focus on aggressive biblical ministry and leave it to the Lord to add to His church (Acts 2:47). Our task is to be faithful in what He has designed for us to do.

Again we return to the principle of the omnipotent and sovereign God. We must not forget that building the church is *His* work. Ours is to "go into all the world and preach the gospel to all creation" (Mark 16:15). Once we begin to think of ourselves as the architects and builders of the church, we usurp God's rightful role, and we redefine our objectives in terms of success, numbers, size, and other artificial standards. A church built merely on that philosophy may seem to flourish for a while, but it is doomed to ultimate spiritual failure.

The key biblical text for this truth is in Matthew 16:18-20. Jesus said to Peter: "You are Peter, and upon this rock I will build My church; and the gates of Hades shall not overpower it. I will give you the keys of the kingdom of heaven; and whatever you shall bind on earth shall be bound in heaven, and whatever you shall loose on earth shall be loosed in heaven."

That passage has been a source of controversy between the Roman Catholic Church and Protestant churches for centuries. It does pose some problems for the interpreter. But at its very heart, it contains simple, profound, rich, glorious truth about the church Christ is building. And it makes a fitting climax to our study.

THE FOUNDATION OF IT—"UPON THIS ROCK"

Let's establish the context of the passage. Jesus spoke these words immediately after Peter's great confession, "Thou art the Christ, the Son of the living God" (Matt. 16:16). The Lord responded by saying, "Blessed are you, Simon Barjona, because flesh and blood did not reveal this to you, but My Father who is in heaven" (v. 17), thus underscoring God's sovereignty in bringing Peter to the truth and faith.

Jesus' next words raise the issue that has stirred so much controversy between Catholics and Protestants: "You are Peter, and upon this rock I will build My church." On the basis of that statement, the Roman Catholic Church teaches that the church is built on Peter, thus making Peter the first Pope, establishing papal succession, and making the papacy the very heart and soul of divine authority on earth.

Most Protestants, on the other hand, take the phrase "upon this rock" as a play on words. The name *Peter* (lit., "small stone") *contrasts* with "this rock" (lit., "large stone"). The "rock," they believe, refers to Peter's confession, and not to Peter himself. They would paraphrase the meaning like this: "You are a little stone, but I will build my church on the solid rock of the truth you have confessed." They also point out that Scripture clearly teaches that Christ is the head of the church (Eph. 5:23; Col. 1:18), and nothing in the Bible speaks of an earthly surrogate who heads the church in Christ's place.

That view is a viable interpretation of this text and is more consistent with biblical truth than the Catholic interpretation. Jesus was certainly not making Peter a pope (or establishing a line of papal succession) in this passage. After all, within a few verses, we read that the Lord rebuked Peter and called him "Satan" (v. 23).

A more natural interpretation of this phrase, however, is that Jesus was addressing Peter as the leader and representative of the Twelve. Scripture *does* say that the church is "built upon the foundation of the apostles and prophets, Christ Jesus Himself being the corner stone" (Eph. 2:20)—so there is a biblical sense in which Peter and all the apostles constituted the foundation on which the church is built. The church Christ is building is raised up on the sure foundation of apostolic doctrine and ministry. Luke records that the earliest church "[devoted] themselves to the apostles' teaching" (Acts 2:42), and building on that foundation, "the Lord was adding to their number day by day those who were being saved" (v. 47). Throughout the rest of the book of Acts, apostolic teaching and ministry continues to be the foundation on which every local congregation is built (e.g., 4:31, 32; 8:12, 35-40; 10:34-48; 12:24, 25; 13:44-49).

The church is a building of "living stones . . . built up as a spiritual house for a holy priesthood, to offer up spiritual sacrifices acceptable to God through Jesus Christ" (1 Peter 2:5). In other words, every Christian is a stone in the structure. Peter and the apostles were the foundation stones. Christ Himself, not Peter, is the chief cornerstone.

THE CERTAINTY OF IT—"I *WILL* BUILD MY CHURCH"

Jesus' statement "I will build my church" is the key to this passage. Everything else in these verses amplifies those words, which are most germane to our theme.

It was, first and foremost, a promise meant to encourage the disciples. They were walking along the dusty roads of Caesarea Philippi, far north of Jerusalem, at the top of Israel near the mountains of Lebanon. They were essentially in exile. Jesus had been rejected by Israel, both in Judea (the southern region) and in Galilee (the northern region). The Jewish religious and political leaders had targeted Jesus and were determined to have Him dead. The people were looking for a political, military, and economic Messiah to deliver them from Roman rule, but Jesus had already disappointed those hopes. The multitudes that once followed Him had turned away as soon as His teaching challenged them (John 6:66). And the messianic experts—the scribes and Pharisees—were the most venomous and hateful of all those who were against Him.

Who could blame the disciples if they were discouraged? The whole concept of the Kingdom as the disciples had understood it seemed far out of reach. Their glorious messianic expectation—with Jesus on an earthly throne, His dominion centered in Israel, and His Kingdom sweeping across the globe—did not appear to be happening. On the contrary, they were a little band of nobodies, ill-equipped, rejected, and seemingly going nowhere. They had retreated into an obscure place in a largely Gentile community to find rest, privacy, and safety. The disciples must have been wondering whether the program was still on schedule. Certainly it looked as if everything was turning out opposite to their plans.

As if all that weren't bad enough, "Jesus Christ began to show His disciples that He must go to Jerusalem, and suffer many things from the elders and chief priests and scribes, and be killed" (v. 21). Peter was so outraged at that suggestion that he "took [Jesus] aside and began to rebuke Him, saying, 'God forbid it, Lord! This shall never happen to You'" (v. 22).

Their confidence was shattered. Their hope was waning. Ominous signs were threatening them. And they must have been very confused and very concerned. It was in the context of all this that Jesus reassured them, "I *will* build my church." He wanted them to know that this was

176

no variation from the original plan. Nothing was lost. The program had not changed.

We can derive comfort in our own time from those words. No matter how beleaguered, persecuted, martyred, rejected, maligned, poor, or ignoble the true church may seem, the Lord will not abandon His chosen ones. When the people of God seem weakest, look again. Jesus is *still* building His church. The original plan is still in operation. Modern times are no threat to His sovereign purposes. The circumstances of our troubled world do not alter His design. And no matter how corrupt and worldly the visible church has been or may become, Jesus Christ is still building *His* church on the original, sure foundation of apostolic teaching and ministry.

When Jesus said "*I* will build My church," He gave the strongest possible guarantee of the church's ultimate success. If it were left only to the people of God, the building would have crumbled long ago. Church history is filled with proof of human failure, worldly corruption, unfaithfulness, doctrinal deviation, compromise, and weakness. Yet the Lord still builds the church. No matter what the church appears to be on the outside, there is at the core of it a body that Christ Himself is building—made of God's elect—and it grows strong and faithful. Even in the bleakest times, there is always "a remnant according to God's gracious choice" (Rom. 11:5).

Paul, at the end of his life and ministry, wrote, "All who are in Asia turned away from me" (2 Tim. 1:15), and, "At my first defense no one supported me, but all deserted me" (4:16). The apostle John, near the end of his life, was in exile on the Isle of Patmos, when the Lord gave him the task of recording the letters to the seven churches of Asia Minor (Rev. 2-3). Five of the seven had severe problems that threatened their very existence.

Yet Christ continues building *His* church, and He personally protects the purity of the believing remnant. Ephesians 5:25-27 says, "Christ . . . loved the church and gave Himself up for her; that He might sanctify her, having cleansed her by the washing of water with the word, that He might present to Himself the church in all her glory, having no spot or wrinkle or any such thing; but that she should be holy and blameless." The church Christ is building will ultimately be holy and blameless. And He will present to Himself a glorious church. In other words, the church is designed as a vehicle through which Christ can eternally manifest His own glory.

That's why we must oppose human wisdom. But that is also why worldliness, carnality, ineptitude, indifference, and apostasy cannot stop the church Christ is building. They may stop a congregation, but the church will go on. Christ will *certainly* build His church. If He is for us, who can be against us?

THE INTIMACY OF IT—"I WILL BUILD *MY* CHURCH"

Jesus' words also speak of a sacred intimacy. Building the church is no impersonal enterprise with Him. The church is His own precious possession. Acts 20:28 speaks of "the church of God which He purchased with His own blood."

Scripture even speaks of the church as His body (Col. 1:24). We are linked inseparably with Him in holy union. Remember when Saul of Tarsus was persecuting the church? Christ arrested him on the Damascus Road and asked, "Saul, Saul, why are you persecuting *Me?*" (Acts 9:4, emphasis added). Those who attack the church attack Christ Himself. "The one who joins himself to the Lord is one spirit with Him" (1 Cor. 6:17).

There is an Old Testament parallel to this truth. Zechariah told the nation of Israel, "He who touches you, touches the apple of [God's] eye" (Zech. 2:8). "The apple of His eye" refers to the pupil. God was saying those who persecute Israel are poking their finger in His eye. That is precisely the same kind of relationship Christ has with the church. He is seriously irritated when anyone offends His chosen ones (cf Matt. 18:6, 10).

THE INVINCIBILITY OF IT—"THE GATES OF HADES SHALL NOT OVERPOWER IT"

The church Christ builds is invincible. "The gates of Hades shall not overpower it" (v. 18). The imagery of this passage is often misunderstood. Jesus was not suggesting that the church would be impervious to attacks from Hades. The word "gates" does not suggest an offensive push. Gates are not weapons; they are barricades. Jesus was picturing Hades like a prison, suggesting that its gates would not be able to contain or imprison the church.

"Hades" is the abode of the dead. It is the Greek equivalent of the Hebrew word *Sheol* (cf Ps. 6:5). The King James Version translates this phrase: "the gates of hell shall not prevail against it," but that is misleading. Jesus was not talking about the torment of eternal hell; He was saying that the grave cannot hold the elect. The gates of death could not hold Jesus Christ, and they cannot hold Christians captive. "O death, where is your victory? O death, where is your sting?" (1 Cor. 15:55).

Actually, "the gates of Hades shall not prevail against it" is a promise of resurrection. The language of death and resurrection were becoming common themes in Jesus' teaching. He knew His disciples were facing treacherous days, and that all of them (except John) would ultimately give their earthly lives as martyrs for Him. He was about to tell them, "Whoever wishes to save his life shall lose it; but whoever loses his life for My sake shall find it" (Matt. 16:25). But first He told them that the grave could never hold the elect.

This theme runs throughout the entire New Testament. Since Christ conquered death, Christians have nothing to fear from it. "Christ, having been raised from the dead, is never to die again; death no longer is master over Him" (Rom. 6:9)—nor can it be master over those who are united to Him by faith. Jesus promised, "Because I live, you shall live also" (John 14:19). In John's apocalyptic vision, Jesus told him, "Do not be afraid; I am the first and the last, and the living One; and I was dead, and behold, I am alive forevermore, and I have the keys of death and of Hades" (Rev. 1:17, 18). Jesus Christ destroyed "him who had the power of death, that is, the devil [so He would] deliver those who through fear of death were subject to slavery all their lives" (Heb. 2:14, 15). He took away the keys to death and Hades, and now the grave cannot contain His elect.

These disciples would one day be in the heat of battle, and the Holy Spirit would call to their minds this promise. It must have brought them great comfort and new vigor. They were ultimately invincible. They would be persecuted—they would even die for their faith—but ultimately they were guaranteed to emerge victors. The gates of Hades could not prevail against them.

THE AUTHORITY OF IT—"I WILL GIVE YOU THE KEYS OF THE KINGDOM OF HEAVEN"

Then Jesus told Peter, "I will give you the keys of the kingdom of heaven; and whatever you shall bind on earth shall be bound in heaven, and whatever you shall loose on earth shall be loosed in heaven" (Matt. 16:19).

The interpretation of that statement has also been a matter of disagreement between Protestants and Catholics over the years. Catholic theology teaches that Christ was instituting the rite of absolution in this promise.

Admittedly, Jesus *does* seem to be granting a tremendous amount of heavenly authority to Peter in this statement. But before we concede that this made Peter the Pope, note that after His resurrection, in John 20:23, Jesus gave similar authority to *all* the apostles. He told them all, "If you forgive the sins of any, their sins have been forgiven them; if you retain the sins of any, they have been retained." Again, it seems that in Matthew chapter 16 our Lord was speaking to Peter as a representative of all the apostles.

But notice that Jesus made a similar statement about "binding and loosing" in the context of his instructions for church discipline in Matthew 18:15-20, a passage we looked at briefly in Chapter 2. You will recall that Jesus told the disciples that if a sinning believer refuses to repent after a private confrontation, a second warning with one or two witnesses, and then public rebuke by the entire congregation, the person is to be treated "as a Gentile and a tax-gatherer" (v. 17). Then Jesus told them, "Whatever you shall bind on earth shall be bound in heaven; and whatever you loose on earth shall be loosed in heaven" (v. 18).

Several truths must be noted from that passage. First, it applies not just to Peter. It is not even limited to the disciples. These are instructions to all believers.

Second, "binding and loosing" has nothing to do with how we handle evil spirits. Verse 19 ("if two of you agree . . . it shall be done for them") is not an instruction about how to gain answers to prayer. Jesus was giving directions on how to deal with sin in the assembly of the redeemed. What is "bound" is the sin of the unrepentant person; what is "loosed" is that person's guilt when he or she repents. Any believer can affirm those conditions on the basis of how someone responds to the call to repentance. The issue on which "two of you agree" is how to handle the sinning member of the flock. Jesus was saying that the authority to deal with sin is granted to *any* assembly as small as "two or three . . . gathered together in My name" (v. 20).

The third truth is that the source of that authority is Christ, not an earthly vicar: "There I am in their midst" (v. 20). He personally mediates His rule through the fellowship of believers acting in accord with His principles.

And fourth, none of this implies authority isolated from the Word of God. Jesus was not authorizing a ruler who could pass down *ex cathedra* edicts. He was not giving anyone authority for literally binding and loosing others. Certainly he was not making Peter head of the church. The authority He spoke of belongs to every believer. And that authority lies in the fact that we have heaven's word on "everything pertaining to life and godliness, through the true knowledge of Him who called us by His own glory and excellence" (2 Peter 1:3). Jesus was commissioning Peter and the other disciples to make the Kingdom message—the Word of God—authoritative in the lives of people. Thus He gave them the keys to the Kingdom.

The keys of the Kingdom are a sacred trust from Christ to His church. Those keys symbolize custody of the very entrance to the Kingdom. He has placed the church in the world and commanded us to preach the gospel so that we can stand as a beacon to point the way to that Kingdom. If we compromise His Word or camouflage the gospel, we cease to be that beacon, and we forfeit the only authority we have to use the keys of the Kingdom.

When the church is faithful to God and His Word, however, we actually enact heaven's decisions here on earth. We can speak with authority to an unbelieving world. When heaven is in agreement with us, the issue is settled in accord with the highest possible authority. But if we compromise God's Word, we forfeit the very source of our authority. That is why it is so crucial for the church to deal seriously with God, to handle His Word with integrity, and to stand apart from the world. And that is what we mean when we pray, "Thy will be done, on earth as it is in heaven" (Matt. 6:10).

MARKS OF AN EFFECTIVE CHURCH

It should be clear that the church is a supernatural work. Christ Himself—not marketing know-how, human cleverness, or church-growth techniques—adds to the church, causes its genuine growth, and blesses the church with health and vitality.

Numerical growth alone does not insure a healthy church. To be sure, growth is one of the signs of life, but as we have seen, size is no proof of God's blessing or of a church's spiritual health.

What are the signs of a healthy church? What are worthy goals for a church to pursue as we seek to let the Lord build His church His way? In closing, let me simply suggest a few marks of a healthy church. I have expanded on this list elsewhere,[2] but perhaps this brief summary will be helpful for those seeking something besides marketing principles that

---

[2]See *The Master's Plan for the Church* (Chicago: Moody, 1991).

can help a struggling church get on target. These, I believe, are the basic biblical principles that provide a blueprint for the church Christ builds:

GODLY LEADERSHIP

Jesus' own earthly ministry was invested primarily in eleven men who would become the core of leadership for the early church. Leadership is primary, and the principal requirement for church leaders is that they must be skilled teachers of the Word of God who are above reproach.

I would venture to say that the chief deficiency in most churches today is in this area of leadership. Too many churches ignore the spiritual requirements for leaders, and choose instead those who seem like strong natural leaders or motivators, are successful in business, have money, or wield influence. But church leaders are above all to be godly teachers, "holding fast the faithful word which is in accordance with the teaching . . . able both to exhort in sound doctrine and to refute those who contradict" (Titus 1:9).

First Timothy 3:1-7 and Titus 1:5-9 contain Paul's profile of the kind of people who should be leading the church. Putting those two passages together, we come up with a comprehensive list of spiritual qualities pastors and elders must possess. They are to be above reproach, devoted to their wife, temperate, prudent, gentle, respectable, just, devout, hospitable, lovers of good, able to teach, not self-centered or self-willed, not quick-tempered or pugnacious, not contentious, free from the love of money, good managers of their own household, men with a good reputation among unbelievers—and mature believers, not recent converts. From that platform of godly example, they teach the Scripture and lead their people to Christlikeness.

Do those seem like extremely high standards? Yet those are the qualifications Scripture establishes. Churches that ignore those guidelines set themselves against God's design and forfeit His blessing. To compromise on the issue of leadership is, as Charles Spurgeon would say, "the most suicidal act that a church can commit."[3]

Surely one of the tragic disasters of American evangelicalism in our generation is the ease with which a man can be restored to leadership after spiritually and morally disqualifying himself. It is not at all uncommon for Christian leaders to scandalize the church through gross moral failure, then step back into leadership almost before the publicity dies

---

[3]"This Must Be a Soldier's Battle," *The Sword and the Trowel* (December 1889), 634.

away. This is a fatal compromise of the biblical standard. It is one of the most pernicious results of modern pragmatism.

Am I saying there should be no restoration for a leader who fails morally and genuinely repents? Certainly there should be restoration to fellowship, but not to the role of an elder or pastor. Churches cannot abandon biblical standards to accommodate their leaders' sin. The biblical requirements for leaders are *purposely* set high, because leadership must be by example. Those who scandalize the church are not above reproach. They are disqualified from leadership as long as their reproach remains. In cases involving sexual scandal or unfaithfulness, that may mean a permanent disqualification (Prov. 6:32, 33). The apostle Paul recognized that possibility. He wrote, "I buffet my body and make it my slave, lest possibly, after I have preached to others, I myself should be disqualified" (1 Cor. 9:27).

If a church's leaders fail in the matter of personal holiness, the church itself is discredited—no matter how orthodox its confession of faith. Those who ignore the biblical prerequisites for church leaders are building a structure with useless materials not in accord with the true foundation (cf 1 Cor. 3:10, 11). No matter how strongly we call for truth and righteousness, if our leaders' lives don't back it up, many will reject their teaching as hypocritical, or simply conclude that genuine godliness is optional.

BIBLICAL GOALS

There is certainly nothing wrong with a church that sets goals. In fact, a church must have some functional goals or it will have no direction.

But our goals for the church must be *biblical*. Wrong goals set a wrong direction, and that is as bad as having *no* direction—maybe even worse. What are biblical goals? They include worship, fellowship, spiritual growth, and evangelism. Those would be primary goals. More specific goals—such as strengthening families, offering biblical counseling, providing childhood education, and similar purposes—must be seen in light of how they help accomplish the primary goals. And they must be kept subordinate to the primary goals. For example, a church might have a notable music ministry or operate a Christian elementary school. If it does so just to boost attendance figures or to make money, those are not worthy goals. But if it sees the ministry as a means to strengthen the church family spiritually or extend the reach of the gospel, that is a legitimate goal. If we can evaluate every church ministry in light of how it promotes the primary goals, that perspective will help keep the church on track.

DISCIPLESHIP

The church is not an arena where a professional minister is cheered on by lay people who are nothing more than spectators. The church should be discipling and training Christians for ministry. Church members, not just staff, are supposed to be ministering. That is the point of Ephesians 4:11, 12. Apostles, prophets, evangelists, and pastor-teachers are given to equip *the saints* to do the work of ministry.

All of this results from discipleship. Discipleship is the ministry of developing deeply spiritual friendships focused on teaching biblical truth, applying Scripture to life, and thus learning to solve problems biblically. It must be reinforced by a godly example, not just delivered as a set of academic precepts. Therefore, discipleship involves time and personal involvement with people. Jesus' earthly ministry to His own disciples is the biblical model. The church must provide an environment that encourages that kind of discipleship at every level, from the pastor to the newest convert.

OUTREACH

The church built by Christ will have a strong emphasis on evangelism, beginning with its own community and extending to the uttermost parts of the earth. The early church turned the world upside down (Acts 17:6). The Jewish leaders told them, "You have filled Jerusalem with your teaching" (Acts 5:28). In a short time their message penetrated the entire community.

Too many Christians think they have fulfilled their responsibility to be witnesses if they drive to church in a car that has a fish sticker on the bumper! Effective churches emphasize the importance of regular, personal outreach on every level.

Our church has been labeled in some circles as non-evangelistic. Yet we have a baptism service for new converts nearly every Sunday night. As they are baptized, people give their testimonies before the entire congregation. Do you know what brings most of these people to a saving knowledge of Christ? Their personal contact with faithful Christians. People in our church witness to their neighbors, co-workers, other parents in Little League, friends at school, people in the markets, their doctors, their attorneys, and everyone they meet. And over the years the

Lord has blessed that one-to-one evangelistic activity to bring more people to faith in Christ than any service, program, or event we have ever sponsored.

If a church lacks this emphasis on outreach, it is doomed to stagnation, decline, and ultimately to failure. The means Christ uses to build His church is the faithful witness of Christians on His behalf.

CONCERN FOR ONE ANOTHER

In the church Christ is building, people are involved in one another's lives. The church is not a theater where people go to watch what happens. People are not supposed to come in, sit down, walk out, and have no other involvement with the fellowship. We are not supposed to encourage anonymity and uninvolvement. Instead, we're commanded to "consider how to stimulate one another to love and good deeds, not forsaking our own assembling together, as is the habit of some, but encouraging one another" (Heb. 10:24, 25).

"One another" is a repeated expression in the New Testament instructions to the church. Here is a sampling of some of these commandments:

- "Be devoted to one another in brotherly love; give preference to one another in honor" (Rom. 12:10).
- "Be of the same [lowly] mind toward one another" (Rom. 12:16).
- Do not judge one another, but determine not to put an obstacle or a stumbling block in a brother's way (Rom. 14:13).
- "Be of the same mind with one another according to Christ Jesus" (Rom. 15:5).
- "Accept one another, just as Christ also accepted us to the glory of God" (Rom. 15:7).
- "Admonish one another" (Rom. 15:14).
- "Through love serve one another" (Gal. 5:13).
- "[Show] forbearance to one another in love" (Eph. 4:2).
- "Be kind to one another, tender-hearted, forgiving each other, just as God in Christ also has forgiven you" (Eph. 4:32).
- "Be subject to one another in the fear of Christ" (Eph. 5:21).
- "Regard one another as more important than himself" (Phil. 2:3).
- "Do not lie to one another" (Col. 3:9).

- Bear with one another and forgive each other (Col. 3:13).

- "Encourage one another, and build up one another" (1 Thess. 5:11).

- "Confess your sins to one another, and pray for one another" (James 5:16).

- "Fervently love one another from the heart" (1 Peter 1:22).

- "Be hospitable to one another without complaint" (1 Peter 4:9).

- "Employ your spiritual gifts in serving one another" (1 Peter 4:10).

- "Clothe yourselves with humility toward one another" (1 Peter 5:5).

That list alone is infinitely more valuable than all the volumes on marketing techniques and user-friendliness that have ever been written. Those are the qualities of the church Christ is building. Like the builder Himself, the church that puts those "one anothers" in practice will be a caring, sensitive, and loving church. Add to that the proper exercise of spiritual gifts (Rom. 12:3-8; 1 Cor. 12:4-11; and 1 Peter 4:10, 11), and what will be produced will be a community conformed to the very image of Christ. But it will not be conformed to the world.

A COMMITMENT TO THE FAMILY

Modern society has unleashed an unprecedented onslaught against the family. Most of the major controversial issues in the news today—such as homosexuality, abortion, feminism, divorce, youth gangs, and so on—are direct attacks against the family. People's families no longer are where their strongest loyalties lie. Few families function as units. This fragmentation of the family has undermined morality and stability throughout all of society.

The church cannot tolerate or accommodate this devastation. It must confront and correct, then train its families. Strong families are the church's backbone. And strong families build strong individuals. We will pay a high price if we don't make the family a priority. That means we must help our people develop solid marriages and sturdy families by teaching husbands to love and lead their wives (Eph. 5:25), wives to submit to their husbands (5:22), children to obey their parents (6:1), and parents not to exasperate their children but to nurture them in the Lord (6:4).

BIBLICAL TEACHING AND PREACHING

No church can remain healthy for long if the pulpit is not strong. And no pulpit is truly strong if the Bible is not the basis of the preaching. That, of course, has been the whole message of this book. But it is certainly worth emphasizing again. As D. Martyn Lloyd-Jones wrote:

> The moment you begin to turn from preaching to these other expedients you will find yourself undergoing a constant series of changes. One of the advantages of being old is that you have experience, so when something new comes up, and you see people getting very excited about it, you happen to be in the position of being able to remember a similar excitement perhaps forty years ago. And so one has seen fashions and vogues and stunts coming one after another in the Church. Each one creates great excitement and enthusiasm and is loudly advertised as *the* thing that is going to fill the churches, the thing that is going to solve the problem. They have said that about every single one of them. But in a few years they have forgotten all about it, and another stunt comes along, or another new idea; somebody has hit upon the one thing needful or he has a psychological understanding of modern man. Here is the thing, and everybody rushes after it; but soon it wanes and disappears and something else takes its place.
>
> This is, surely, a very sad and regrettable state for the Christian Church to be in, that like the world she should exhibit these constant changes of fashion. In that state she lacks the stability and the solidity and the continuing message that has ever been the glory of the Christian Church.[4]

Biblical preaching cannot be geared toward meeting felt needs, solving psychological problems, amusing the audience, making people feel good about themselves, or any of the other hollow fads that have commandeered pulpits in this entertainment-oriented age. Biblical preaching must uphold the truth of God and demand that it be heeded. There is plenty of room for innovation and creativity within those guidelines, but the message itself cannot be altered or abridged in any way without prostituting the church's responsibility. Truth proclaimed powerfully

---

[4]*Preaching and Preachers* (Grand Rapids, Mich.: Zondervan, 1971), 35.

from the Scriptures is the sine qua non of the church. Any other kind of preaching is not worthy of the church Christ is building.

A WILLINGNESS TO CHANGE

Healthy churches must be willing to change.

Wait a minute! someone says. *Aren't you appealing for traditionalism in churches?* No. There's nothing sacred about human tradition. I'm not in favor of staid formalism or hackneyed custom. I agree with those who warn that stagnation can be fatal to a church. I just don't believe the church needs to abandon the centrality of the Word of God, the primacy of preaching, and the fundamentals of biblical truth in order to be fresh and creative.

Someone has said that the seven last words of the church are, "We've never done it that way before!" An inflexible attitude is the bane of a healthy church. We must be willing to grow and adapt and try new things—but never at the expense of biblical truth, and never to the detriment of the gospel message.

WORSHIP

I've saved worship for last, certainly not because it is least crucial but because it sums up all the others. Several years ago I wrote a book on worship titled *The Ultimate Priority*.[5] I do believe that worship is the church's—and the individual Christian's—highest priority. True worship comprises and fulfills all these other characteristics of the church Christ builds. The church that sets its focus on God will find that all other things fall naturally into place.

Here is precisely the problem with the market-oriented, user-friendly, pragmatic approach to ministry: it is man-centered, not God-centered. Its concern is what people desire, not what God demands. It sees the church as existing for people's sake rather than for God's sake. It works from a faulty blueprint rather than fulfilling the plan of the Master Builder.

User-friendly, entertainment-oriented, market-driven, pragmatic churches will probably continue to flourish for a while. Unfortunately, however, the whole movement is based on current fashion and therefore cannot last long. When the fickle winds finally change, one of three things may happen. These churches will fall out of vogue and wane; or they will

---

[5](Chicago: Moody, 1983).

opt to change with the spirit of the age and very likely abandon any sem-blance of biblical Christianity; or they will see the need to rebuild on a more sure foundation. My prayer, of course, is that they will take the third course of action and not wait until worldliness and compromise have so permeated their fellowships that it becomes impossible to change.

Charles Spurgeon wrote, "It is hard to get leaven out of dough, and easy to put it in. . . . Oh that those who are spiritually alive in the churches may look to this thing, and may the Lord himself baffle the adversary!"[6]

---

[6]"Notes," *The Sword and the Trowel* (October 1888). Reprinted in *The "Down Grade" Controversy* (Pasadena, Tex.: Pilgrim, n.d.), 67.

10

Epilogue

*On the "Down-Grade" the train travels very fast: another station has
been passed. What next? And what next?*

CHARLES HADDON SPURGEON[1]

WHAT IS the future of evangelicalism? In a perceptive series of
articles on the church-growth movement, Os Guinness points
out that traditional evangelicalism not only resisted worldly
influences, but also stressed "cognitive defiance" of the world spirit.
Evangelicals historically have understood that their calling is to be in the
world but not of the world. Now, however, "at the high noon of moder-
nity, the world has become so powerful, pervasive, and appealing that the
traditional stance of cognitive defiance has become rare and almost
unthinkable."[2] Somewhere along the line evangelicals decided to make
friends with the world.

Guinness points out that although we are called to be in the world
but not of the world (John 17:14-18), many Christians have reversed the
formula, becoming *of* the world while not really being *in* the world. They
did this by allowing cable television, VCRs, radio, and other forms of communication to infuse worldly values into their thinking, while isolating
themselves from any personal involvement with the people in the world
who most desperately need the gospel.

"Evangelicals are now outdoing liberals as the supreme religious
modernizers—and compromisers—of today," Guinness writes.[3] He suggests that the market-driven philosophy so popular among modern evan-

---

[1]"Notes," *The Sword and the Trowel* (May 1889). Reprinted in *The "Down Grade"
Controversy* (Pasadena, Tex.: Pilgrim, n.d.), 76.
[2]"Recycling the Compromise of Liberalism," *Tabletalk* (May 1992), 51.
[3]*Ibid.*

191

gelicals is nothing more than "a recycling of the error of classical liberalism."[4]

We noted earlier that the reason most evangelicals were caught unaware by modernism a hundred years ago is that liberals rose from within evangelical ranks, used evangelical vocabulary, and gained acceptance through relentless appeals for peace and tolerance. The new modernism is following precisely the same course, and that tactic seems likely to take evangelicals by surprise once again.

Most of the market-driven megachurches insist they would never compromise doctrine. They are attractive to evangelicals precisely because they claim to be as orthodox in their doctrine as they are unorthodox in their methodology. Multitudes are sufficiently reassured by such promises and simply abandon their critical faculties, thus increasing their vulnerability. Unfortunately, real discernment is in short supply among modern evangelicals.

The truth is, it wouldn't matter much *what* doctrinal position some of these churches took, because doctrine is simply a non-issue with them. A friend of mine wanted to learn how the user-friendly churches integrate doctrine into their ministries. He selected one of the largest and best-known churches in the movement and ordered several cassettes from their tape ministry. He asked for tapes that focused on biblical doctrine and was sent several tapes and a catalogue. A survey of the catalogue revealed that the sermons preached in the church—by a ratio of more than thirty to one—usually dealt with contemporary topics, psychological issues (depression, eating disorders, self-image), personal relationships, motivational themes, and other matters à la mode. Messages dealing with doctrine—even sermons based on any biblical text—were rare. A tape titled "The Cost of Commitment" dealt not with commitment to Christ, but with the personal sacrifice required to build strong personal relationships with others. After listening to hours of tapes from this pastor, my friend concluded that it was impossible to tell what the man's positions were on any basic doctrinal issues. Most of the messages would have been immediately transferrable to any context—a sales convention, a school assembly, or a businessmen's luncheon. They simply avoided doctrinal or biblical issues altogether, using Scripture for illustrative purposes only, often reserving the scant biblical allusions for the very end.

---

[4]*Ibid.*, 51.

Like the modernists a century ago, churches in the user-friendly movement have decided that doctrine is divisive and that peace is more important than sound teaching. Wanting to appeal to a modern age, they try to frame their message as a friendly, agreeable, and relevant dialogue. Unfortunately, it is often the most "relevant" topics that the church can ill afford to agree on. The pet doctrines of our modern age—radicalism, abortion, feminism, homosexuality, and other politically charged moral issues—pose the most obvious problems for user-friendly churches. Their undefined theology and seeker-sensitive philosophy do not permit them to take a firm biblical stance on such matters, because the moment they defy the spirit of the age, they forfeit their marketing appeal. They are therefore forced to keep mum or capitulate. Either way, they compromise the truth.

If a church is not even willing to take a firm stand against abortion, how will that church deal with erosion of crucial doctrine? If a church lacks discernment enough to condemn such overt errors as homosexuality or feminism, how will that church handle a *subtle* attack on doctrinal integrity?

The landscape of evangelicalism is rapidly changing. The 19 February 1990 issue of *Christianity Today* included an article by Robert Brow entitled "Evangelical Megashift," reporting on a recent wave of radical thinking among evangelical theologians. "New-model" evangelicalism, as the article labeled the movement, turns out to be nothing more than "old-model" liberalism. By redefining key terms, this new-model theology seeks to fashion a kinder, gentler Christianity.

For example, new-model evangelicalism redefines *hell*. "No one could possibly be in hell who would rather be in heaven," the new view claims.[5] So hell is no longer thought of as a place of eternal torment. Instead, it is an exclusive refuge from God's presence, open only to those determined to get there.

There's more:

> In new-model theology . . . *wrath*—specifically God's wrath—similarly means something different from the old-model understanding. Wrath connotes not angry punishment, but the bad consequences God assigns, as any loving parent might, to destructive or wrongful behavior. The word *wrath* as used in the Old Testament, it is argued,

---

[5]"Evangelical Megashift," 13.

is not primarily a law-court term. It never means sending people to an eternal hell. In fact, it can simply be translated "bad consequences"—the bad consequences of pestilence, drought, and famine, or the ravages of wild animals and invading armies, experienced in the here and now.[6]

That's still not all. "*Sin*, also changes meaning. . . . In old-model theology, even one sin would be sufficient to condemn us to hell. New-model evangelicals, on the other hand, cannot think about sin without reference to the fatherly care of God. For loving parents, sin or bad behavior requires discipline and correction, with a view to helping the child change. But the purpose is never to exclude the child from home."[7] That is, God would never cite sin as a reason for sending anyone to hell.

In new-model theology God's primary attribute is benevolence. It overrides and supersedes His holiness, justice, wrath, and sovereignty. The new-model God is a *judge* only in the sense of being a "defender of His people." His sole concern is "the freedom and peace of the people."[8] Moreover, the new-model church is called not to confront the world, but "to make known the love of God, to say, 'your sins are forgiven,' as Jesus did, and to offer the resources of the Spirit to all who want to learn how to love and enjoy God and their neighbors."[9]

If ever there was a user-friendly theology, this is it. But it is not biblical, and there is nothing really new about it. It is simply retreaded liberalism. These are the same arguments and the same teachings that liberals have promoted for years—only now they are designated "evangelical." Don't let the label fool you. Spurgeon wrote, "It is mere cant to cry, 'We are evangelical; we are all evangelical,' and yet decline to say what evangelical means."[10] "You may believe anything, everything, or nothing, and yet be enrolled in the 'Evangelical' army—*so they say*. Will there arise no honest, out-spoken evangelicals among Dissenters to expose and repudiate this latitudinarianism? Are all the watchmen asleep? Are all the churches indifferent?"[11]

---

[6]*Ibid.*

[7]*Ibid.*

[8]*Ibid.*

[9]*Ibid.*, 14.

[10]"Notes," *The Sword and the Trowel* (October 1888). Reprinted in *The "Down Grade" Controversy*, 66.

[11]"Notes," *The Sword and the Trowel* (January 1889), 40.

According to new-model theology, "The cross was not a judicial payment, but the visible expression in a space-time body of his eternal nature as Son."[12] That is simply a new way of stating the central tenet of liberal theology: that Christ's saving work was not substitutionary atonement, but His moral example. It is an attack on the central truth of evangelical theology. It proves beyond question that some who like to think of themselves as evangelicals have already passed the warning signs and are now freewheeling heedlessly down the slope.

User-friendly churches lack means of defense against trends like new-model theology. Their market-driven philosophy does not easily permit them to take firm enough doctrinal positions to oppose these teachings. Their outlook on leadership drives them to hire marketers who can sell rather than biblically qualified pastors who can teach. Their approach to ministry is so *un*doctrinal that they cannot educate their people against subtle errors. Their hatred of controversy puts them in a position where they cannot oppose false teaching that masquerades as evangelicalism. In fact, new-model theology seems *ideally suited* to the user-friendly philosophy. Why would the user-friendly church oppose such doctrines?

But oppose them we must, if we are to remain true to God's Word and maintain a gospel witness. Pragmatism does not hold answers to the dangers confronting biblical Christianity. Pragmatism is carnal wisdom—spiritually bankrupt and contrary to the Word of God. (See Appendix 3 for an eighteenth-century contrast between carnal and spiritual wisdom that applies particularly well to twentieth-century pragmatism.)

Marketing techniques offer nothing but the promise of popularity and worldly approval. They certainly offer no safeguard against the dangers of the down-grade.

The only hope is a return to Scripture and sound doctrine. We evangelicals desperately need to recover our determination to be biblical, our refusal to comply with the world, our willingness to defend what we believe, and our courage to defy false teaching. Unless we collectively awaken to the current dangers that threaten our faith, the adversary will attack us from within, and we will not be able to withstand. History will repeat itself, and the same disaster that ravaged the church a hundred years ago will also strike our generation.

---

[12]"Evangelical Megashift," 14.

Yet, surely, there must be some who will fling aside the dastard love of peace, and speak out for our Lord, and for his truth. A craven spirit is upon many, and their tongues are paralyzed. Oh, for an outburst of true faith and holy zeal!

(CHARLES HADDON SPURGEON)[13]

---

[13]"Notes," *The Sword and the Trowel* (May 1889). Reprinted in *The "Down Grade" Controversy*, 76.

APPENDIX 1

Spurgeon and the Down-Grade Controversy

[At the end of the Puritan age] by some means or other, first the ministers, then the Churches, got on "the down grade," and in some cases, the descent was rapid, and in all, very disastrous. In proportion as the ministers seceded from the old Puritan godliness of life, and the old Calvinistic form of doctrine, they commonly became less earnest and less simple in their preaching, more speculative and less spiritual in the matter of their discourses, and dwelt more on the moral teachings of the New Testament, than on the great central truths of revelation. Natural theology frequently took the place which the great truths of the gospel ought to have held, and the sermons became more and more Christless. Corresponding results in the character and life, first of the preachers and then of the people, were only too plainly apparent.

THE SWORD AND THE TROWEL[1]

I N MARCH 1887, Charles Spurgeon published the first of two articles entitled "The Down Grade" in his monthly magazine, *The Sword and the Trowel*. The articles were published anonymously, but the author was Robert Shindler, Spurgeon's close friend and fellow Baptist pastor. Shindler wrote the articles with input from Spurgeon, who footnoted the first article with a personal endorsement: "Earnest attention is requested for this paper. We are going down hill at breakneck speed."[2]

Tracing the state of evangelicalism from the Puritan age to his own era, Shindler noted that every revival of true evangelical faith had been followed within a generation or two by a drift away from sound doctrine,

---

[1]Robert Shindler, "The Down Grade," *The Sword and the Trowel* (March 1887), 122.
[2]*Ibid.*, 122n.

197

ultimately leading to wholesale apostasy. He likened this drifting from truth to a downhill slope, and thus labeled it "the down-grade."

DOWN-GRADE I

In that first article, Shindler recounted the history of the major Protestant denominations in England since the beginning of Puritanism's decline in 1662. He noted that in the first generation after the Puritan era, virtually every non-conformist (non-Anglican Protestant) denomination in England drifted from orthodoxy toward an ancient form of theological liberalism called *Socinianism* (which denies original sin and Christ's deity). Shindler recounted how hundreds of post-Puritan churches had abandoned sound doctrine in favor of rationalistic skepticism, Unitarianism, and other liberal beliefs. The downward slide usually began slowly, almost imperceptibly. He suggested that denominations often "got on the down-grade" when they abandoned Calvinism (which emphasizes God's sovereignty in salvation) in favor of Arminianism (which makes human will the decisive factor). Other groups embraced *Arianism* (which denies the full deity of Christ). Still others simply became enamored with scholarship and worldly wisdom; consequently they lost their zeal for truth.

"The Presbyterians were the first to get on the down line," Shindler wrote. They took the route of worldly wisdom: "They paid more attention to classical attainments and other branches of learning. . . . It [was therefore] an easy step in the wrong direction to pay increased attention to academical attainments in their ministers, and less to spiritual qualifications; and to set a higher value on scholarship and oratory, than on evangelical zeal and ability to rightly divide the word of truth."[3]

Shindler further stated:

As is usual with people on an incline, some who got on "the down grade" went further than they intended, showing that it is easier to get on than to get off, and that where there is no brake it is very difficult to stop. Those who turned from Calvinism may not have dreamed of denying the proper deity of the Son of God, renouncing faith in his atoning death and justifying righteousness, and denouncing the doctrine of human depravity, the need of Divine renewal, and the necessity for the Holy Spirit's gracious work, in order that men

---

[3]*Ibid.*, 123.

might become new creatures; but, dreaming or not dreaming, this result became a reality.[4]

Some who abandoned the faith did so openly, Shindler said. But many purposely concealed their skepticism and heresy, preferring to sow seeds of doubt while posing as orthodox believers. "These men deepened their own condemnation, and promoted the everlasting ruin of many of their followers by their hypocrisy and deceit [cf Matt. 23:15]; professing to be the ambassadors of Christ, and the heralds of his glorious gospel, their aim was to ignore his claims, deny him his rights, lower his character, rend the glorious vesture of his salvation, and trample his crown in the dust."[5]

Many of those who remained true to the faith were nevertheless reluctant to fight for what they believed in. Evangelical preaching was often cold and lifeless, and even those who held to sound doctrine were careless about where they drew the line in their associations with others: "Those who were really orthodox in their sentiments were too often lax and unfaithful as to the introduction of heretical ministers into their pulpits, either as assistants or occasional preachers. In this way the Arian and Socinian heresies were introduced into the Presbyterian congregations in the city of Exeter."[6]

Thus within only a few decades, the Puritan fervor that had so captured the soul of England gave way to dry, listless, apostate teaching. Churches became lax in granting membership privileges to the unregenerate. People who were, in Shindler's words, "strangers to the work of renewing grace" nevertheless claimed to be Christians and were admitted to membership—even leadership—in the churches. These people "chose them pastors after their own hearts, men who could, and would, and did, cry 'Peace, peace,' when the only way of peace was ignored or denied."[7]

Shindler concluded that first paper on "The Down Grade" with these words: "These facts furnish a lesson for the present times, when, as in some cases, it is all too plainly apparent men are willing to forego the old for the sake of the new. But commonly it is found in theology that that which is true is not new, and that which is new is not true."[8]

---

[4]*Ibid.*, 124.
[5]*Ibid.*, 125.
[6]*Ibid.*
[7]*Ibid.*, 126.
[8]*Ibid.*

DOWN-GRADE II

In April, *The Sword and the Trowel* carried a second article entitled "The Down Grade." In it, Robert Shindler continued his overview of the history of the decline of Puritanism. He laid the blame for the downhill slide at the feet of the church leaders. Even those who were orthodox in their teaching were not earnestly contending (Jude 3), but were weak in defending the faith, Shindler said. As one example, he cited Philip Doddridge (1702-1751), best known today as the hymn writer who penned "O Happy Day" and "Grace, 'Tis a Charming Sound." Doddridge, according to Shindler, "was as sound as he was amiable; but perhaps he was not always judicious; or more probably still, he was too judicious, and not sufficiently bold and decided."[9]

Doddridge had been principal of the academy where most non-conformist ministers went for training in the mid-1700s. Shindler's judgment was that "[Doddridge's] amiable disposition permitted him to do what men made of sterner stuff would not have done. He sometimes mingled in a fraternal manner, even exchanging pulpits, with men whose orthodoxy was called in question. It had its effect on many of the younger men, and served to lessen in the estimate of the people generally the growing divergence of sentiment."[10] In other words, Shindler felt that Doddridge's tolerance of unorthodox teachers obscured from his ministerial students the awful reality that these men were guilty of serious error, and left the students exposed to the deadly effects of their heresy. But, Shindler hastened to add, no one could "insinuate even the suspicion of heresy" against Doddridge himself.

Because of the attitude of tolerance implanted by Doddridge, the academy at last succumbed to Socinianism, then was dissolved in the generation after Doddridge's passing.[11]

Shindler paraphrased Hosea 4:9: "Like priest, like people," and wrote, "Little good can be expected of such ministers, and little hoped for of the hearers who approve their sentiments."[12] He warned against such tolerance, suggesting it is better to err on the side of caution:

---

[9]"The Down Grade" (second article), *The Sword and the Trowel* (April 1887), 166.
[10]*Ibid.*, 167.
[11]*Ibid.*
[12]*Ibid.*, 168.

In too many cases sceptical daring seems to have taken the place of evangelical zeal, and the husks of theological speculations are preferred to the wholesome bread of gospel truth. With some the endeavour seems to be not how steadily and faithfully they can walk in the truth, but how far they can get from it. To them divine truth is like a lion or a tiger, and they give it "a wide berth." Our counsel is—Do not go too near the precipice; you may slip or fall over. Keep where the ground is firm; do not venture on the rotten ice.[13]

He gave specific examples of how tolerance had led to disaster, noting that the "tadpole of Darwinism was hatched. . . [in a pew] of the old chapel in High Street, Shrewsbury," where Charles Darwin had first been introduced to skepticism by a pastor who was enthralled with Socinianism. Also the chapel once pastored by Matthew Henry, author of the famous commentary on the whole Bible, had for years been teaching "full-blown Socinianism."[14]

The Baptists, Shindler noted, had seen their share of churches on the down-grade. He named several churches in the county of Kent that had embraced Socinianism: those at Dover, Deal, Wingham, and Yalding.

But, he added, there were a few notable exceptions to the rule. Those churches willing to fight for the faith and uphold the doctrines of grace and God's sovereignty had managed to avoid the fate of those on the down-grade. They were singular illustrations of the up-grade, Shindler said, showing the down-grade in bold relief.

How did so many Bible-believing churches go astray? And why does this happen again and again in human history? Shindler raised these questions:

In the case of every errant course there is always a first wrong step. If we can trace that wrong step, we may be able to avoid it and its results. Where, then, is the point of divergence from the "King's highway of truth"? What is the first step astray? Is it doubting this doctrine, or questioning that sentiment, or being sceptical as to the other article of orthodox belief? We think not. These doubts and this scepticism are the outcome of something going before.[15]

---

[13] *Ibid.*
[14] *Ibid.*
[15] *Ibid.*, 170.

What was that "something"? What was the common denominator between all those who started on the down-grade?

> The first step astray is a want of adequate faith in the divine inspiration of the sacred Scriptures. All the while a man bows to the authority of God's Word, he will not entertain any sentiment contrary to its teaching. "To the law and to the testimony," is his appeal concerning every doctrine. He esteems that holy Book, concerning all things, to be right, and therefore he hates every false way. But let a man question, or entertain low views of the inspiration and authority of the Bible, and he is without chart to guide him, and without anchor to hold him.
>
> In looking carefully over the history of the times, and the movement of the times, of which we have written briefly, this fact is apparent: that where ministers and Christian churches have held fast to the truth that the Holy Scriptures have been given by God as an authoritative and infallible rule of faith and practice, they have never wandered very seriously out of the right way. But when, on the other hand, reason has been exalted above revelation, and made the exponent of revelation, all kinds of errors and mischiefs have been the result.[16]

Shindler noted a correlation between Calvinistic doctrine and a high view of Scripture, suggesting that the great majority of those who remained committed to the authority of Scripture were "more or less Calvinistic in doctrine."[17] In the "Notes" section of that same issue of *The Sword and the Trowel*, Spurgeon added this: "We care far more for the central evangelical truths than we do for Calvinism as a system; but we believe that Calvinism has in it a conservative force which helps to hold men to the vital truth."[18] The clear implication to both Spurgeon and Shindler was that a high view of Scripture goes hand in hand with a high view of divine sovereignty. Moreover, Shindler noted, those churches that held firmly to sound doctrine remained healthy and flourished, while those that embraced Socinianism inevitably began to dwindle and die. Shindler quoted the Rev. Job Orton, a man who evidently had Socinian leanings himself but nonetheless wrote a warning to pastors flirting with liberal theology:

---

[16] *Ibid.*
[17] *Ibid.*
[18] *Ibid.*, 195.

"I have long since found," says [Orton], "(and every year that I live increases my conviction of it), that when ministers entertain their people with lively and pretty things, confine themselves to general harangues, insist principally on moral duties, without enforcing them warmly and affectionately by evangelical motives; while they neglect the peculiars of the gospel, never or seldom display the grace of God, and the love of Christ in our redemption; the necessity of regeneration and sanctification by a constant dependence on the Holy Spirit of God for assistance and strength in the duties of the Christian life, their congregations are in a wretched state; some are dwindling to nothing, as is the case with several in this neighbourhood, where there are now not as many scores as there were hundreds in their meeting-places, fifty years ago. . . . There is a fatal deadness spread over the congregation. They run in 'the course of this world,' follow every fashionable folly, and family and personal godliness seems in general to be lost among them. There is scarcely any appearance of life and zeal."[19]

Shindler wryly added, "It would seem that Orton had seen the folly of 'the down grade' course, and was anxious to bear his testimony, to deter others."[20]

Then he closed that article with an appeal to the centrality and sufficiency of God's Word:

But leaving men and their opinions, the Word of the Lord standeth fast forever; and that Word to every one who undertakes to be God's messenger, and to speak the Lord's message to the people, is "He that hath my word, let him speak my word faithfully. What is the chaff to the wheat? saith the Lord."

The Lord help us all to be "steadfast, immovable, always abounding in the work of the Lord, forasmuch as we know our labour shall not be in vain in the Lord."[21]

With that the two-part series ended.

Shindler appended it with a third article for the June *Sword and Trowel*. The June article offered an analysis of a heresy trial in America involving some professors from Andover Theological Seminary, Andover,

---

[19] *Ibid.*, 171-72.
[20] *Ibid.*, 172.
[21] *Ibid.*

New York. Andover had been founded less than a hundred years earlier in response to Socinianism at Harvard. Andover's founders, Shindler wrote, "were sound Calvinists of the Cotton Mather type, and the College was instituted for the special purpose of training men in that faith."[22] Shindler accused "the five gentlemen who now fill professorial chairs" with having "seriously departed from the faith of the founders." They did this by deceit, Shindler said. Having subscribed to the school's doctrinal statement, they were now undermining it by their teaching, which had been labeled "Progressive Orthodoxy" by some. Shindler had his own assessment: "Indeed the *progression* is so considerable that the 'orthodoxy' is lost sight of."[23] He went on to chronicle the heresies taught by these men, which, though considered subtle in the late nineteenth century, were indeed serious defections from the faith.

Shindler saw the Andover disaster as an object lesson on the dangers of the down-grade, and he did not hesitate to make the point, using American Baptists as an illustration, that The Baptist Union in England was headed down the same road.

Three months later, Charles Haddon Spurgeon himself would write about "the down-grade." The controversy was only beginning to heat up.

DOWN-GRADE III

In August *The Sword and the Trowel* carried an article by Spurgeon entitled "Another Word Concerning the Down-Grade." The tone of this article was more urgent than Shindler's had been. The earlier articles had evidently provoked two basic responses—displeasure from those who believed Shindler's analysis was too pessimistic, and hearty agreement from many who were also troubled about the trends in British evangelicalism.

Those who agreed with Shindler's warning blasts responded by offering more proof of apostasy and compromise in formerly sound churches. Spurgeon read these responses, and his outrage grew. One man reported that "two ministers had derided him because he thought we should pray for rain." A woman told Spurgeon that "a precious promise in Isaiah which had comforted her had been declared by her

---

[22]Robert Shindler, "Andover Theology," *The Sword and the Trowel*, Vol. 23 (June 1887), 274.
[23]*Ibid.*

minister to be uninspired."[24] The editorial office of *The Sword and the Trowel* was inundated with such accounts.

From the opening paragraph, Spurgeon's tone was more militant, more intense than Shindler had been in the earlier articles. In the weeks since those first two articles were published, Spurgeon had evidently come to feel that *The Sword and the Trowel* had underestimated the gravity of "The Down-Grade":

> Our solemn conviction is that things are much worse in many churches than they seem to be, and are rapidly tending downward. Read those newspapers which represent the Broad School of Dissent, and ask yourself, How much farther could they go? What doctrine remains to be abandoned? What other truth to be the object of contempt? A new religion has been initiated, which is no more Christianity than chalk is cheese; and this religion, being destitute of moral honesty, palms itself off as the old faith with slight improvements, and on this plea usurps pulpits which were erected for gospel preaching.[25]

In place of gospel preaching, this "new-and-improved" variety of Christianity was substituting amusements. Spurgeon warned that many were turning the church into a "play-house," allowing the values and techniques of the theater to invade the sanctuary of the Lord.

Spurgeon noted that many churches were no longer having prayer meetings. Spiritual fervor was dwindling, congregations were thinning, and enthusiasm for the gospel was quickly becoming extinct. "Alas! many are returning to the poisoned cups which drugged that declining [post-Puritan] generation. . . . Too many ministers are toying with the deadly cobra of 'another gospel,' in the form of 'modern thought.'"[26]

Who was chiefly to blame for the decline? Spurgeon believed it was the preachers: "The case is mournful. Certain ministers are making infidels. Avowed atheists are not a tenth as dangerous as those preachers who scatter doubt and stab at faith. . . . Germany was made unbelieving by her preachers, and England is following in her tracks."[27]

---

[24]"Another Word Concerning the Down-Grade," *The Sword and the Trowel* (August 1887), 399.
[25]*Ibid.*, 397.
[26]*Ibid.*, 398.
[27]*Ibid.*, 399.

Spurgeon made no effort to disguise his contempt for the modernists: "These destroyers of our churches appear to be as content with their work as monkeys with their mischief. That which their fathers would have lamented they rejoice in: the alienation of the poor and simple-minded from their ministry they accept as a compliment, and the grief of the spiritually-minded they regard as an evidence of their power."[28]

To those who might be put off by such frankness, Spurgeon wrote, "A little plain-speaking would do a world of good just now. These gentlemen desire to be let alone. They want no noise raised. Of course thieves hate watch-dogs, and love darkness. It is time that somebody should spring his rattle, and call attention to the way in which God is being robbed of his glory, and man of his hope."[29]

At the end of the article, Spurgeon fired this shot, which for the first time raised the issue that would become the focus of all the subsequent controversy:

> It now becomes a serious question how far those who abide by the faith once delivered to the saints should fraternize with those who have turned aside to another gospel. Christian love has its claims, and divisions are to be shunned as grievous evils; but how far are we justified in being in confederacy with those who are departing from the truth? It is a difficult question to answer so as to keep the balance of the duties. For the present it behooves believers to be cautious, lest they lend their support and countenance to the betrayers of the Lord. It is one thing to overleap all boundaries of denominational restriction for the truth's sake: this we hope all godly men will do more and more. It is quite another policy which would urge us to subordinate the maintenance of truth to denominational prosperity and unity. Numbers of easy-minded people wink at error so long as it is committed by a clever man and a good-natured brother, who has so many fine points about him. Let each believer judge for himself; but, for our part, we have put on a few fresh bolts to our door, and we have given orders to keep the chain up; for, under colour of begging the friendship of the servant, there are those about who aim at robbing the Master.[30]

---

[28] *Ibid.*, 399-400.
[29] *Ibid.*, 400.
[30] *Ibid.*

Spurgeon was now suggesting that true believers might have reason to sever their organizational ties with those who were promulgating the new theology. In his estimation the truth of the Word had been so seriously compromised that true Christians needed to consider the command of 2 Corinthians 6:17: "'Come out from their midst and be separate,' says the Lord. 'And do not touch what is unclean.'"

This was not a call for a new denomination. Spurgeon clearly distrusted earthly organizations:

> We fear it is hopeless ever to form a society which can keep out men base enough to profess one thing and believe another; but it might be possible to make an informal alliance among all who hold the Christianity of their fathers. Little as they might be able to do, they could at least protest, and as far as possible free themselves of that complicity which will be involved in a conspiracy of silence. If for a while the evangelicals are doomed to go down, let them die fighting, and in the full assurance that their gospel will have a resurrection when the inventions of "modern thought" shall be burned up with fire unquenchable.[31]

The article rocked the evangelical world. Spurgeon, who for decades had been almost universally revered by evangelicals, was suddenly besieged with critics from within the camp. What he was proposing was diametrically opposed to the consensus of evangelical thought. All the trends were toward unification, harmony, amalgamation, and brotherhood. Suddenly here was a lone voice—but the most influential voice of all—urging true believers to become separatists. The church was neither prepared nor willing to receive such counsel—not even from the Prince of Preachers.

DOWN-GRADE IV

Despite pleas from some of the brethren that he soften his rhetoric or tone down his complaints, Spurgeon ratcheted up the intensity in a September *Sword and Trowel* article. Reader response to the earlier articles vindicated his position, Spurgeon believed. Letters had been pouring in to corroborate his worst allegations. In fact, he was now wondering if his alarm had been too little, too late:

---

[31] *Ibid.*

According to the best of our ability we sounded an alarm in Zion concerning the growing evils of the times, and we have received abundant proof that it was none too soon. Letters from all quarters declare that the case of the church at this present is even worse than we thought it to be. It seems that, instead of being guilty of exaggeration, we should have been justified in the production of a far more terrible picture. This fact causes us real sorrow. Had we been convicted of misstatement we would have recanted with sincerely penitent confessions, and we should have been glad to have had our fears removed. It is no joy to us to bring accusations; it is no pleasure to our heart to seem to be in antagonism with so many.[32]

Instead of answering Spurgeon's charges, the critics had declared them vague (although both Shindler and Spurgeon had been anything but vague). Spurgeon was now struggling with recurring kidney ailments and had been absent from the pulpit. Some insinuated that the Down-Grade articles were the rantings of someone who was desperately sick. Clearly, Spurgeon was personally grieved by that allegation:

Our opponents have set to work to make sneering allusions to our sickness. All the solemn things we have written are the suggestions of our pain, and we are advised to take a long rest. With pretended compassion, but with real insolence, they would detract from the truth by pointing to the lameness of its witness. Upon this trifling we have this much to say:—In the first place, our article was written when we were in vigorous health, and it was in print before any sign of an approaching attack was discoverable. In the second place, if we were in a debate with Christians we should feel sure that, however short they might run of arguments, they would not resort to personalities.[33]

His opponents had attacked him personally, though he and Shindler both had taken extreme care to avoid making personalities the subject of their censures. What is more, Spurgeon's adversaries utterly ignored the substance of his strictures. "No one has set himself to disprove our allegations," Spurgeon wrote.[34] No one had denied any of his charges. Indeed,

---

[32]"Our Reply to Sundry Critics and Enquirers," *The Sword and the Trowel* (September 1887), 461.
[33]*Ibid.*, 462.
[34]*Ibid.*, 461.

no one could. Though few wanted to admit it, English evangelicalism was indeed on the down-grade.

Employing the vivid imagery that was the hallmark of Spurgeon's preaching, he wrote, "The house is being robbed, its very walls are being digged down, but the good people who are in bed are too fond of the warmth, and too much afraid of getting broken heads, to go downstairs and meet the burglars; they are even half vexed that a certain noisy fellow will spring his rattle, or cry, 'Thieves!'"[35]

Spurgeon was beginning to think more seriously and speak more explicitly about breaking fellowship with those whom he believed were opposing the gospel. For several decades Spurgeon had been the most visible and influential member of the Baptist Union. Yet it seemed he was now seriously pondering withdrawal from the Union as a matter of conscience.

> The divergence is every day becoming more manifest. A chasm is opening between the men who believe their Bibles and the men who are prepared for an advance upon Scripture. Inspiration and speculation cannot long abide in peace. Compromise there can be none. We cannot hold the inspiration of the Word, and yet reject it; we cannot believe in the atonement and deny it; we cannot hold the doctrine of the fall and yet talk of the evolution of spiritual life from human nature; we cannot recognise the punishment of the impenitent and yet indulge the "larger hope." One way or the other we must go. Decision is the virtue of the hour.
>
> Neither when we have chosen our way can we keep company with those who go the other way.[36]

Spurgeon apparently hoped the evangelical leaders of the Baptist Union would see his side and opt for reform. The Union had never required adherence to a doctrinal statement of any kind. From the beginning, it had more or less been the assumption that members of the Union were all evangelical. The only point of doctrine required for membership, therefore, dealt with the mode of baptism. Spurgeon believed that was an insufficient guard against the erosion of truth, so he appealed to the

---

[35]*Ibid.*, 465.
[36]*Ibid.*

Baptist Union to affirm a new structure that would ensure doctrinal integrity among its members.

Faced with the possibility of losing Spurgeon versus the certainty of splitting the Union, denominational leaders began looking for a way of compromise.

But Spurgeon refused to compromise:

> Let those who will keep the narrow way keep it, and suffer for their choice; but to hope to follow the broad road at the same time is an absurdity. What communion hath Christ with Belial?
>
> Thus far we come, and pause. Let us, as many as are of one mind, wait upon the Lord to know what Israel ought to do. With steadfast faith let us take our places; not in anger, not in the spirit of suspicion or division, but in watchfulness and resolve. Let us not pretend to a fellowship which we do not feel, nor hide convictions which are burning in our hearts. The times are perilous, and the responsibility of every individual believer is a burden which he must bear, or prove a traitor. What each man's place and course should be the Lord will make clear unto him.[37]

And thus Spurgeon ended his article. He had thrown down the gauntlet. His mind and heart were set. He would not be moved.

DOWN-GRADE V

The October issue of *The Sword and the Trowel* carried the third of Spurgeon's articles about the down-grade. This article, entitled "The Case Proved," consisted mostly of excerpts from letters and reviews Spurgeon had received in response to the earlier articles. These fell into two categories. The first were from readers who saw controversy brewing and wanted to still the storm. Spurgeon characterized them as "esteemed friends" who wanted to "rush in between the combatants, and declare that there was no cause for war, but that our motto might continue to be 'Peace, peace!'"[38] Spurgeon accused such people of being "so supremely amiable that they see all things through spectacles of tinted glass."[39]

The second category included responses from people affirming

---

[37]*Ibid.*
[38]*The Sword and the Trowel* (October 1887), 509.
[39]*Ibid.*, 510.

Spurgeon's assessment of the dismal state of affairs. Many described specific examples of compromise and false teaching among those who classified themselves as evangelical.

Again Spurgeon asked the question, *"Are brethren who remain orthodox prepared to endorse such sentiments by remaining in union with those who hold and teach them?"*[40] Believing that the Baptist Union would take up these issues at their annual autumn meetings at Sheffield, Spurgeon made his position clear one final time:

> What action is to be taken we leave to those who can see more plainly than we do what Israel ought to do. One thing is clear to us: we cannot be expected to meet in any Union which comprehends those whose teaching is upon fundamental points exactly the reverse of that which we hold dear. . . . To us it appears that there are many things upon which compromise is possible, but there are others in which it would be an act of treason to pretend to fellowship. With deep regret we abstain from assembling with those whom we dearly love and heartily respect, since it would involve us in a confederacy with those with whom we can have no communion in the Lord.[41]

But at Sheffield the issue never even came up.

WITHDRAWAL FROM THE UNION

On October 28, 1887, Spurgeon wrote to Samuel Harris Booth, General Secretary of the Baptist Union:

> Dear Friend,—I beg to intimate to you, as the secretary of the Baptist Union, that I must withdraw from that society. I do this with the utmost regret; but I have no choice. The reasons are set forth in *The Sword and the Trowel* for November, and I trust you will excuse my repeating them here. I beg you not to send anyone to me to ask for reconsideration. I fear I have considered too long already; certainly every hour of the day impresses upon me the conviction that I am moving none too soon.
>
> I wish also to add that no personal pique or ill-will has in the least degree operated upon me. I have personally received more respect than I desired. It is on the highest ground alone that I take this step,

---

[40]*Ibid.,* 513.
[41]*Ibid.,* 515.

and you know that I have long delayed it because I hoped for better things.—Yours always heartily,

C.H. Spurgeon[42]

Spurgeon evidently had already written his November *Sword and Trowel* article when he wrote the letter to Booth. He began the article, "A Fragment upon the Down-Grade Controversy," with these words: "By this time many of our readers will be weary of the Down-Grade controversy: they cannot be one-tenth so much tired of it, or tried by it, as we are."[43] The controversy had consumed Spurgeon's thoughts and emotions as he deliberated whether to withdraw from the Union. But Spurgeon felt he was left no choice. Severing ties with the enemies of the gospel was no option as far as he was concerned: "*Fellowship with known and vital error is participation in sin.*"[44] The force of his rhetoric is an insight into Spurgeon's heart: "To be very plain, we are unable to call these things Christian Unions, they begin to look like Confederacies in Evil. Before the face of God we fear that they wear no other aspect. To our inmost heart this is a sad truth from which we cannot break away."[45]

Spurgeon saw no reason true Christians should accommodate those who doubted the authority and sufficiency of Scripture. "If these men believe such things, let them teach them, and construct churches, unions, and brotherhoods for themselves! Why must they come among us?"[46]

He felt he had no choice other than the course of action he had taken: "During the past month many have put to us the anxious question, *'What shall we do?'* To these we have had no answer to give except that each one must act for himself after seeking direction of the Lord. In our own case we intimated our course of action in last month's paper. We retire at once and distinctly from the Baptist Union."[47]

That announcement must have come as a jolt to many readers. Few had believed Spurgeon would carry through with his threats. Peace and unity were almost universally esteemed as the highest of Christian

---

[42]Cited in G. Holden Pike, *The Life and Work of Charles Haddon Spurgeon*, 6 vols. (London: Cassell and Company, n.d.), 6: 287.
[43]*The Sword and the Trowel* (November 1887), 557.
[44]*Ibid.*, 559.
[45]*Ibid.*, 558.
[46]*Ibid.*, 559-60.
[47]*Ibid.*, 560.

virtues. It was unthinkable that Charles H. Spurgeon, the most visible and popular British evangelical of his day, would become a schismatic. Yet that was the popular perception of the course Spurgeon had pursued.

SPURGEON AND THE BAPTIST UNION

But Spurgeon had not withdrawn capriciously or hastily. On November 23 he wrote from the south of France to explain his actions to a fellow pastor, Mr. Mackey: "It was encumbent upon me to leave the Union, as my private remonstrances to officials, and my repeated pointed appeals to the whole body, had been of no avail. My standpoint had become one from which, as an earnest man, I could see no other course but to withdraw."[48]

The private letter to Mackey was shared with the hundred-member Council of the Baptist Union. Eighty of these men met December 13 to discuss Spurgeon's charges. Most of them were outraged at Spurgeon's charges and his subsequent withdrawal from their group. They accused him of making charges based on inaccurate information, and the officers of the Union flatly denied that Spurgeon had ever come to them with "private remonstrances" or concerns of any kind about the doctrinal state of the Union.

One officer in particular, General Secretary Booth, knew better. Booth and Spurgeon had had many private conversations and exchanged many letters about the deplorable state of the Union. In fact, Booth himself had urged Spurgeon to speak out against the modernism that was running rampant in the Union. Booth evidently had even given Spurgeon details about the widespread compromise and names of men whose orthodoxy he had reason to doubt.[49] But Booth had sworn Spurgeon to secrecy about their correspondence. "My letters to you were not official but in confidence," Booth wrote when he thought Spurgeon was about to blow the whistle on him. "As a matter of honor you cannot use them."[50]

The Council minutes show that Booth misled the Council as to the nature of his conversations with Spurgeon. He told them, "Again I say that whatever conversations I have had with Mr. Spurgeon were not of a kind to formulate charges against brethren in order that I might submit

---

[48]*Letters of Charles Haddon Spurgeon* (Edinburgh: Banner of Truth, 1992), 183.

[49]Lewis Drummond, *Spurgeon: Prince of Preachers* (Grand Rapids, Mich.: Kregel, 1992), 671.

[50]*Ibid.*, 697.

them to this council. It never entered my mind that Mr. Spurgeon intended the things which passed in conversation to be brought here and formulated as charges."[51] While strictly speaking that was true, it was far from the whole truth. Booth, after all, had first come to Spurgeon with concerns. Their dialogue on the issues was far more than passing conversation. Booth more than anyone else had known about—and as far as Spurgeon believed, shared—the great preacher's profound concern over the drift of the Union.

But even when the Baptist Union Council—including Booth himself—accused Spurgeon of misrepresenting the truth, Spurgeon honored Booth's wishes to keep their correspondence confidential. "Spurgeon could have summarily proved the extent of his prior consultation with Union officials by producing correspondence from Booth."[52] Instead, he bore the abuse and false accusations—even when Booth himself became one of the accusers.

"For Dr. Booth to say I never complained, is amazing," Spurgeon wrote his wife. "God knows all about it, and He will see me righted."[53]

But as one biographer pointed out, "Spurgeon was never righted. The impression in many quarters still remains that he made charges which could not be substantiated, and when properly called upon to produce his evidence he resigned and ran away. Nothing is further from the truth. Spurgeon might have produced Dr. Booth's letters. I think he should have done so."[54]

The Baptist Union Council accused Spurgeon of having breached Jesus' instructions in Matthew 18 by failing to go privately first to those with whom he had grievances. In another letter to his wife, Spurgeon responded to that charge: "What a farce about my seeing these brethren, privately, according to Matt. xviii. 15! Why, I saw the Secretary and the president again and again; and then I printed my plaint, and only left the Union when nothing could be done."[55]

To Dr. James Culross, president of the Union, Spurgeon wrote,

---

[51] *Ibid.*

[52] Iain Murray, *The Forgotten Spurgeon* (Edinburgh: Banner of Truth, 1966), 145.

[53] Susannah Spurgeon and J. W. Harrald, eds., *C. H. Spurgeon's Autobiography*, 4 vols. (London: Passmore and Alabaster, 1897), 4:257.

[54] J. C. Carlisle, *C. H. Spurgeon—An Interpretive Biography* (London: Religious Tract Society, 1933), 247.

[55] *Autobiography*, 4:256.

I have followed out our Lord's mind as to private remonstrances by seeing Presidents and Secretary on former occasions, and I have written my remonstrances again and again without avail. I had no course but to withdraw. Surely, no sane person thinks that I should have made a tour to deal with the individual errorists. I have no jurisdiction over them, and should have been regarded as offensively intrusive if I had gone to them; and justly so. My question is with the Union, and with that alone. I have dealt with it all along.[56]

By raising the Matthew 18 question, and by accusing Spurgeon of failure to bring his concerns properly before the Union's leaders, the Council was clearly evading the real issues. They proposed sending a delegation of four men to confront Spurgeon and wrote him to try to arrange a visit while Spurgeon was in France. Spurgeon declined, saying he would meet with the men when he returned to England.

Spurgeon saw the Council's response as a transparent attempt to make *him* the issue, and to draw the controversy away from the doctrinal drift within the Union. Furthermore, he had carefully avoided making any of his attacks personal, and now the Council was using even that against him, claiming that since he had not mentioned specific names and details, his charges were too vague for them to address. In an uncharacteristically defensive letter, Spurgeon sent a letter to the editor of the main publication of the Union:

To the Editor of "The Baptist."
DEAR SIR—I would not occupy your columns with a personal matter were it not of considerable importance that I should do so. In the letter to Mr. Mackey I wrote: "It was incumbent upon me to leave the Union, as my private remonstrances to officials, and my repeated pointed appeals to the whole body, had been of no avail." This is not untrue, nor inaccurate. After a painful occurrence at Leicester [in 1883 a Unitarian minister was permitted to preach at the Baptist Union meetings there] I made serious complaint to the secretary, the president (Mr. Chown), and others of the Council. At the Orphanage, to which he kindly came, Mr. Chown made to me a pathetic appeal to regard it as a solitary incident, and hoping that I had been mistaken.

---

[56]*Ibid.*, 4:263.

I did not go further with this matter, for which, possibly, I am blame-worthy.

Since then I have repeatedly spoken to the secretary [Booth] upon the subject, as he will willingly admit. I think each year either him-self or Mr. Baynes has waited upon me to preach for the Union, or to preach at the mission services connected with the Union gatherings. On each occasion one or other has heard my complaints till they must, I fear, have been wearied. Here I beg to add that I do not confound the mission with the Union; but it so happens that these good secre-taries call upon me while making arrangements for the same series of meetings, and therefore I have regarded that which I said to one as said to both. The fact has remained that I have declined to take a pub-lic part in the meetings, because I could not feel sure that I should not be compromised thereby. This is surely an action which spoke more loudly than words. With Mr. Williams and Dr. Maclaren I had considerable correspondence, which on their part, at any rate, was most admirable.

My friend Mr. Williams says my letters were marked "Private," and that is just what I said to Mr. Mackey. Mr. Booth did not regard my communications as made to him *officially*, neither did I ever say that he did. The complaints were, however, made by me to him, while I tried to compromise the matter with my judgment by joining in the *work*, and not in the *talk*, of the Union, and I wish it could have been a possible middleway. I will not venture to say definitely how many of the Council knew my views and feelings by hearing me utter them at various times, but more than enough to justify my statement to Mr. Mackey.

Please note that the first clause of the sentence only is taken, and it is made to be more prominent than I intended by the remainder being left out—"my repeated pointed appeals to the whole body." My letters on "The Down-grade" do not deal exclusively with the Baptist denomination, which I have all along admitted to be far less tainted than another; but they did so far concern it that the republished arti-cles were submitted to the entire ministry and posted to all. "The organ of the Baptist denomination" likened the affair to a "big goose-berry," and stated that certain ministers on the road to Sheffield regarded it as a "great joke." At the meetings no public notice was taken except to assail me before a public meeting, where there was no opportunity of reply. Of other expressions of an unkind character then used by individuals I will not write; but the whole together made it clear to me that no one thought my appeals worthy of notice. Had any one of the brethren judged them to be serious he could have mentioned them to the Council, and could have asked that private statements should become public ones; but no one thought this wise. Of this I am not complaining; but it must not be said that I have not spoken the truth in the lines quoted above.

The fact seems to be that the question asked was not, "Is that statement made by Mr. Spurgeon true?" but the real inquiry made was, *"Has he so written that the officials felt bound to lay the matter before the Council?"* This is quite another subject, as anyone can see with half an eye. Thus I can exonerate questioners, repliers, and others by the theory that *they* meant one thing and *I* meant another; and I at once do so.

But this is a sad beginning for a brotherly conference. The charge was not that I was knowingly untruthful, but that I said what was not true—I suppose through the failure of my mental powers. The inference should be that it is a waste of time to send a deputation to confer with so imbecile a person. I will not, however, draw the inference. I have not descended, I trust, to personalities. I do not even impute motives; but I hope I may write thus much without seeming to be disrespectful to the honoured brethren who request a conference with me.—Yours truly,

C. H. Spurgeon.
Menton, December 19.[57]

The magazine never published Spurgeon's letter.

THE BAPTIST UNION CENSURE

Spurgeon's reluctance to meet with the Union delegation in France stemmed from his fear that they were simply trying to make him appear disagreeable and obstinate. He wrote Susannah, "Think of four doctors of divinity coming all this way to see me! I was in great perplexity, and knew not what to reply. I don't quite see what it all means. I lay awake till one o'clock. . . . I do not fear four doctors, but I think it a very wise move on their part. If it means they will surrender, it is well; but if it is meant to fix on me the odium of being implacable, it is another matter."[58]

On January 13, 1888, Spurgeon was back in London and met with the Union delegation at the Tabernacle. The group included General

---

[57]Cited in Pike, 6: 292-93.
[58]*Autobiography*, 4: 257.

Secretary Booth, outgoing President James Culross, and President-elect John Clifford. Alexander Maclaren, the fourth member of the appointed panel—and the most likely to be sympathetic to Spurgeon—was ill and did not attend.[59] The men asked Spurgeon to reconsider his withdrawal. Spurgeon proposed that the Union adopt an evangelical statement of faith. The delegation refused. Neither side felt anything was accomplished by the meeting.

Five days later the full Baptist Union Council met again. This time they voted to accept Spurgeon's withdrawal. Then they voted to censure him by passing a resolution condemning his actions.

A surprisingly lopsided majority approved the censure against their best-known member; only five of the nearly one hundred members supported Spurgeon in the vote. The Council passed this resolution:

> The Council recognises the gravity of the charges which Mr. Spurgeon has brought against the Union previous to, and since, his withdrawal. It considers that the public and general manner in which they have been made reflects on the whole body, and exposes to suspicion brethren who love the truth as dearly as he does. And as Mr. Spurgeon declines to give the names of those to whom he intended them to apply, and the evidence supporting them, those charges in the judgment of the council, ought not to have been made.[60]

One writer at the time, Richard Glover, accurately assessed the issues in the *Evangelical Nonconformist*:

> The policy which they adopted was to attempt to put the responsibility for disturbing the peace of the Union back on Spurgeon. They took the position that his charges were too vague to merit serious investigations, that he had failed to substantiate them by naming any ministers who were guilty. However useful this policy might have been politically, it can only be described as dishonest trifling with the subject.[61]

The fact is, as we have seen, Spurgeon *could* have named names. He could have produced Booth's letters and thereby not only exonerated

[59]"Brief Notes," *The Baptist* (February 1888), 84.
[60]*Ibid.*, 85.
[61]Cited in Drummond, 700-1.

himself but also forced Booth into the role of a second witness against the heretics. Moreover, Spurgeon could have simply cited the published works of some of his fellow Baptists. "Spurgeon had plenty of evidence; there were the utterances of well-known men which had been published in the pages of the *Christian World*, and the *Independent*, the *Freeman*, the *British Weekly*, and the *Baptist*. Reference to the files of these journals for 1887 and 1888 can still be made, and will provide ample proof of the truth of Spurgeon's general charge."[62]

Why didn't Spurgeon simply name those who had abandoned evangelicalism? For one thing, he did not want to wage a dispute over individuals. He feared that the debate would degenerate into a personal war: "If we were not extremely anxious to avoid personalities, we could point to other utterances of some of these esteemed writers which, if they did not contradict what they have now written, would be such a supplement to it that their entire mind would be better known."[63] "The warfare has been made too personal; and certain incidents in it, upon which I will not dwell, have made it too painful for me to feel any pleasure in the idea of going on with it."[64]

But more important, Spurgeon felt the clamoring for names was simply an attempt to deflect from the real issue, which was the policy of the Baptist Union. As he pointed out, the Union had no doctrinal statement, and therefore no authority to discipline anyone for false teaching: "No one can be heterodox under this constitution, unless he should forswear his baptism."[65] So even if he had named names, nothing could be done about the heretics unless the Union was willing to adopt an evangelical statement of faith and require all members to abide by it. That is precisely what the Union had heretofore refused to do.

Spurgeon sincerely hoped that the Down-Grade Controversy would stir the Union's rank and file membership to demand that the Council institute such a policy.

THE FINAL COMPROMISE

"No creed but Christ" was a popular sentiment among evangelicals in Spurgeon's day. There were many who felt creeds and doctrinal state-

---

[62]Carlisle, 248.
[63]"The Case Proved," 27.
[64]"The Baptist Union Censure," *The Sword and the Trowel* (February 1888), 83.
[65]*Ibid.*, 81.

ments were somehow sub-Christian. And there is a legitimate sense in which we ought to guard against elevating any creed above Scripture. When that happens, the creed itself can become an idol, something that actually hinders true worship.

But Spurgeon pointed out that if the creed itself is *true*—that is, if it is in harmony with Scripture and subject to Scripture—no such danger exists:

> To say that "a creed comes between a man and his God," is to suppose that it is not true; for truth, however definitely stated, does not divide the believer from his Lord. So far as I am concerned, that which I believe I am not ashamed to state in the plainest possible language; and the truth I hold I embrace because I believe it to be the mind of God revealed in his infallible Word. How can it divide me from God who revealed it? It is one means of my communion with my Lord, that I receive his words as well as himself, and submit my understanding to what I see to be taught by him. Say what he may, I accept it because he says it, and therein pay him the humble worship of my inmost soul.
>
> I am unable to sympathize with a man who says he has no creed; because I believe him to be in the wrong by his own showing. He ought to have a creed. What is equally certain, he has a creed—he must have one, even though he repudiates the notion. His very unbelief is, in a sense, a creed.
>
> The objection to a creed is a very pleasant way of concealing objection to discipline, and a desire for latitudinarianism. What is wished for is a Union which will, like Noah's Ark, afford shelter both for the clean and for the unclean, for creeping things and winged fowls.[66]

In the theological climate of late nineteenth-century England, it was impossible not to see that Spurgeon had a point. Even after their censure of Spurgeon, the Union Council knew it would have to deal with the issue of a creed at the April 23 Assembly meeting.

Spurgeon had guarded hopes for the Union Assembly meeting. In the April *Sword and Trowel* "Notes," he wrote,

> Prayer should be continually offered by the people of God at this time. The Baptist Union meets in full assembly on April 23, and the great

---

[66]*Ibid.*, 82.

question then before it will be—"Is this Union to have an Evangelical basis or not?" We trust the question will be discussed with good temper, and that the decision will be of the right kind. Surely, as every other body of Christians avows its faith, the Baptist Union should do the same. Whatever its belief is, let it own it.[67]

Spurgeon appealed for clarity above all. He sent a letter to the editor of the *Baptist* that said in part, "Whatever the Council does let it above all things avoid the use of language which could legitimately have two meanings contrary to each other. Let us be plain and outspoken. *There are grave differences*—let them be avowed honestly."[68]

In Iain Murray's words, "This was almost precisely the policy which the council did not follow."[69] Meeting before the April Union Assembly, the Council prepared a brief, somewhat vague, but essentially evangelical, doctrinal statement. When the statement was read at the Assembly meeting, however, it was introduced with a statement disclaiming that the Union had any authority to enforce doctrinal standards on its members. Worse, a footnote had been appended that said some "brethren in the Union . . . have not held the common interpretation" on passages regarding the resurrection and final judgment.[70]

Nevertheless, many evangelicals at the Assembly meetings—Spurgeon's brother James included—believed the statement as read was an acceptable compromise. Certainly it was clear that the Union would go no further.

A proponent of the "New Theology," Charles Williams (not the famous novelist) moved that the Assembly adopt the compromised statement. Williams took the opportunity to deliver a passionate plea in favor of liberal ideas. James Spurgeon "seconded Mr. Williams's resolution, but not his speech."[71] *The Baptist* reported that "The sincerity, the courage, and manliness of Mr. Spurgeon's speech deeply impressed the audience, and did much towards gaining substantial unanimity in the subsequent vote."[72] The resolution passed 2,000 to 7.

---

[67]*Ibid.*, 197-98.
[68]"Notes," *The Sword and the Trowel* (March 1888), 148.
[69]*The Forgotten Spurgeon*, 147.
[70]Cited in Drummond, 704.
[71]"A Welcome Conclusion," *The Baptist* (May 1888), 230.
[72]*Ibid.*, 231.

A man named Henry Oakley was there that day. Years later, he recalled the bedlam in the auditorium:

> I was present at the City Temple when the motion was moved, seconded, and carried. Possibly the City Temple was as full as it could be. I was there very early, but found only a "standing seat" in the aisle of the back gallery. I listened to the speeches. The only one of which I have any distinct remembrance was that of Mr Charles Williams. He quoted Tennyson in favour of a liberal theology and justification of doubt. The moment of voting came. Only those in the area were qualified to vote as members of the assembly. When the motion of censure was put, a forest of hands went up. "Against," called the chairman, Dr Clifford. I did not see any hands, but history records that there were *seven*. Without any announcement of numbers the vast assembly broke into tumultuous cheering, and cheering and cheering yet. From some of the older men their pent-up hostility found vent; from many of the younger men wild resistance of "any obscurantist trammels," as they said, broke loose. It was a strange scene. I viewed it almost with tears. I stood near a "Spurgeon's [College] man," whom I knew very well. Mr Spurgeon had welcomed him from a very lowly position. He went wild almost with delight at this censure of his great and generous master. I say it was a strange scene, that that vast assembly should be so outrageously delighted at the condemnation of the greatest, noblest, and grandest leader of their faith.[73]

It is almost certain, however, that most evangelicals present that day did not see as clearly as Oakley. They could not have understood the vote as another censure of Spurgeon. Certainly James Spurgeon intended no affront to his brother when he seconded the motion. But like most of the evangelicals there that day, James was so eager for reconciliation that he mistakenly believed a doctrinal statement—any statement at all—was something of a victory for their side.

Charles Spurgeon knew otherwise. He wrote to a friend, "My brother thinks he has gained a victory, but I believe we are hopelessly sold. I feel heart-broken. Certainly he has done the very opposite of what I should have done. Yet he is not to be blamed, for he followed his best judgment. Pray for me, that my faith fail not."[74]

---

[73]Cited in Murray, 149-50.
[74]*Ibid.*, 148.

THE AFTERMATH

G. Holden Pike wrote, "As the sequel proved, the peace gained [by the Assembly vote] was not that abiding peace which many had anticipated. The rupture with the Union . . . was never to be repaired."[75] Just as Charles Spurgeon had warned all along, nothing was to be gained by compromising with the enemies of the gospel. The Baptist Union's decline was, if anything, accelerated. Those who embraced the "New Theology" were emboldened after the Union Assembly. They now held the reins of the Union.

Spurgeon wrote,

> The resolution, with its footnote, with the interpretation of its mover, and the re-election of the old council, fairly represent the utmost that would be done when everybody was in his best humour. Is it satisfactory? Does anybody understand it in the same sense as anybody else? Does not the whole virtue of the thing lie in its pleasing both sides a little? And is not this the vice and the condemnation of it?[76]

Spurgeon understood what most evangelicals who voted at the Assembly meeting did not: that the last-minute modifications utterly negated the whole point of having a doctrinal statement:

> The points mentioned were certainly elementary enough, and we did not wonder that one of the brethren exclaimed, "May God help those who do *not* believe these things! Where must they be?" Indeed, little objection was taken to the statements which were tabulated, but the objection was to a belief in these being made indispensable to membership. It was as though it had been said, "Yes, we believe in the Godhead of the Lord Jesus; but we would not keep a man out of our fellowship because he thought our Lord to be a mere man. We believe in the atonement; but if another man rejects it, he must not, therefore, be excluded from our number."[77]

Spurgeon hated schism. He did not want to be divisive. But his conscience would not permit him to align with the enemies of the gospel. In the end he concluded that separating from the Union was actually the

---

[75]Pike, 302.
[76]"Notes," *The Sword and the Trowel* (June 1888). Reprinted in *The "Down Grade" Controversy* (Pasadena, Tex.: Pilgrim, n.d.), 56.
[77]"Attempts at the Impossible," *The Sword and the Trowel* (December 1888), 618.

best way to promote true unity: "Nothing has ever more largely promoted the union of the true than the break with the false."[78]

Spurgeon saw separation as a biblical *necessity* for himself. "Whether others do so or not, I have felt the power of the text, 'Come out from among them, and be ye separate,' and have quitted both Union and Association once for all. . . . This is forced upon me, not only by my convictions, but also by the experience of the utter uselessness of attempting to deal with the evil except by personally coming out from it."[79]

Spurgeon did not actively seek to pull others out of the Union, but he could not understand why men who wanted to remain faithful to the Scriptures would continue to belong to an organization that was so obviously barreling down the down-grade:

> Numbers of good brethren in different ways remain in fellowship with those who are undermining the gospel; and they talk of their conduct as though it were a loving course which the Lord will approve of in the day of his appearing. We cannot understand them. The bounden duty of a true believer towards men who profess to be Christians, and yet deny the Word of the Lord, and reject the fundamentals of the gospel, is to come out from among them. If it be said that efforts should be made to produce reform, we agree with the remark; but when you know that they will be useless, what is the use? Where the basis of association allows error, and almost invites it, and there is an evident determination not to alter that basis, nothing remains to be done inside, which can be of any radical service. The operation of an evangelical party within can only repress, and, perhaps, conceal, the evil for a time; but meanwhile, sin is committed by the compromise itself, and no permanently good result can follow. To stay in a community which fellowships all beliefs in the hope of setting matters right, is as though Abraham had stayed at Ur, or at Haran, in the hope of converting the household out of which he was called.
>
> Complicity with error will take from the best of men the power to enter any successful protest against it. . . . Our present sorrowful protest is not a matter of this man or that, this error or that; but of principle.[80]

---

[78]"Notes," *The Sword and the Trowel* (May 1888). Reprinted in *The Down Grade Controversy*, 55.

[79]"Notes" *The Sword and the Trowel* (June 1888), 56.

[80]"Notes," *The Sword and the Trowel* (October 1888). Reprinted in *The "Down Grade" Controversy*, 66.

The Down-Grade Controversy was a perpetual grief to Spurgeon until his death on January 31, 1892. Close friends, and even some of the students from his Pastors' College, turned against him. But Spurgeon declared to the end that he did not regret the stand he had taken.

It was surely difficult for Spurgeon himself, and even his early biographers, to assess the value of the Down-Grade Controversy. In those last years of Spurgeon's life, the strife was so much in the foreground that it obscured for most observers the real importance of the stand Spurgeon had taken. Spurgeon was the first evangelical with international influence to declare war on modernism. The Baptist Union was never the same. But the Evangelical Alliance, an interdenominational fellowship, stood with Spurgeon and gained strength. Spurgeon's actions helped alert evangelicals worldwide to the dangers of modernism and the down-grade.

Robert Shindler, author of those original "Down Grade" articles in *The Sword and the Trowel*, wrote a biography of Spurgeon which was published the year of the great preacher's death. Recalling a scene in those final, tumultuous years when Spurgeon was invited to address the Evangelical Alliance, Shindler wrote,

> The reception given by the audience to Mr. Spurgeon when he rose to speak was almost overpowering in its fervor and heartiness. We occupied a seat on the platform near enough to witness the powerful emotions that agitated his soul, and the tears that streamed down his cheeks as he listened to previous speakers; and though only a very few of his Baptist brethren were present, there was not wanting such a display of hearty sympathy as must have been cheering to his heart, and comforting to his soul. Since then time has revealed much; and following months and years will, no doubt, make more and more evident how needful was the protest which fidelity to God and to the gospel would not allow him to withhold.
>
> The Lord graciously purge His Church of all false doctrine, all false teachers, and all who are traitors in the camp of Israel! And may the Spirit from on high be poured out upon all flesh, that all the ends of the earth may see, and own, and rejoice in, the salvation of our God![81]

---

[81]*From the Usher's Desk to the Tabernacle Pulpit: The Life and Labors of Charles Haddon Spurgeon* (New York: A. C. Armstrong and Son, 1892), 274.

APPENDIX 2

Charles Finney and American Evangelical Pragmatism

CHARLES FINNEY was born in 1792 in Connecticut but lived most of his childhood in Oneida County, New York. His parents were not Christians, and Finney grew up largely ignorant of Christian doctrine. He remembered no preaching or gospel witness in that part of New York (which he called "a wilderness")—though the historical records indicate there was at least one strong evangelical church in the community.[1]

The religion Finney remembered as a child was, he said later, "of a type not at all calculated to arrest my attention."[2] He described the only preacher he remembered from his youth:

> I sat in the gallery, and observed that he placed his manuscript in the middle of his Bible, and inserted his fingers at the places where were to be found the passages of Scripture to be quoted in the reading of his sermon. This made it necessary to hold his Bible in both hands, and rendered all gesticulation with his hands impossible. As he proceeded he would read the passages of Scripture where his fingers were inserted, and thus liberate one finger after another until the fingers of both hands were read out of their places. When his fingers were all read out, he was near the close of the sermon. His reading was altogether unimpassioned and monotonous; and although the people attended very closely and reverentially to his reading, yet, I must confess, it was to me not much like preaching.[3]

---

[1] B. B. Warfield, *Perfectionism,* 2 vols. (New York: Oxford, 1932), 2: 10.
[2] *Charles G. Finney: An Autobiography* (Old Tappan, N.J.: Revell, n.d.), 78.
[3] *Ibid.,* 6.

Finney characterized the pastor's content as "a dry discussion of doctrine," then added, "and this was really quite as good preaching as I had ever listened to in any place. But any one can judge whether such preaching was calculated to instruct or interest a young man who neither knew nor cared anything about religion."[4]

Finney decided to study law and took an apprenticeship in Adams, New York, where for the first time he became actively involved in a church. The local Presbyterian pastor, George W. Gale, a young man about two years Finney's senior, took an interest in the law student. Gale made Finney choir director in the church, and began to visit him in the law office to converse about spiritual matters.

Then Finney began to notice references to the Bible in his elementary law textbooks, so he acquired a Bible and began to study it. But again, Finney says, the preaching was a stumbling-block to him. "[Gale] seemed to take it for granted that his hearers were theologians, and therefore that he might assume all the great and fundamental doctrines of the Gospel. But I must say that I was rather perplexed than edified by his preaching."[5]

Finney pressed the young pastor with doctrinal questions during their conversations in the law office: "What did he mean by repentance? Was it a mere feeling of sorrow for sin? Was it altogether a passive state of mind, or did it involve a voluntary element? If it was a change of mind, in what respect was it a change of mind?"[6] and so on. One gets the impression from the nature of Finney's inquiries that Gale's preaching could not have been as thoroughly tedious as Finney later portrayed it. The evidence suggests Pastor Gale's ministry was having the desired effect on Finney.

FINNEY'S DRAMATIC CONVERSION

Indeed, while Finney was in Adams, he was spectacularly converted. Ironically, though Finney's conversion was dramatic, overwhelming, and revolutionary, he never came to understand that conversion is wholly a work of God. In Finney's telling of the story, it becomes clear that he believed his own will was the determinative factor that brought about his salvation: "On a Sabbath evening in the autumn of 1821, *I made up my mind that I would settle the question of my soul's salvation* at once, that if it were pos-

---

[4]*Ibid.*, 6-7.
[5]*Ibid.*, 7.
[6]*Ibid.*, 8.

sible *I would make my peace with God.*"[7] Evidently under intense conviction, Finney went into the woods, where he made a promise "that I would give my heart to God or die in the attempt."[8]

Finney was converted there in the woods. At first it seemed a normal conversion. Finney himself was unsure of what had occurred, except that he had yielded himself to the Lord. His mind was "wonderfully quiet and peaceful." The overwhelming conviction of sin he had felt was entirely gone. He even wondered if he had somehow "grieved the Holy Ghost entirely away."[9] But then later that evening, in the law office, Finney had an experience that he described as "a mighty baptism of the Holy Ghost. . . . The Holy Spirit descended upon me in a manner that seemed to go through me, body and soul. I could feel the impression, like a wave of electricity, going through and through me."[10]

Even after all that, however, Finney's state of mind that night was so confused that years later he wrote, "Notwithstanding the baptism I had received . . . I went to bed without feeling sure my peace was made with God."[11]

Finney's doubts were suddenly, mystically erased the next morning, however, and later that same day he decided God wanted him to preach, and that he must begin immediately. "After receiving these baptisms of the Spirit I was quite willing to preach the gospel. Nay, I found that I was unwilling to do anything else. I had no longer any desire to practice law. . . . My whole mind was taken up with Jesus and His salvation; and the world seemed to me of very little consequence."[12]

CALLED TO PREACH?

It was, I believe, extremely unfortunate that Finney chose to pursue a preaching ministry immediately after his conversion. Devoid of any solid Christian influence in his early life, he was almost completely ignorant of the Scriptures and of theology. Finney had a brilliant mind, however, and had always been able to hold his own in a theological debate—even with a trained man like Pastor Gale. His legal training had conditioned Finney

---

[7] *Ibid.*, 12 (emphasis added).
[8] *Ibid.*, 16.
[9] *Ibid.*, 17.
[10] *Ibid.*, 20.
[11] *Ibid.*, 22.
[12] *Ibid.*, 25-26.

to think logically, but it had also saddled him with a world of wrong pre-suppositions. Finney's notions of justice, guilt, righteousness, transgression, forgiveness, responsibility, sovereignty, and a host of other terms were drawn from his legal studies, not from Scripture.

Wherever Finney preached, people responded enthusiastically. Immediate evidences of revival seemed to follow his wake. As his reputation spread, so did his influence. Finney boldly challenged conventional doctrine and persuasively championed his own rather novel set of doctrines. Finney began preaching wherever he could gather an audience, and it wasn't long before he began to make an impact on the established churches. "Here was this young man, but two years a minister, but four a Christian, with no traditions of refinement behind him, and no experience of preaching save as a frontier missionary, suddenly leading an assault upon the churches. He was naturally extravagant in his assertions, imperious and harsh in his bearing, relying more on harrowing men's feelings than on melting them with tender appeal."[13]

It must be noted that when Finney came on the scene many churches had drifted from true orthodoxy to a cold hyper-Calvinism. *Hyper-Calvinism* is the belief that the gospel invitation is for the elect only. Hyper-Calvinists do not believe the gospel should be preached indiscriminately or that salvation should be offered freely to all. In essence, they oppose the very idea of evangelism. Many of the churches in Finney's day were stymied by hyper-Calvinist tendencies. Finney's own pastor, George Gale, may have had hyper-Calvinist leanings. Finney described Gale's preaching: "He never seemed to expect, nor even to aim at converting anybody, by any sermon that I ever heard him preach."[14]

Finney concluded that his pastor's belief in human depravity and divine sovereignty were incompatible with evangelism. He wrote: "The fact is, these dogmas were a perfect straight-jacket to him. If he preached repentance, he must be sure before he sat down, to leave the impression on his people that they could not repent. If he called them to believe he must be sure to inform them that, until their nature was changed by the Holy Spirit, faith was impossible to them. And so his

---

[13]Warfield, 2: 21.
[14]*Autobiography*, 59.

orthodoxy was a perfect snare to himself and to his hearers. I could not receive it."[15]

FINNEY'S AVERSION TO ORTHODOXY

Finney did not distinguish between Calvinist orthodoxy and hyper-Calvinism.[16] Consequently, he distrusted orthodox doctrine and rejected Calvinism altogether. He studied doctrine only superficially and invented a unique system of theology that satisfied his own sense of logic. He applied nineteenth-century American legal standards to every biblical doctrine. "I had read nothing on the subject [of the atonement] except my Bible," he wrote; "and what I found on the subject, I had interpreted as I would have understood the same or like passages in a law book."[17] He concluded that God's justice demanded that He extend grace equally to all. He reasoned that God could not righteously hold mankind guilty for Adam's disobedience. In his opinion, a just God would never condemn people for being sinners by nature: "The Bible defines sin to be a transgression of the law. What law have we violated in inheriting this [sin] nature? What law requires us to have a different nature from that which we possess? Does reason affirm that we are deserving of the wrath and

---

[15]*Ibid.*, 59-60.

[16]Finney wrote, "I have everywhere found, that the peculiarities of hyper-calvinism have been a great stumbling-block, both of the church and of the world. A nature sinful in itself, a total inability to accept Christ, and to obey God, condemnation to eternal death for the sin of Adam, and for a sinful nature, and all the kindred and resultant dogmas of that peculiar school, have been the stumbling-block of believers and the ruin of sinners" (*ibid.*, 368-69). But the doctrines Finney enumerates are not doctrines unique to hyper-Calvinism; they are simple Calvinist orthodoxy—and in most cases, plain biblical teaching. Finney jettisoned them all—and thus repudiated the heart of biblical theology.

The unique theology Finney devised was fraught with problems—particularly in the area of sanctification. Finney developed a radical form of perfectionism, which in turn spawned many other fanatical ideas among his followers. B. B. Warfield wrote a thorough and devastating critique of Finney's theology in his two-volume work, *Perfectionism*, 2: 1-215.

What Finney failed to consider carefully enough is that the most robust revivals in eighteenth-century America—including the Great Awakening—all originated with Calvinist teaching. Jonathan Edwards, George Whitefield, David Brainerd, and the early Baptists were all strongly Calvinistic, yet zealously committed to aggressive evangelism. Unfortunately, Finney was all too eager to shed that heritage and devise his own brand of theology. The pragmatic approach that was part and parcel of Finney's system has endured through today, even among many Christians who would deplore Finney's doctrinal innovations.

[17]*Autobiography*, 42.

curse of God for ever, for inheriting from Adam a sinful nature?"[18] Thus Finney discarded the clear teaching of Scripture (Rom. 5:16-19) in favor of human reason.

Worse yet, Finney denied that a holy God would impute people's sin to Christ or impute Christ's righteousness to believers. Finney concluded that those doctrines—clearly taught in the third, fourth, and fifth chapters of Romans—were "theological fiction."[19] In essence, he denied the core of evangelical theology.

Unfortunately, Finney's early success in preaching obscured the serious flaws in his theology. Finney himself admitted that when he was being examined by his church to be licensed to preach, the presbytery "avoided asking any such questions as would naturally bring my views into collision with theirs."[20] They were evidently intimidated by Finney's growing popularity as a revivalist. But one of the examiners did ask Finney if he accepted the Westminster Confession of Faith. Finney admitted later that he had never even read the Confession. But he answered the presbytery in a way that indicated affirmation of their doctrinal standards. "I replied that I received it for substance of doctrine, so far as I understood it."[21] Afterward, when Finney read the Confession, he was shocked to discover that it contradicted much of what he believed. "As soon as I learned what were the unambiguous teachings of the confession of faith . . . I did not hesitate on all suitable occasions to declare my dissent from them," he wrote.[22]

In rejecting hyper-Calvinist tendencies, Finney swung wildly to the opposite extreme. "There is nothing in religion beyond the ordinary powers of nature," he wrote.[23] "A revival is not a miracle, nor dependent on a miracle, in any sense. It is a purely philosophical result of the right use of the constituted means—as much so as any other effect produced by the application of means. . . . A revival is as naturally a result of the use of means as a crop is of the use of its appropriate means."[24]

---

[18] *Ibid.*, 339.
[19] *Ibid.*, 56-58.
[20] *Ibid.*, 51.
[21] *Ibid.*, 51.
[22] *Ibid.*, 59.
[23] *Revivals of Religion* (Old Tappan, N.J.: Revell, n.d.), 4.
[24] *Ibid.*, 5.

THE END JUSTIFIES THE MEANS?

Finney was the first influential evangelist to suggest that the end justifies the means: "The success of any measure designed to promote a revival of religion, demonstrates its wisdom. . . . When the blessing evidently follows the introduction of the *measure itself*, the proof is unanswerable, that the measure is wise. It is profane to say that such a measure will do more harm than good. God knows about that. His object is, to do the *greatest amount* of good possible."[25]

Finney's influence on the American evangelical movement was profound. He was the first to ask converts to "come forward" in evangelistic meetings to indicate their acceptance of Christ. He is the one who first applied the term "revival" to evangelistic campaigns. It was Finney who popularized the after-meeting for inquirers seeking salvation. He also left his mark on the American preaching style, encouraging young preachers to be extemporaneous, anecdotal, more conversational and less doctrinal than preachers traditionally had been. All of those ideas—pretty much standard fare in evangelicalism today—were part of the "new measures" Finney introduced.

Not all Finney's innovations were wrong, of course. He urged preachers to be direct, clear, cogent, earnest, and confrontational in their messages. He advised them not to speak about sinners in the third-person, but to address them as "you" in order to target their consciences more directly. He stressed the need for immediate conversion, in contrast to the prevailing notion of that day, in which sinners were often counseled to wait on God to give them repentance and faith. Echoing Scripture and Jesus' own preaching, Finney called sinners to repent and believe—not to remain passive and hope God would convert them.

Finney's ministry was centered in western New York state. Even during Finney's lifetime, the area was known as "the burned-over district,"[26] because repeated waves of religious fervor had seemed to erase any real

---

[25] *Ibid.*, 211 (emphasis in original).

[26] Oddly, Finney himself may have helped coin this expression. In his memoirs, he referred to the area as "a burnt district," because of the resistance to his own revivalism he found there. *Autobiography*, 78.

A fascinating secular analysis of the region and its history of revivalism has been written by Whitney R. Cross, *The Burned-Over District: The Social and Intellectual History of Enthusiastic Religion in Western New York, 1800-1850* (New York: Harper Torchbooks, 1950).

concern for the gospel. But in his younger days Finney always seemed to be able to fan the flames at least one more time.

Before long, however, the excitement and fervor of the supposed "revival" gave way to hardened unbelief and widespread agnosticism. The "burned-over district" was scorched again and became harder than ever. In fact, since Finney's time that part of the country has *never* experienced another revival.

One of the workers who labored alongside Finney in the revivals wrote to him in 1834:

> Let us look over the fields where you and others and myself have labored as revival ministers, and what is now their moral state? What was their state within three months after we left them? I have visited and revisited many of these fields, and groaned in spirit to see the sad, frigid, carnal, contentious state into which the churches had fallen—and fallen very soon after our first departure from among them.[27]

B. B. Warfield wrote,

> No more powerful testimony is borne . . . than that of Asa Mahan [Finney's longtime friend and fellow worker], who tells us—to put it briefly—that everyone who was concerned in these revivals suffered a sad subsequent lapse: the people were left like a dead coal which could not be reignited; the pastors were shorn of all their spiritual power; and the evangelists—"among them all," he says, "and I was personally acquainted with nearly every one of them—I cannot recall a single man, brother Finney and father Nash excepted, who did not after a few years lose his unction, and become equally disqualified for the office of evangelist and that of pastor."
>
> Thus the great "Western Revivals" ran out into disaster. . . . Over and over again, when he proposed to revisit one of the churches, delegations were sent him or other means used, to prevent what was thought of as an affliction.[28]

"Even after a generation had passed by," Warfield notes, "these burnt children had no liking for the fire."[29]

---

[27] Cited in Warfield, 2: 26.
[28] *Ibid.*, 2: 26-27.
[29] *Ibid.*, 2: 28.

A DISAPPOINTING END

Finney became discouraged when his methods failed. He accepted the pastorate of Broadway Tabernacle Congregational Church in New York City, and later the presidency of Oberlin College in Ohio. He turned his energies to the development of his perfectionist doctrines and to the work of the college.

Later assessing his own evangelistic career, Finney wrote, "I was often instrumental in bringing Christians under great conviction, and into a state of temporary repentance and faith. . . . [But] falling short of urging them up to a point, where they would become so acquainted with Christ as to abide in Him, they would of course soon relapse into their former state."[30] Realizing his evangelistic methodology had failed, Finney, ever the pragmatist, concluded that his perfectionist teachings were the *real* key to successful ministry. In retrospect, he felt he would have been successful if he had preached a strong perfectionist message based on fear. But had he lived long enough, he would have discovered that perfectionism planted seeds of spiritual disaster worse than shallow evangelism.

A contemporary of Finney's said,

> During ten years, hundreds, and perhaps thousands, were annually reported to be converted on all hands; but now it is admitted, that [Finney's] real converts are comparatively few. It is declared, even by himself, that "the great body of them are a disgrace to religion"; as a consequence of these defections, practical evils, great, terrible, and innumerable, are in various quarters rushing in on the Church.[31]

So Finney's most enduring and far-reaching influence, unfortunately, is not from multitudes of souls saved or sinners reached with the gospel. Those effects, it seems, were almost wholly superficial, often vanishing as soon as Finney left town. Finney's real legacy is the disastrous impact he had on American evangelical theology and evangelistic methodology. The church in our generation is still seething with the leaven Finney introduced, and modern evangelical pragmatism is proof of that.

---

[30]Cited in Warfield, 24.
[31]*Ibid.*, 23.

APPENDIX 3

Carnal v. Spiritual Wisdom

This appendix is excerpted and adapted into modern English from "A Soliloquy on the Art of Man-Fishing," by Thomas Boston. Boston was an evangelical pastor in Ettrick, Scotland in the early 1700s. He was a prolific author in the Puritan tradition, remembered for several important works, including Human Nature in Its Fourfold State *and* The Crook in the Lot, or The Sovereignty and Wisdom of God Displayed in the Afflictions of Men, *both of which books are currently in print. The endurance of Boston's works is ample testimony to the timeless nature of the truths he dealt with, as is especially evident in this excerpt. Although the word* pragmatism *would not be invented for two hundred years, in this piece Boston delivers a powerful assault against the pragmatic approach to ministry.*

OUR LORD'S command *"Follow Me*, and I will make you fishers of men" (Matt. 4:19, emphasis added) implies a renouncing of our own wisdom. Human wisdom cannot be our guide (Matt. 16:24); we must deny ourselves. Paul refused to preach with the wisdom of words (1 Cor. 1:17)—nor did he follow the rules of carnal wisdom. Therefore, oh my soul, renounce your own wisdom. Seek the wisdom that is from above; seek to preach the words of the living God, and not your own. When you determine to take this direction, praying that you might not preach according to your own wisdom and natural reason, you receive God's signal blessing.

Do not take the way of natural reason or follow the rules of carnal wisdom. Its language will always be, "Spare yourself. Guard your honor and your reputation among others. If you speak freely, they will call you a troublemaker and call your preaching reactionary. Every church will be frightened of you as a monster that would preach them all to hell; and so you shall never be settled. Such and such a man, who has a great influence in the church, will never like you. After all, direct preaching is not the way to win people; it unnerves them from the very beginning. Instead, you should bring them on little by little, being somewhat smooth—at least at first. For this generation is not able to abide such doctrine as what you preach."

But hear and follow the rules of the wisdom that is from above: "The wisdom of this world is foolishness before God" (1 Cor. 3:19). That which is in high esteem among men is nothing in God's sight. The wisdom that is from above tells us we must deny ourselves (Matt. 16:24; Luke 14:26). We cannot seek honor, reputation, acclaim, or other such earthly entice-ments. Heavenly wisdom tells us people may call us what they will, we must nevertheless "cry loudly, do not hold back; raise your voice like a trumpet, and declare to My people their transgression, and to the house of Jacob their sins" (Isa. 58:1). Divine wisdom says, "Not many wise according to the flesh, not many mighty, not many noble" are called (1 Cor. 1:26). "But God has chosen the foolish things of the world to shame the wise, and God has chosen the weak things of the world to shame the things which are strong, and the base things of the world and the despised, God has chosen, the things that are not, that He might nullify the things that are" (vv. 27, 28). "But you shall speak My words to them whether they listen or not, for they are rebellious" (Ezek. 2:7). God's wis-dom will show you rules quite contrary to those of carnal wisdom. Consider then what carnal wisdom says, and what the wisdom from above says:

CARNAL WISDOM	SPIRITUAL WISDOM
Your body is weak; don't weary it. It cannot abide toil, labor, and stress. So spare yourself.	Your body is God's as well as your spirit; don't safeguard it from glorify-ing God: "You have been bought with a price: therefore glorify God in your body" (1 Cor. 6:20). Paul said, "I have been in labor and hardship, through many sleepless nights, in hunger and thirst, often without food, in cold and exposure" (2 Cor. 11:27). But God "gives strength to the weary, and to him who lacks might He increases power" (Isa. 40:29). This you have experienced.

CARNAL WISDOM	SPIRITUAL WISDOM
Work diligently for fluent and eloquent speech; fine style very much appeals to the learned. Without it they will think nothing of your preaching.	Christ sent you "to preach the gospel, not in cleverness of speech" (1 Cor. 1:17). Do not preach "with superiority of speech or of wisdom" (1 Cor. 2:1). Your message and preaching should not be "in persuasive words of wisdom" (v. 4).
Attempt to be somewhat smooth and calm in your preaching. Do not attack the particular sins of the land, or of the persons to whom you preach.	"Cry loudly, do not hold back; raise your voice like a trumpet, and declare to My people their transgression, and to the house of Jacob their sins" (Isa. 58:1). "Better is open rebuke than love that is concealed" (Prov. 27:5). "Be diligent to present yourself approved to God . . . handling accurately the word of truth" (2 Tim. 2:15).
If you are not subtle, your hearers will be irritated against you and may create trouble for you. And what a foolish thing would it be for you to speak boldly to such a generation as this, whose very looks are disagreeable!	"He who rebukes a man will afterward find more favor than he who flatters with the tongue" (Prov. 28:23). I have experience of this. "Behold, I have made your face as hard as their faces. . . . Do not be afraid of them or be dismayed before them, though they are a rebellious house" (Ezek. 3:8, 9). Experience confirms this, too.
It is dangerous to speak freely and deal with specifics: there may be more hazard in it than you are aware of.	"He who walks in integrity walks securely" (Prov. 10:9). "He who walks blamelessly will be delivered" (Prov. 28:18).
You will be perceived as a fool, as a monster; you will be called a railer and so lose your reputation and prestige. You need to preserve that. People will hate and abhor you; why	"If any man among you thinks that he is wise . . . let him become foolish that he may become wise" (1 Cor. 3:18). "We have become a spectacle to the world. . . . We are fools for Christ's

CARNAL WISDOM

should you expose yourself to such things?

Great people especially will be offended unless you speak charmingly to them and court and caress them. And if you are looked down upon by great people who are wise and mighty, how will you have any self-respect?

Our people have just come out from under the oppressive hierarchy of a state church. They would not desire to have certain sins disclosed or especially old sores to be ripped open. They cannot abide certain doctrines. More agreeable doctrine will be better for them. Hold off negative things. Such doctrine may do them harm; it will do them no good.

SPIRITUAL WISDOM

sake" (4:9, 10). "'A slave is not greater than his master.' If they persecuted Me, they will also persecute you" (John 15:20). Who cares what people say about you? After all, many said of Jesus, "He has a demon and is insane" (John 10:20). He said, "If anyone wishes to come after Me, let him deny himself, and take up his cross, and follow Me" (Matt. 16:24). "If the world hates you, you know that it has hated Me before it hated you," says our Lord (John 15:18).

"Let me now be partial to no one; nor flatter any man. For I do not know how to flatter, else my Maker would soon take me away" (Job 32:21, 22). "No one of the rulers or Pharisees has believed in Him, has he?" (John 7:48). "Not many wise according to the flesh, not many mighty, not many noble" are called (1 Cor. 1:26). "I will also speak of Thy testimonies before kings, and shall not be ashamed" (Ps. 119:46). "If you show partiality, you are committing sin" (Jas. 2:9).

"You shall speak My words to them whether they listen or not, for they are rebellious" (Ezek. 2:7). "Whenever you hear a word from My mouth, warn them from Me. When I say to the wicked, 'You shall surely die'; and you do not warn him or speak out to warn the wicked from his wicked way that he may live, that wicked man shall die in his iniquity, but his blood I will require at your

CARNAL WISDOM	SPIRITUAL WISDOM
	hand" (3:17, 18). "What the Lord says to me, that I will speak" (1 Kings 22:14).
If you *do* preach such things, prudence requires that you speak of them very cautiously. If conscience says you must speak, do it somewhat covertly, so that you do not offend people too badly. This is especially important with respect to people who are young in the faith. Take your time exposing them to the hard truths and soften them as much as possible; you don't want to turn young believers away.	"Cry loudly, do not hold back" (Isa. 58:1). "Cursed be he that doeth the work of the Lord deceitfully" (Jer. 48:10, KJV). "[We] have renounced the hidden things of dishonesty, not walking in craftiness, *nor handling the word of God deceitfully;* but by manifestation of the truth commending ourselves to every man's conscience in the sight of God" (2 Cor. 4:2, KJV, emphasis added). Peter, preaching to unbelievers in the first sermon of the Christian era, told the Jewish inquirers, "You nailed [this Man] to a cross by the hands of godless men and put Him to death" (Acts 2:23). "We must work . . . as long as it is day; night is coming, when no man can work" (John 9:4).
Be especially pleasant to those who have the most influence in the church—at least until you are settled and secure with a comfortable salary. Otherwise, you may be always looking for work; for churches will be frightened away from you, and will not call you. How then will you live? Forthright preaching, therefore, may be detrimental to your livelihood. A more subtle approach might also afford you a broader ministry.	"To show partiality is not good, because for a piece of bread a man will transgress" (Prov. 28:21). "The will of the Lord be done!" (Acts 21:14, 15). God has "determined [your] appointed times, and the boundaries of [your] habitation" (Acts 17:26). "My purpose will be established, and I will accomplish all My good pleasure" (Isa. 46:10). "God makes a home for the lonely . . . only the rebellious dwell in a parched land" (Ps. 68:6). "A faithful man will abound with blessings, but he who makes haste to be rich will not go

CARNAL WISDOM   **SPIRITUAL WISDOM**

unpunished" (Prov. 28:20). "The fear of man brings a snare, but he who trusts in the Lord will be exalted" (Prov. 29:25).

Thus you see how carnal wisdom—although it speaks convincingly and with a good deal of seeming reason—is quite contrary to the wisdom that is from above (cf Jas. 3:15-18). It promises great advantages to those who follow it, but its promises are not always performed. It threatens great calamity for those who defy it, but neither do its threatenings always come to pass. It makes molehills mountains, and mountains molehills. Therefore reject the wisdom of the world, for it is foolishness with God.

Carnal policy would make us fear those who can only kill the body— and they can hardly do even that much these days. Worldly wisdom would make us cast off the true fear of God. But remember this and use it to strengthen yourself: *"The fear of man brings a snare, but he who trusts in the Lord will be exalted"* (Prov. 29:25). Never seek temporal profit by putting your soul in hazard, but *"Wait for the Lord, and keep His way, and He will exalt you to inherit the land; when the wicked are cut off, you will see it"* (Ps. 37:34). For His way is the safest way, though carnal wisdom may speak otherwise and call His way mere folly. Above all, remember that *"the foolishness of God is wiser than men, and the weakness of God is stronger than men"* (1 Cor. 1:25).

"God has chosen the foolish things of the world to shame the wise, and God has chosen the weak things of the world to shame the things which are strong" (v. 27). *"Your faith should not rest on the wisdom of men, but on the power of God"* (2:5).

"The word of the cross is to those who are perishing foolishness, but to us who are being saved it is the power of God. For it is written, 'I will destroy the wisdom of the wise, and the cleverness of the clever I will set aside.' Where is the wise man? Where is the scribe? Where is the debater of this age? Has not God made foolish the wisdom of the world? For since in the wisdom of God the world through its wisdom did not come to know God, *God was well-pleased through the foolishness of the message preached to save those who believe"* (1 Cor. 1:18-21, emphasis added).

"Do not fear, for I am with you; do not anxiously look about you, for I am your God. I will strengthen you, surely I will help you, surely I will

242

uphold you with My righteous right hand. Behold, all those who are angered at you will be shamed and dishonored; those who contend with you will be as nothing, and will perish" (Isa. 41:10, 11).

SCRIPTURE INDEX

SUBJECT INDEX

Abortion, the dilemma of user-friendly churches regarding, 193
Absolution, rite of, 179
Academic respectability, coveting, 106-18, 137-51, 237-43
America, religious decline of, 86
Ananias and Sapphira, sin of, 52-66
Andover Theological Seminary, theological drift of, 203-4
Annihilationism, 64-66
Arianism, 198
Arminianism, 198
Attendance figures, preoccupation with church *See* Growth

Baby Boomers, ministering to, 119-21, 132
Baptist Union *See* Down-Grade Controversy
Bar, the church viewed as a, 83-84
Barna, George, his disclaimer regarding compromise, 48
on the apostle Paul as a marketer, 90
on the church as a tavern, 83
on marketing the church, 23-24, 125
on meeting felt needs, 48-49, 76
on target marketing, 125
Booth, Samuel Harris, his dubious involvement in the Down-Grade Controversy, 211-19
Boston, Thomas, on carnal v. spiritual wisdom, 237-43
Bowling alleys, in churches, 70
Brow, Robert, on the evangelical megashift, 193
Brown, Dr. David, on altering the gospel, 159-60
Buckingham, Jamie, on long sermons, xi-xii

Calvin, John, on 1 Corinthians 9:19-23, 96
Calvinism, hyper-, 230-32

value of, 160, 198, 202
Carlisle, J. C., his biography of Spurgeon, 214, 219
Carnality, 237-43
Chandler, Russell, his article on church marketing, 50
Christianity, evangelical *See* Evangelicalism
Church, attendance, xviii
building the, 66, 173-90
growth, xviii, 51-66, 72-88, 173-90
large churches, 69-76, 173
leadership, 182-83
marks of an effective, 181-89
purpose of the, 83, 183-84
unbelievers at, 83-84
the user-friendly, 45-66, 191-96
Clowns, used in churches, 46, 70, 85
Comedy routines, used in churches, 46
Commitment, tape on, 192
Compromise, sin of, 34-36, 48, 106-7, 191-93
theological v. acceptable, 89-107
Conditional immortality, 64-66
Contextualization, 90-104, 137-51
Controversy, confronting, xix-xx, 40-42
Creeds *See* Doctrine
Crime, inability of worldly wisdom to deal with, 113
Cross, the *See* Gospel
Cross, Whitney R., on the "burned-over district," 233
Culross, Dr. James, Spurgeon's letter to, 214-15

Dale, R. W., his endorsement of Spurgeon, 159
Dancing, in church, 70, 85, 90
Dart, John, his article on Saturday church services, 46

251

Ashamed of the Gospel was typeset by the Creative Services
Department of Crossway Books, Wheaton, Illinois.

Compositor: Raymond J. Elliott

Manuscript editor: Leonard G. Goss

Production editor: Ted Griffin

Graphic designer: Mark Schramm

The text was set in 11 point Caslon 540